9-13-62

59-11702

WHAT MANNER OF MEN

What Manner of Men

FORGOTTEN HEROES OF
THE AMERICAN REVOLUTION

BY

Fred J. Cook

WILLIAM MORROW & COMPANY

NEW YORK · 1959

Copyright © 1959 by Fred J. Cook

Published simultaneously in the Dominion of
Canada by George J. McLeod Limited, Toronto.

Printed in the United States of America.

Library of Congress Catalog Card Number 59-11702

For my son,
Frederick P. Cook II,
whose help in research made
this book possible

Contents

WHAT MANNER OF MEN

CHAPTER I

★

★　★　★

★

The Divine Right of Man

THE "LITTLE" MEN WHO DO the dirty work of the fighting and dying are almost universally overlooked in history. The heroes in our history books are usually the generals and admirals, not the lowly cavalry captains, not the privates in the ranks. Greatness, the kind of greatness that preserves a man's name for posterity, is all too often the by-product of fortuitousness, the fusion of that lucky combination of personal ability with the sweepstakes chance of a spotlight command. Yet the little men whose fate it is to remain lost and forgotten often possess the qualities of greatness for which only the great are noted. Frequently, they exhibit a courage and devotion, either to their cause or to their comrades caught in the luckless straits of battle, that for purity of motive can't be matched by the general bedecked with medals, eyes fixed on immortality. This, then, is a book dedicated to the memory of some of the little men who were truly great men in the first and most desperate of our wars, the Revolution.

Every war produces its unsung heroes, and to them we owe both the existence and the preservation of our nation. Yet about the men of the Revolution there was a unique quality. For one thing, the Revolution was an amateur's war. The Thirteen Colonies plunged into it with no professional army or navy; with no commanders perfected in tactics at a West Point or an Annapolis; with no drilled rank-and-file, nothing more than a raw militia yet to hear shots fired in anger; without even the *esprit de corps* that comes from a bright tradition of battle and success.

The commanders of the patriots came from farm and plantation, from a bookseller's shop, an apothecary's cubicle, a smith's forge; the troops they commanded were men like themselves—clerks, farmers, artisans, riflemen from the exposed frontier. Both the leaders and the led were novices pitted against the greatest military power of their day, an army and a navy battle-tested in the almost ceaseless succession of Europe's wars; an army and a navy that stood at a pinnacle of power, all opposition crushed, even mighty France stripped of her colonial possessions.

Cold reason said that, against such overwhelming force, the patriots in homespun stood not the slightest chance if England made an all-out effort. And England did. She met rebellion with a massive flexing of muscle. One of the least appreciated facts of the Revolution today is the sheer magnitude of Great Britain's endeavor. Few realize that the invasion fleets she sent to the American coast in the spring of 1776 were the largest the world had ever seen. They dwarfed both in numbers and power the one hundred twenty sails that had comprised the famed Spanish Armada.

A mere recital of the day-by-day massing of warships, troopships, and supply ships off Staten Island for the invasion of New York conveys a vivid impression of the overwhelming odds the patriots faced. In one day, forty-five ships hove into sight; in another, eighty-two more were counted. Soon one hundred thirty ships of war and transports were disembarking ninety-three hundred soldiers on Staten Island, and this was only the advance force. Day by day, the sails of other fleets grew large above the eastern horizon until finally "five hundred dark hulls" clustered off the Staten Island shore, and thirty-two thousand trained and disciplined professional soldiers, fully armed, equipped and supplied, were ready to march against the rebels. It was the greatest fighting force that Great Britain had ever sent to sea, and in the years that followed—despite the French alliance and renewed war in Europe —huge convoys comparable for their day and age to those of World War II continued across the Atlantic, bringing more Hessians, more British regiments, more equipment and supplies.

Such was the power with which, for eight seemingly endless years, the patriots had to contend. Looking back, it is amazing that they could have withstood the odds for a week, a month, or a year. That they could have stuck it out for the full, grueling course seems incredible, especially when one realizes that the rebelling Colonies were far from united in their own cause.

Most historians today estimate that the Colonists were divided into three distinct classes: one-third militant patriots; one-third equally staunch Tories; one-third fence-sitters. This last contingent was motivated by a single passion, the desire to wind up on the winning side; and throughout the long course of the war, as a major battle or enveloping campaign would appear to have been decisive, the fence-sitters were at times lured into premature decision. This led to much hopping off the fence, much scrambling back again, much hopping off in the opposite direction. Literally thousands changed sides more than once.

Such selfish and fickle adherents, of course, did not decide the outcome. The war was won in the end by the dedicated one-third who, in defiance of all common sense, of all logistics, held stubbornly steadfast to the cause to which they had committed themselves. It does not detract from their accomplishment to say that without the repeated stupidities and blunders of British generalship they could not possibly have won. The miracle is that, despite the almost astronomical odds for which the blunders barely compensated, they stood the gaff; they remained dedicated to a cause that seemed, even to them, in a constant repetition of dark hours, the most hopeless of forlorn causes. We who live in an age when massive force, when the sheer weight of men and matériel and industrial production determines the fate of battles, are inevitably led to wonder: What manner of men were these?

They were, if I read their story right, men who were guided by a special inspiration, fired by a personal dedication to a cause in which they passionately believed. They were fighting for something new in the world. They had glimpsed a new dimension of freedom, and they were determined to possess it and make it eternally their own.

In Europe, for centuries, monarchies had ruled the destinies of men. The Colonies had been settled in large part by religious and political rebels, by men who had broken with the autocracies of Church and State. They had sought escape, and in a hostile wilderness, they had escaped. They had learned to rely largely on themselves and their neighbors; they had perfected their own rough rural democracy; and when England demanded that they help bear the burdens of empire without any voice in its direction, they rebelled.

This is not to say that all of their motives were pure and lofty. The Revolution was supported, at the outset at least, by many men of essentially conservative cast who were primarily concerned in striking off the business and commercial shackles by which Britain kept the Colonies in the dependent status of poor relations. Ideals at times were less important than money. But the ideals were there, deep in the channel of a mainstream composed of many currents.

Perhaps the simplest way to phrase it is to say that the centuries-old tradition of the divine right of kings was being challenged by a new concept of the divine right of man. It was an age of new and revolutionary political thought. In France and England, philosophical cults had been built up about what we today would consider the myth of an overriding Natural Law. This new philosophy held that Nature, in a perfect wisdom all her own, had created all men equal, with equal rights to liberty and justice and, inevitably, to participation in the social and political order that would realize these ideals. In Europe, the worship of Nature and Nature's way was at first little more than a drawing-room fad; but in America, where the harsh experiences of frontier life had proved a great leveler between man and man, the idea of social and political equality struck a responsive chord.

It found expression in the philippics of Samuel Adams, the agitator who made the Revolution possible. Adams, in a propaganda effort that lasted for years and in the end proved persuasive throughout the Colonies, pictured the mother country as attempting to reduce the Colonists to a state of "slavery, poverty, and misery," and he harped constantly on the theme that England in so doing was violating the inherent rights of man. He held that "the natural liberty of man is to be free from any superior power on earth, and not to be under the will or legislative authority of man, but only to have the law of nature for his rule."

The potency of the theme was best illustrated by the enthusiastic reception accorded that strange mixture of logic and passion that was Thomas Paine's "Common Sense." It was the most explosive document of its age; its circulation was tremendous; and the phrases that leaped from its pages spread through the Colonies with the rapidity of a gale-fanned fire. Paine saw government as "a necessary evil," its only justification lying in the need to curb lawless impulse, and he attacked the entire concept of monarchy. "One of the strongest natural proofs of the folly of the hereditary right of kings," he wrote, "is that nature disapproves it, otherwise she would not so frequently turn it into ridicule by giving mankind an *ass for a lion.*"

Paine called for the formation of a republic as the least restrictive form of government, he called for the severance of all ties with England, and he proclaimed: "The sun never shined on a cause of greater worth. 'Tis not the affair of a city, a county, a province or a kingdom; but of a continent—of at least one-eighth part of the habitable globe. 'Tis not the concern of a day, a year, or an age; posterity are virtually involved in the contest, and will be more or less affected even to the end of time by the proceedings now." And he closed on a high note of exhortation, writing words that once read or heard were forever memorable: "O ye that love mankind! Ye that dare oppose not only tyranny but the tyrant, stand forth! Every spot of the old world is overrun with oppression. Freedom hath been hunted round the globe. Asia and Africa have long expelled her. Europe regards her like a stranger, and England hath given her warning to depart. O receive the fugitive, and prepare in time an asylum for mankind!"

This, then, was the vision and the dream. Not all men saw it. Not all men who saw had the strength to act. The warriors of the Revolution were not all heroes. Many served their six-month enlistment, got a quick bellyful and went home. Others simply deserted. Others still, switched to what they thought must prove the winning side. Even the steadfast, beaten down at times by the hammer strokes of a never-ceasing sequence of misfortunes, despaired of victory, and for them Thomas Paine again was the oracle who wrote in *The American Crisis* the unforgettable lines: "These are the times that try men's souls: The summer soldier and the sunshine patriot will, in this crisis, shrink from the service of his country; but he that stands it Now, deserves the love and thanks of man and woman. Tyranny, like hell, is not easily conquered; yet we have this consolation with us, that the harder the conflict the more glorious the triumph."

This book is about those who stood it and who have been largely forgotten. It includes both men and women, for in this citizens' war, the women also fought. It includes cavalrymen and Indian scouts and sea fighters. They were individuals inspired by different motives, driven by different compulsions; yet in many respects they were alike. They were novices and amateurs in the business of war, reacting with a mixture of idealism, instinct and desperation to the demands of their day. They were volunteers all. There was no draft, no hard inescapable summons to compel them to go out and risk and die. They could have quit at any time. But they stuck it out, the best of them, through the cruel winter of Valley Forge with its bloody footprints on the snow and, after Valley Forge, through the ordeal of Morristown, a winter less-publicized but actually just as bad. They defied a succession of perils, they bounced back from repeated wounds, and of their own free will, they joined up again and fought once more. They ignored the fact that they were the underdogs, perhaps simply because they *had* to ignore it if they were to hope at all, and they made almost a fetish of attempting the superhuman and the seemingly impossible. If they had not, almost certainly this nation never would have been created.

From the crucible of great perils and terrible tensions there came astounding individual performances. Some of the feats of these forgotten men of the Revolution, defying the kind of odds that we have been taught to respect, may seem almost unbelievable to our more cynical modern eyes. An age that is preoccupied with the looming horror of intercontinental ballistic missiles capable of obliterating entire cities is an age that is preoccupied with man in the mass, not man the individual. In the Revolution, fortunately for us, the reverse was true. The fate of an entire army might rest on the incessant activity of an Allan McLane riding the forward lines; the safety of an entire frontier could hinge on the woodland skill of a Timothy Murphy. The times were not yet so complex that man as an individual had lost all control of his fate; indeed, they called on him to exert himself, they challenged him with the need of supreme effort to save himself and his fellows. What follows are the stories of some who heeded the call, who met the challenge and who, in the process, performed some almost incredible exploits.

The cavalrymen of the Revolution were an especially hard-riding and dashing breed. Yet, peculiarly enough, when the war began, the patriots had virtually no cavalry. The men who fought at Lexington and Concord were farmers who fired at the redcoats from the shelter of rock fences, and the early battles were waged almost exclusively by an amateur infantry.

Even among the officers there were few who had any conception of the vital role an alert cavalry could play as the eyes and ears of an army. Most of those who had had training in warfare had fought on the frontiers, and they were more familiar with the technique of Indian fighting than they were with the large-scale maneuvering of armies in the open field. George Washington himself had been a frontier hero, and he was handicapped at the outset by the limitations of his own knowledge and experience. He did not realize at once how essential it was to have a mobile cavalry screen riding the forward lines to feel out the movements of the enemy and to guard against surprise. The result was that time and again in the early going the British struck where they were least expected and inflicted defeats that would have crushed a less resilient and determined army.

It was not until the patriots had lost their capital city of Philadelphia, not until the grim winter of 1777–78 had clamped its icy hand on the snow-shrouded misery of Valley Forge, that Washington began to employ cavalry as it should be used. Then one of the most dashing figures of the war became, almost overnight, the hero of the army.

He was Allan McLane, the first great cavalryman of the Revolution. Though he was destined to suffer cruel eclipse and to fade virtually forgotten from the pages of history, Allan McLane was the kind of man whose fire and fervor still stir the pulses. He was one of those rarities in any time, a dedicated idealist—a man so enwrapped in a cause that he sacrificed to it both personal fortune and personal glory. In Allan McLane were all the qualities of the crusader, passionate hatred mingling with passionate belief.

The combination was a double-edged sword. The fervor of conviction spurred the man to incessant action. He rode the forward lines with such relentless purpose that it seemed he never rested, he never slept. The British, penned up in Philadelphia, quickly found it was almost impossible to stick their heads outside the city without encountering the rough riders of Allan McLane. Yet the same fervor that made McLane an incomparable commander in the field was destined, with a kind of preordained inevitability, to bring him into conflict with those among his own comrades who were less possessed by ideals than he. In Allan McLane, the seed of triumph and the seed of personal tragedy were the same seed —the seed of his own impassioned and incorruptible fervor. It is this perhaps, as much as the flaming quality of his deeds, that makes Allan McLane today seem a unique and challenging figure.

★

★ ★ ★

★

CHAPTER II

Allan McLane

CAPT. ALLAN MCLANE WAS a handsome man of medium height, lithe, agile, intense. In the winter of Valley Forge, he had earned his reputation as the crack cavalryman of the Continental Army. Incessantly on the move, he had roamed the countryside around the patriots' conquered capital of Philadelphia; he had swooped down upon British foraging parties, snatching from them the supplies they had so carefully gathered; he had developed a spy network that kept George Washington informed of events inside the city, where the British dined and danced and wenched as the patriots froze, sickened, starved. It was now the spring of 1778, and rumors spread that the British were about to evacuate Philadelphia and return to their major base at New York. The rumors spurred Allan McLane to keep the forward lines by day, by night, driving men and horses to the brittle edge of exhaustion. Information was what he sought, and on the morning of June 16, 1778, he rode to a prearranged rendezvous—and to what he well recognized might be a carefully laid British trap.

The plot had begun to develop the previous day. In a journal in which he later recorded some of his more exciting adventures, McLane, writing of himself in the third person as was his habit, described the preliminaries.

"On the 15th the Daughter of a Citizen residing in the City informed the Capt. that her father would meet him at . . . the Horse House near the Rising Sun Tavern between daybreak and sunrise in the morning of the 16th and give him intelligence of importance," McLane wrote.

It is obvious from the tenor of the journal that McLane suspected the possibility of treachery. His activities had marked him as a dangerous man, the British naturally would want his scalp, and he was being lured by a tempting promise. Information was being dangled before his nose, and he must ride alone to get it. All the possibilities of a trap were there, and McLane, recognizing this, decided that he had better not go unprepared.

Turning out his entire troop, he left the vicinity of Chestnut Hill in that darkest hour before the dawn. As he rode toward the rendezvous, he made his dispositions. He kept just two dragoons near him, ordering the rest of the troop to follow at a distance and to halt out of sight in the rear of the Rising Sun, a tavern located in the countryside near Germantown. The two dragoons, he posted as vedettes on a road linking the Frankfort Road and the Old York Road, and he ordered them to fire their pistols one after the other as a signal to the waiting troop at the first sign of the enemy. Then, having guarded as well as he could against surprise, McLane rode on alone to his rendezvous.

A furtive-acting man was waiting, and McLane began talking to him just inside the gate of the yard. They had hardly met when a patrol of thirteen British horse rode up quietly from the south, circled a small hill and a patch of woods, and then launched themselves at a gallop straight at the two men in the horse pen.

McLane's informant—whether a patriot or tool of the British,

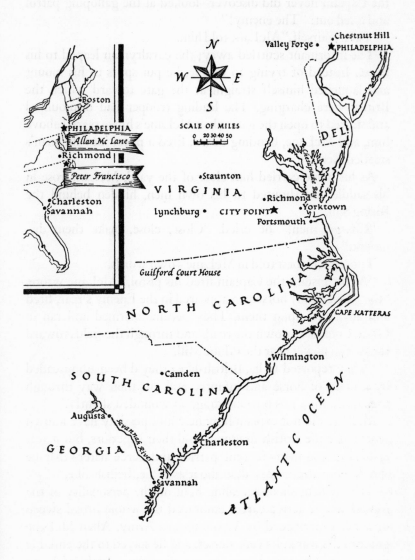

the Captain never did discover—looked at the galloping patrol and cried out: "The enemy!"

"Save yourself," McLane told him.

The informant scuttled away; the cavalryman leaped to his horse. Instead of trying to escape, he put spurs to his mount and launched himself straight at the gate toward which the British were charging. The leading trooper had dismounted and started to open the gate when McLane's horse reared above him, and McLane, bending down, fired a pistol into the man's startled face.

As his horse carried him clear of the yard, McLane rose in his saddle and shouted to his own men, hidden behind the Rising Sun.

"Charge, men!" he cried. "Close, close, make them dismount."

The sequel is best told in McLane's own words.

"At the instant the Captain fired his pistol," McLane wrote, "the [American] horsemen appeared in the Enemy's rear, fired and advanced upon them. They became alarmed and ran in Grate Confusion down the roads and through the fields toward the British picket near the Globe Mill.

"They reported (a lie, British-like) they'd been ambuscaded by a body of horse and infantry and cut their way through them without a loss but one dragoon wounded slightly."

McLane did not explain how he could possibly have known what story the British dragoons told their superiors, but it was typical of the man—fervent patriot and fierce hater—that he should contemptuously describe it as a "lie, British-like."

The incident sheds revealing light on the personality of the fighter whose active career embraced the whole broad sweep of battle experienced by Washington's Army. Allan McLane got into the war at its very outset, and he stayed to the end. He was one of the rare heroes in the disastrous Battle of Long Island that sealed the downfall of New York; he was a master scout whose intelligence more than once saved an army; he was a spy who passed through the British lines before the bloody battle of Monmouth and who gathered the information that led to the midnight bayonet charge at Stony Point. And finally, most importantly, he was the secret agent who, on a long-forgotten mission, carried the dispatches and advanced the clinching arguments that determined the strategy of Yorktown.

Few men played a greater role in the events leading to the climactic surrender of Cornwallis and American independence —yet the very name of Allan McLane has been consigned to almost total oblivion. It is a fate that McLane foresaw, a fate against which he bitterly and futilely rebelled.

For the man who had no doubts that the dragoons fleeing from the horse yard of the Rising Sun had told "a lie, British-like" was a man who had all the defects of his virtues. He was one of those rare and priceless and difficult individuals who are too dedicated. He was a zealot in the cause of liberty and democracy. As well as fighting like a madman for the cause he believed in so passionately, he sacrificed his considerable private fortune to it and impoverished his family. Almost inevitably, he was embittered by repeated discoveries that not all his brothers-in-arms, not all the leaders of the rebellion, were so selfless or so loftily inspired. In disillusionment, he clashed repeatedly with the glory-hunters, though he himself could not refrain from bitterness at being deprived of his just share of glory; he despised the self-serving politicians; he worshiped only Washington and even Washington, he sometimes complained, was duped and misled. In the end, having made himself as famous among his comrades for his acerbic disposition as he was among the enemy for his hard-riding valor in battle, he wrote on his retirement from the army that he had "Received nothing but abuse and Insults from the people then in power as a reward for his sacrifices and faithful services from 1775."

Self-pity and resentment of personal injustices run through the disconnected writings of Allan McLane. Strong emotion he sometimes committed to paper with such an angry slash of the quill that the result is partly indecipherable; but that same strong passion, finding vent in the field, led him to perform such deeds in the grim winter of Valley Forge that Washington, wholeheartedly grateful, confided to one of his headquarters staff, "I would not do without him in the light corps—no, not for a thousand pounds."

The man whose services were rated at such a price by his commander-in-chief was born in Philadelphia on August 8, 1746. His parents, whose names he failed to record in his diary, were "of the middling grade," he said. Patently, they were persons of some affluence, for McLane made an educational tour of Europe when he was twenty-one and when his father died in 1775 McLane inherited more than fifteen thousand dollars worth of property in Philadelphia, an estate that was considered quite ample in those days.

When he was twenty-three, McLane married Rebecca Wells, the daughter of the Sheriff of Kent County, Delaware. In 1774, he settled near Smyrna in Kent County, and with the outbreak of the Revolution less than a year later, he was off to war. He joined Virginia patriots who were rebelling against their much-hated Royal Governor, Lord Dunmore, and he fought against Dunmore's forces at Great Bridge and in the vicinity of Norfolk. Returning to his home in Delaware in late summer, he was commissioned on September 11, 1775 as an adjutant in a company of volunteers raised by Caesar Rodney, one of Delaware's leading patriots. With this company, Allan McLane joined the Continental Army under Washington. Early in the game, McLane showed the verve and dash which were to become his trademark.

The war was about to enter upon its most critical phase. After the first clash at Lexington and Concord, the British had been penned up in Boston, and in the spring of 1776, with cannon placed on Dorchester Heights, Washington had driven them out. Even as the sails of the British fleet vanished over the horizon, Washington began to worry about where the next blow would fall. He sensed that the target would be New York, with its spacious harbor and its wide-open route up the Hudson to Canada, and he moved his army south to block the way.

By late summer, the five hundred ships in the invasion fleet sprouted a forest of masts off the shores of Staten Island. Washington correctly deduced that the British would hop from this staging area across the Narrows to Long Island. Rashly, since he had no sea power to oppose a fleet more than four times the size of the Spanish Armada, he crossed the East River and committed his army to battle in a disjointed defense line strung out along Brooklyn Heights.

Sir William Howe, the British commander, could have cut off the patriots and perhaps ended the war at one stroke if he had had the elementary common sense to thrust his powerful fleet up the East River, severing communication with the Manhattan shore. But Howe ignored the obvious and ideal strategy. Instead, he concentrated on the problem of smashing the American defenses. These ran in a wavering and irregular line from Wallabout Bay, jutting in from the East River on the north, to Gowanus Bay bellying off the harbor near the Narrows on the south. The American right, composed of Maryland and Delaware troops, including McLane's company, was solidly based on Gowanus Bay, but was only loosely linked to the more advanced center. And on the left the line tailed off in air.

Howe, a devotee of the type of pincer movement World War II was to make famous, split his army to take advantage of this faulty alignment. He left a mere holding force in front of the American right and center. Then, placing himself at the head of a column of ten thousand troops, backed by twenty-eight pieces of artillery, he set out on a long and circuitous night march. The movement was undetected by the Americans, who had yet to learn the uses of cavalry reconnaissance, and on the early morning of August 27th, Howe debouched through the gap on the left, whirled and struck at the ill-prepared, surprised patriots, most of whom were getting their initiation in battle. The shock was irresistible, the rout almost instantaneous.

The American front splintered into fleeing fragments. The entire center and left were swept away; only the rear behind redoubts in Brooklyn and the right in an exposed angle by Gowanus Bay still stood firm. Lord Stirling commanded the Marylanders and Delawares on the right, a post of desperate isolation as British and Hessian regiments swept across the battlefield and converged upon it. Stirling, bending back his line to prevent complete envelopment, met the shock of overwhelming odds, his nine hundred fifty men a tiny island almost smothered by waves of seven thousand British regulars and two thousand Marines. In the midst of this unequal battle, Allan McLane scored a success unique on this day of universal disaster.

The Delaware troops wore uniforms of blue, faced with red. These, as it happened, were the identical colors of the Hessians, who had been thrown into battle on this same general sector of the front. The Colonel of the Second British Grenadiers, finding his men under heavy fire from the blue-and-red uniformed troops, assumed that they were Hessians firing upon him by mistake, and so he dispatched a small detachment, composed of a lieutenant, a sergeant, a corporal and twenty men, to contact the troublesome marksmen and rectify the supposed error.

The British lieutenant led his party close to the American front. Only then did he discover the real nature of the mistake. And as he did, Allan McLane at the head of a small detachment of fighting Delawares came charging out of the American lines. McLane and his men quickly surrounded the British band, and after a brief, sharp clash, captured the lieutenant and eighteen of his soldiers. Placing the prisoners in the middle of his little force, McLane wheeled to rejoin his regiment. The advancing British Grenadiers thrust between, trying to cut him off, but McLane kept his men together, slashed his way through and brought off his prisoners.

This success on a day of bloody reverses showed the caliber of the man. The swift pounce on the enemy, the short sharp fight, the slashing getaway—all were characteristic of the raider who, in the black days ahead, was to become Washington's favorite commander in the light corps.

Ferried across the East River with the remnants of the shattered Long Island forces, McLane rejoined Washington's Army and participated in the succession of defeats that seemed to have no end. He fought at White Plains, fought again in rear guard actions as the beaten and disheartened Continentals straggled across New Jersey and fled beyond the Delaware. He was in the thick of the stunning, about-face victory at Trenton that saved the rebellion from quick collapse, and he was conspicuous at Princeton in the desperate fighting that opened the new year, 1777. Here his gallantry attracted Washington's personal attention, and he was promoted to captain on the field of battle. His formal commission, dated January 13, 1777, assigned him to Col. John Patton's regiment of foot, but he was soon detached and sent to Delaware to raise a company of his own. McLane returned with ninety-four men enlisted and equipped at his own expense, "every shilling of the bounty money being drawn from his pocket."

Now, with a command of his own, with the attention of the commander-in-chief focused upon him, Allan McLane was ready to gallop into history. His emergence in his own characteristically individual role coincided with a series of new disasters. Howe attacked and took Philadelphia, scattering the Continental Congress in flight. Washington fought a futile battle in defense of the capital along a little stream known as the Brandywine. Beaten, he fell back, regrouped and launched another attack on the British army in Germantown. Allan McLane and his light horse, riding in the van of the lead column, charged the first British pickets, killed two at the loss of one of his own men and captured two British field pieces. The Continental Army, pouring along the road behind McLane's raiders, caught the British by surprise and drove them hard, but the battle quickly bogged down in a mélange of errors and missed chances. Washington, beaten again, retreated to the country-side north of Philadelphia, hovering still within striking dis-tance, and Howe settled himself and his army in the city that was now securely his.

In these circumstances, with the winter of Valley Forge almost upon him, Washington decided to give McLane a free hand to rove the countryside around the fallen capital, cutting off supplies flowing to the British troops and gathering in-formation regarding the enemy's dispositions and intentions. The commander-in-chief's decision was made known to Mc-Lane in an order from headquarters dated November 7, 1777 and still preserved in the McLane papers in the New York Historical Society. The order read:

"Sir, You being acquainted with the country in the neighbor-hood of Philadelphia will take the post most advantageous for watching the enemy, sending out the necessary parties and patriots for that end. . . . You are to prevent as far as possible all intercourse between Philadelphia and the country, suffering none to go to the city without papers given by the authority of the commander-in-chief."

Never were orders more expeditiously executed. On his very first night of service, according to Alexander Garden, an officer in Lee's Legion who knew and admired McLane, the hard-riding light cavalry Captain "took three spies, fifteen British soldiers who had quitted the city in search of plunder, and twelve Tories carrying in supplies to the enemy."

In the weeks that followed, McLane rode hard and in-cessantly. He wore out troopers and horses. On November 15, 1777, just eight days after he had been given his roving com-mission on the forward lines, an additional one hundred troop-ers with supplies for four days were ordered to join him at the Rising Sun Tavern in the countryside north of Germantown. And on November 27th, still another one hundred were dis-

patched, whether as reinforcements or relief for troopers exhausted by McLane's constant raiding is not clear. One thing
is certain: McLane and his fast-moving troop blanketed the
countryside outside Philadelphia. They raided supply trains,
they cut off communications, they halted and questioned all
travelers, they set up their own spy system. In less than a
month, they made themselves the indispensable eyes and ears
of the Army—and it was good for Washington that they did.

The Continental Army, which had missed victory by the
narrowest of margins in the counterattack at Germantown, was
still strong enough to be dangerous. It was encamped at Whitemarsh, some dozen miles from Philadelphia, close enough so
that it could strike suddenly, close enough to represent a
menace. Howe, nettled by its hovering presence, decided to
eliminate the threat. He would surprise Washington and end
the war at a single stroke. Careful plans were laid—plans that
might have succeeded except for a courageous Quaker matron
and Allan McLane.

On Second Street in Philadelphia, directly opposite Howe's
headquarters, lived a Quaker couple, William and Lydia Darrah. Sometimes Howe's officers rented an apartment from
Lydia for a quiet party or extremely private consultation. On
December 2, 1777, Howe's adjutant general told Lydia he
wanted the apartment for that night and advised her to send all
her family to bed early.

"When we are ready to depart, we will let you know so that
you can let us out and extinguish the fire and candles," he told
the landlady.

Lydia Darrah pretended to agree, but her curiosity was
aroused by the strange order, especially by the injunction that
she should send all her family to bed early. She reasoned that
the meeting must be one of more than ordinary importance,
and she resolved to eavesdrop on the gathering, if she could,
and find out the reason for the exceptional secretiveness.

Obeying the adjutant's orders, she bundled her family off

to bed before eight o'clock. Then she waited. When the British officers were all assembled, she took off her shoes and felt her way along the hall to the room in which the conference was being held. Stooping and putting her ear close to the keyhole, she listened—and was shocked by what she heard. The British officers were discussing plans for an attack on Washington at Whitemarsh. Repeating the maneuver that Howe had worked so successfully on Long Island, the troops were to leave at midnight December 4th, and they were to march in two columns, striking the unsuspecting Continentals in the gray of dawn.

Lydia Darrah retreated to bed with the secret she had surprised. What was she to do? She feigned sleep while her mind worried toward a decision. When the staff conference broke up and the British adjutant general came to waken her, she made him knock on her door several times before at last, seemingly arousing herself from slumber, she let him and his friends out. In the dark hours of the night, she finally determined on a course of action: she must try to warn Washington.

When morning came, without letting even her husband know her real purpose, she announced that the family's supply of flour was getting low and that she would have to go to the miller in Frankfort, outside the city, to purchase some. She crossed the street to Howe's headquarters, requested and obtained a pass, and went through the lines carrying her empty flour bag. She left the bag at the miller's to be filled, then hurried on into the countryside to the north, seeking contact with the patriot forces. Soon Allan McLane and a troop of his light horse, who were stopping everything that moved upon the roads, came riding up, and Lydia delivered her message.

While the Quaker matron retrieved her filled flour bag from the miller and returned unsuspected through the British lines to her home in Philadelphia, McLane galloped to warn Washington at Whitemarsh. With several precious hours to make preparations, Washington promptly alerted his camp and prepared his defenses. McLane, with one hundred picked cavalry-men, was sent back to maintain a night-long watch on the roads from Philadelphia and to keep Washington informed of the movements of the enemy.

Howe, unaware that his carefully laid plans were no longer secret, moved at midnight with virtually his entire army. The British veterans filed in two long and massive columns along the Manatawny and Skippack Roads. McLane quickly spotted the movement and dispatched a courier to Washington. Then he gathered his troopers into one compact, hard-riding unit, and when the British advance on the Skippack Road had reached Three Mile Run, he charged out of the night, slashing through the head of the column, wheeling and charging back again.

The sudden onslaught surprised and stunned the British. The leading division was thrown momentarily into confusion. It halted and formed in line of battle, expecting an attack by Washington's force. By the time it was ready to fight, McLane was gone like a ghost in the night. Slowly, more cautiously, the British pressed forward, and as they did, McLane repeatedly led his heroic handful back to the charge, striking now at the flank, now at the front of the bewildered British column.

Galled severely by McLane's pestiferous troopers, the British Army finally reached Chestnut Hill. Before them, on a ridge three miles away, was the American Army, alert, drawn up in line of battle behind strong abatis and entrenchments. All hope of surprise was gone, and so strong was the American position that Howe sat down in camp for two days, cogitating what to do about it.

He finally decided on a night maneuver, attacking in two columns and attempting to roll up the left wing of the American Army. Major General Charles Grey led a feint against the right, while Howe himself personally pressed the major attack on the left. There a fierce charge dislodged a regiment of Pennsylvania militia and another of Continentals, stationed in a wood. Generals John Cadwalader and Joseph Reed had been posted with these troops as observers, and at the first fire, Reed's horse was shot and fell, pinning Reed to the ground. The British charged with the bayonet; the Americans fled in confusion. General Reed lay helpless. The bayonets of the first rank of the charging British were almost at his breast when there was a thunder of galloping hoofs and Allan McLane's hard-riding troopers swirled upon the scene, sabering all in their path, momentarily blunting the forward surge of the British—and rescuing the general.

This fierce skirmish virtually ended the abortive battle of Whitemarsh. The Americans, their outposts caved in, withdrew into their main lines, and Howe, finding these too strong to pierce, folded his tents and retreated to Philadelphia.

To the British, the complete miscarriage of their best-laid plans was both a mystery and a humiliation. The British adjutant general questioned Lydia Darrah closely. Had everybody been in bed on the night of the conference? he asked.

"I sent all the family to bed before eight o'clock, just as you instructed," Lydia told him.

The British officer shook his head. "You, I know, Lydia, were asleep," he said, "for I knocked at your door three times before you heard me, yet, though I am at a loss to conceive who gave the information to General Washington, it is certain that we were betrayed."

The death and destruction the British could not accomplish were now about to be imposed on the patriot cause by one of the most rigorous winters of the war. Washington, unable to keep the field in bitter cold and snow, withdrew to Valley Forge and an ordeal worse than battle. His army was nearly naked, ill-shod, starving; and all he got from the politicians in the Continental Congress were promises that were not fulfilled and complaints that he had not driven the British from Philadelphia. In these circumstances, the army had to rely largely upon itself, and one of Washington's main reliances was Allan McLane.

In the early days of that harsh winter, McLane's little band, never much more than one hundred men, roved constantly across the countryside outside of Philadelphia. His troopers were in such desperate straits for breeches that McLane's wife, Rebecca, ripped up her white linen tablecloths to make them. Clad in these, beaver hats and rough hunting shirts, minus great-coats and boots, McLane's ragtag riders were a ubiquitous force, snapping at the heels of every British party that ventured outside the city. They became known as "the market stoppers." A British foraging party, well-guarded by troops, would be winding along a country road back to Philadelphia when suddenly, out of a woods, down the slope of a hill, there would come a compact knot of wild, hard riders. The headlong impact of their charge, accompanied by sharp deadly shots and the clash of steel, would scatter the protective screen of British troopers along the road like leaves scuttling before the fierce winter wind, and the supplies and livestock the British had gathered would wind up eking out the scanty rations of Washington's impoverished army at Valley Forge.

This harassment was important, but it couldn't feed an army. In January Washington, in desperation, ordered McLane to take his troop on a foraging expedition into Delaware and the Eastern Shore of Maryland. McLane was gone most of January and all of February, and his success as a forager is attested by his own tally, which laconically records "1500 fat hogs, 500 head of Cattle, 200 head of Horses and 50 head of horses for the army at Valley Forge and a full supply for General Smallwood at Wilmington."

Despite such supplies, privation and disease whittled the ranks of the army to the last thin, irreducible line. Colonel Patton's regiment, to which McLane originally had been attached, was typical. A friend in camp wrote McLane on February 15,

1778: "Your regiment have very few officers in camp. It is commanded by Lieutenant Joseph Davis. I have often inquired amongst your company how they were treated, and they have no complaints, but that of being naked, which must be endured as it is a general Calamity."

The end of the winter saw McLane, his foraging completed, back with the main army, roving the forward lines around Philadelphia. He became once again the eyes and ears of Washington. At the head of a troop of one hundred to one hundred fifty horsemen, sometimes reinforced by fifty Oneida Indians, he added almost daily to his reputation as scout and raider. Washington noted in one letter that "Captain McLane frequently employs Spies to bring him intelligence," and McLane himself, in disguise, sometimes penetrated the British lines and entered Philadelphia. Little that happened in the city or in Howe's headquarters escaped him. He developed an almost uncanny knack for being omnipresent, on hand for every crisis.

Typical was his uninvited and certainly unwanted contribution to the Mischianza, the elaborate festival given on May 18, 1778 in honor of Howe, who had been recalled to England and was to be succeeded in command by Sir Henry Clinton. The fete was planned and directed by the handsome and dashing Major John André, later to be executed as Benedict Arnold's partner in espionage but then the darling of the pretty Tories of Philadelphia.

Military magnificence was André's motif in this farewell to his chief. The day began with a colorful regatta on the Delaware, with some of the Quaker City's most famous beauties floating down the stream in colorfully bedecked barges, squired by British officers in vivid scarlet uniforms. Guns of the British warships in the harbor thundered in salute as the flotilla landed opposite the Wharton house, now the site of the Pennsylvania Railroad Station. Here a great amphitheater had been laid out with triumphal arches at either end. A mock tournament was held, and then the entire company passed through an avenue

three hundred yards in length, flanked with troops and decorated with regimental colors. At the end of this human lane,
the British officers and their fair companions mounted the steps
of the mansion for an evening of dining, drinking and dancing,
followed by elaborate fireworks.

At midnight, when the gaiety was at its height, Allan Mc-
Lane added a scene not included in the brilliant André's script.
Creeping up close to the British lines, he injected a deeper, more
explosive note into the cheery popping of the Mischianza's
fireworks. McLane had one hundred and fifty men with him,
and they were backed up by a company of dragoons. McLane's
men carried a number of crude, homemade bombs—camp
kettles filled with powder and scrap iron. Dividing his troop
into small parties, McLane spread them out along the line of
abatis in front of the British works, and just when the festivi-
ties at the Wharton house were at their merry best, he gave the
signal that sent the camp kettles hurtling into the British lines,
there to explode in a whirring of deadly shrapnel. The detona-
tions, coming fast one upon the other, rattled the windows of
the Wharton mansion, and many an officer of the line was
summoned from the dance floor and hurried to the front in
pursuit of the brash McLane.

"The British," wrote Benson J. Lossing, early authority on
the Revolution, "beat the long alarm roll, and the assailants
were attacked and pursued by the strong guard along the line.
The officers at the fete managed to keep the ladies in ignorance
of the tumult without."

McLane, with his usual agility, eluded the pursuit and slipped
away in the night. This audacious foray probably prompted
the letter written to him in May, by Col. Alexander Scammell
from Washington's headquarters, which says: "I am very glad
you made so lucky and narrow an escape. Hope they will ever
fail in the same manner. However, as you can't but be sensible,
they'll use every method to entrap you possible, I nothing
doubt you will keep your usual good lookout."

Before this letter reached McLane, he had given headquarters and the entire Continental Army additional cause for
rejoicing.

Just at the time of Howe's Mischianza, Washington had
committed himself to a maneuver filled with potential disaster.
He had thrown the forces commanded by the Marquis de
Lafayette far forward in an exposed position at Barren Hill on
the Schuylkill River, only eleven miles from Philadelphia and
only two miles from the British outposts at Chestnut Hill. The
ostensible reason for the move was that Washington wanted a
protective screen in front of him, and he also wanted information on the possible evacuation of Philadelphia, reported imminent. But he gave Lafayette twenty-two hundred men, one-
third of the entire effective Continental Army—a force too
small to fight a major battle and far too large to have the fluidity
of movement necessary for scouting, a function much better
performed by McLane's troopers. Historians since have the-
orized that Lafayette, eager to distinguish himself, had persuaded Washington to let him have this independent command
and that the commander-in-chief, in this instance, had been
ruled not by his head but by his heart. In any event, one fact
was indisputable: Lafayette and his tiny force were thrust
perilously close to the British lines, almost like a nut resting
in the jaws of a nutcracker.

Howe, an experienced if dilatory general, could hardly believe his good fortune when word of Lafayette's exposed position was brought to him. It was daylight of May 19th, and
Howe had just been climbing into bed after a day-long, night-
long revel. When he heard the news, even the charms of his
favorite mistress, Mrs. Loring, couldn't keep him from the business of war. He promptly climbed out of bed, summoned his
staff, and ordered a new round of drinks. Then he sent out
invitations to his friends to come to dinner that night to meet
"the Boy," as he termed Lafayette.

To insure the presence of the guest of honor at his dinner

party, Howe turned out almost the entire British Army. His battle plan was drafted in the sound and familiar Howe pattern that, so far, had worked only on Long Island—a night march in three columns, a surprise at dawn with the Americans boxed in and backed up against the impassable Schuylkill in their rear. Confronted with overwhelming force, his escape routes to fords across the Schuylkill cut off, "the Boy" would have only one choice as Howe envisioned it—abject surrender.

The British march from Philadelphia began at ten-thirty on the evening of May 19th. At the outset, the sweeping envelopment proceeded with precision. General Grant with five thousand men and fifteen guns swept around to the north and rear of Lafayette, cutting the only known roads that led to the fords of the Schuylkill. A second force of two thousand men under General Grey gained their allotted post on Lafayette's left flank, prepared to attack at dawn. Both movements were completed successfully, with no alarm given. American troops whom Grant had encountered on the Whitemarsh Road as he marched to cut off the fords had simply retired before him— and hadn't even bothered to notify Lafayette, still serenely encamped on Barren Hill, unaware of his danger.

Fortune needed to favor Howe just once more, and Lafayette would be snared. It was only necessary for the third column, led by Howe and Clinton in person, to get into position unobserved for the surprise to be complete, for the trap to snap irrevocably shut.

This third column, comprising the bulk of the British force, was driving up the Ridge Road, intent on gaining position to smash in the front of Lafayette's lines in the dawn. But— British grenadiers had been sent up the road as patrols in advance of the main body, and at Three Mile Run, the ever alert Allan McLane, who hadn't even paused for rest after his bomb-throwing adventure the previous night, swooped out of the darkness and cut off and captured two of the grenadier scouts. McLane realized instantly that their presence on the road at that hour was unusual; he questioned them closely, and from them he learned enough to sense the massive movement of troops advancing up the road behind them. McLane immediately sensed the magnitude of the British plan, and his reaction was swift and spontaneous. He detached a Captain Parr, with a company of riflemen to skirmish with the head of the British column when it came into sight. Then, with the rest of his troop, he set out at a breakneck gallop to carry the warning to Lafayette at Barren Hill.

McLane's hard-pounding riders came thundering up the road from the south just as day was breaking. Hardly taking time to swing from the saddle, McLane started to inform Lafayette of his danger. As he did so, rifle shots from Parr's company crackled out along the Ridge Road in the distance, underlining the warning; and, at almost the same instant, a panting countryman came running into the camp to inform Lafayette that he had seen British troops on the Whitemarsh Road, circling toward the American rear, cutting off the escape to the fords.

The desperate nature of Lafayette's plight was instantly obvious, but the young marquis did not panic. Calmly, confidently, he drew up his troops in battle order; quietly, he sent out scouts in all directions, seeking a way out of the trap. Soon the scouts returned. They had found a way, a small opening in the tightening British net.

There was a road that didn't show on the maps of the day. It was little more than a narrow trace that popped over the edge of the bluff behind Lafayette's camp on Barren Hill. It dropped steeply to the river, and there it wound along concealed, out of sight of the main roads along which the British were advancing, until it reached Matson's Ford over the Schuylkill.

Lafayette seized his slim chance immediately. Actually, at that moment Grant with his five thousand British regulars was a lot closer to the ford than was Lafayette; but Grant was looking for the Americans, if they tried to escape, to come at him along the roads on the high ground. He might not even know about the sunken road along the very lip of the river, and he certainly could not see, because the high banks would veil it, the escape of troops moving along this trace to Matson's Ford.

Masking his intentions beautifully, Lafayette drew up a portion of his force on the heights as if prepared to offer desperate resistance to the attacking British; then, while the British formed in line of battle, he peeled companies off, one by one, and sent them scuttling over the brow of the bluff to the rear and along the hidden road to Matson's Ford. So swiftly and skillfully was the maneuver executed that Lafayette himself, bringing up the rear, had melted away with all his men and all his guns before the British snapped the jaws of their pincers and found the wings of their army advancing upon each other unopposed through a deserted camp.

In this final surge, one ludicrous incident occurred that seems to epitomize the entire adventure. A body of Clinton's dragoons, advancing up the Ridge Road toward the American lines, encountered a band of McLane's Oneida Indians. Both parties were mutually surprised. The Indians, unaccustomed to battling cavalry, leaped up in alarm, emitted terrifying warwhoops and yells—and fled. The dragoons, unaccustomed to fighting Indians, were equally alarmed at the frightful outburst of sound; their horses stampeded—and *they* fled. The two parties had struck mutual terror into each other and had taken to their heels in opposite directions without either having fired a shot.

Such was the inglorious end to Howe's grandiose plan. He had no "Boy" to entertain his guests at dinner. Instead, weary and bedraggled from their futile march, his troops returned to Philadelphia "ashamed and . . . laughed at for their ill success," as Lafayette noted exultantly in his memoirs. In the American camp, the mere fact that the British had been made to look ridiculous was cause for much rejoicing. Again Colonel Scammell wrote from headquarters, congratulating McLane.

"I am happy that you with your little party have conducted with so much honor to yourself," he wrote. "The Marquis effected a glorious retreat as well as a difficult one."

Such praise from headquarters became an almost daily routine in those frenetic weeks in the spring of 1778 when the British were about to evacuate Philadelphia and Allan McLane rode the forward lines constantly watchful, constantly on the prowl. He was a man who thrived on danger—and met it every day. Typical of the period was McLane's account in his journal of a "party of observation" on which he set out on June 8, 1778 with two dragoons.

Referring to himself in the third person, his invariable custom, McLane gave this description of the manner in which he suddenly found himself riding into a British trap:

"On his approach to the notorious place called The Rock, he encountered an Ambuscade of British Infantry, covered by a Troop of British Dragoons then posted between Bustletown and the road leading to Oxford Church. The two Horsemen following the Capt. Discovered the British Infantry. After the Capt. had passed to the right of the Enemy Ambuscade, [they] turned out of it, received a fire from the Enemies Infantry and retired, leaving the Capt. to his fate.

"The Infantry rose up from their concealment, ordered the Capt. to Dismount, but he put spurs to his Horse, preferring Death to being a prisoner."

Now began a series of desperate maneuvers on McLane's part, all aimed toward one end—escape.

The British infantry, seeing McLane galloping away, poured out a volley, and musket balls whizzed all around him. One came close enough to graze the rump of his horse, but McLane was lucky. Still determined to get away, he turned into an open field. On the opposite side of the field, however, the British cavalry was drawn up. And the infantry, reloading their muskets, streamed out of the underbrush, ran across the road

McLane had been riding on, and straggled out along the near edge of the field, cutting off his escape in that direction.

McLane was hemmed in. At this point, he rode toward the dragoons, as if he were about to surrender to them. As he went, he edged himself away from the infantry, out of range of another musket volley, and almost imperceptibly, he cantered to the left, toward the end of the dragoons' line. He maintained the pretense of being about to surrender until he was certain that he was well beyond the range of the infantry's fire; then, he suddenly clapped spurs to his horse and at a furious gallop shot through the gap at the end of the file of dragoons.

This daring, surprise maneuver carried him into the clear, and he gained the Oxford Road, with the dragoons pounding hard in pursuit. "This Squadron followed him in a Body to the Oxford Road," McLane wrote, "but Disparing of overtaking him with the troop, the Commander Detached two of the Seventeenth Regiment of British Light Horse. The Capt. Immediately lost sight of the Squadron, but the two gained on him . . ."

The chase continued for two miles along the Oxford Road, but with each thundering stride, the British troopers drew closer. Only by desperate stratagem could he now escape. The pursuit had pounded along the road to the vicinity of Shoemaker's Mills. Here was country hilly and wooded. McLane swerved suddenly from the road, bending low in his saddle as he galloped across broken ground and into the trees. The British troopers followed, close behind his laboring horse. Swords drawn, they shouted to him to surrender or be cut down.

McLane spurred his horse across the crest of a wooded hill. Momentarily concealed from his pursuers, he drew his pistols and thrust them out of sight in the breast of his coat. Then, down the flank of the hill, he pulled his horse to a sharp halt, and the animal stood, head down, puffing and blowing as if all but foundered. This was the tableau that greeted the eyes of the

British troopers as they charged across the brow of the hill and plunged downward, waving their swords and yelling in triumph.

Quietly, offering no resistance, McLane sat his horse, obviously waiting for the inevitable, his unused sword dangling against his hip. Sure that now, at last, he was ready to surrender, the British troopers galloped up on either side. The one on the left let his sword slip back into the sword strap. The one on the right followed suit, and as he came abreast of McLane, he reached out with his sword hand and grasped the Captain's right shoulder. Then, at the last possible second, McLane acted.

He whipped out one of the pistols concealed under his coat and fired its ball directly into the chest of the dragoon on his left. Whirling in his saddle, he used his free hand to grasp the sword of the dragoon on his right, and while this startled trooper struggled to grip the handle and wrench the blade clear, McLane rose in his stirrups and put the whole weight of his body behind two savage blows, crushing the skull of the dragoon with the lock and barrel of his discharged pistol, wielded like a club. The man crumpled forward, hanging insensible over the pommel of his saddle, and McLane rode clear.

Having disposed of both his enemies, he could easily have taken possession of their horses and accoutrement, had not he too been injured. In the struggle with the second dragoon, a deep gash had been inflicted on his hand by the sword he had grasped, and McLane began to feel faint from loss of blood. His horse was winded and somewhere far to the rear was the pursuing squadron, still perhaps doggedly on the trail. McLane needed quick refuge. Near him was a millpond, and McLane, dropping in exhaustion from his horse, tottered to this and immersed himself in the cold water. The iciness of the current eventually stopped the flow of blood from his wound, and in a little while a troop of his own horse, alerted by the two troopers who had fled, came looking for him.

The hairbreadth escape became one of the most celebrated of McLane's exploits. Added to his other recent adventures, it helped to make him a romantic figure, the hero of the army. Lafayette wrote him on June 12th: "I give you joy for your escape the other day, and the cleverness with which you dispatched two English Dragoons." And James Peale, one of the leading artists of the Revolution, commemorated the event with a colorful if not totally accurate canvas showing McLane clubbing the second dragoon over the head with the pursuing British squadron coming into sight around a bend in the road.

Just eight days after his clash with the dragoons, McLane ventured into the trap in the horse yard of the Rising Sun and galloped out, firing his pistol in a dragoon's face. And just two days after this, he was in Philadelphia—the first American soldier to re-enter the capital on the heels of the departing British.

It was an honor for which, apparently, he had been angling for some time. On June 3rd, James McHenry, an aide-de-camp of Washington, had written him that Washington had given permission for McLane to enter Philadelphia and check on his personal property there as soon as the British withdrew. But McHenry added two strange conditions: McLane was to turn over his command to "a proper officer" before he entered the city, and he was not to mention the fact that he had obtained this permission to anyone. Whatever the purpose of these seemingly pointless restrictions, it is obvious that McLane paid little attention to them.

He was still in command of his light horse, perhaps having found no "proper officer" to whom to turn over his men and perhaps not having tried very hard, when the hour came to return to Philadelphia. McLane got the first intimation of the British evacuation at daybreak on June 18th as he was scouting with his cavalry along the Schuylkill, almost in the environs of the city. One of his contacts in Philadelphia, a man named George Roberts, crossed by the Middle Ferry with the information that Sir Henry Clinton, the new British commander, had transported the last of his army across the Delaware to New Jersey for the march to New York. Through his glasses, from a rise of ground, McLane could see barges ferrying the last of the British regulars across the river in the bright morning light. He wasted no time waiting for orders. Gathering his entire troop, some hundred men, he crossed the Schuylkill and entered the city.

Galloping with drawn swords through Second Street, McLane's raiders surprised a group of British laggards. In an instant, McLane had the British penned in a ring of pistols and steel. The haul included a captain, a provost marshal, one of the army guides, and thirty enlisted men. All were captured without resistance, without the loss of a man. His prisoners secured, McLane pressed rapidly on, searching the streets; and at Ninth and South Streets, he came upon a second small body of British troops, snapped them up and then sat down to pen a hasty note to Washington.

This message evidently reached Valley Forge shortly after Roberts had brought first word of the evacuation; for Washington, who had been writing a short letter to the President of Congress about his plans for following the British into Jersey, appended a postscript: "A letter from Capt. McLane, dated in Philadelphia, this minute came to hand confirming the evacuation."

Washington had assigned the command of the American forces entering their reoccupied capital to Benedict Arnold, the hero of Saratoga. The choice was a fateful one as far as McLane personally was concerned.

Benedict Arnold's reputation as a field leader outshone that of any other general in the Continental Army. More than any other man, he had been responsible for Saratoga, the greatest victory of the war, the triumph that had resulted in the surrender of Gentleman Johnny Burgoyne and his entire army and that had led directly to the all-important alliance with France. Arnold, in achieving the victory, had had one leg shattered by a British musket ball at the Second Battle of Freeman's Farm. He was still incapacitated for the field, unable to stand without assistance; but there were cogent reasons for his being given the command of Philadelphia.

It was an honor intended to atone for multiple wrongs. Though Arnold's genius on the field had made him the Patton of his day and had won him the admiration of the army, he had been shabbily treated by some of the time-serving politicians in Congress. Lesser men of nondescript, indeed imperceptible talents, had been promoted over his head; and Arnold, whose fatal defect was that he could never rise above his own interests, had been mortally wounded in that most tender of his qualities, his self-esteem. Only his supreme achievement at Saratoga had at last brought him deserved recognition, and Washington, recognizing the unpalatability of grudging and long-delayed reward, understandably sought to atone by salving with honor the ego of a general whose unique talents meant so much to the patriot cause.

For these reasons, he had appointed Arnold to the command of Philadelphia on May 28, 1778, and Arnold had taken the oath of office as military governor two days later. It is not known just when the two tempestuous fighters, Benedict Arnold and Allan McLane, first met and clashed. But the aversion each felt for the other appears to have been instinctive.

Ironically, both were men who suffered the same neglect, the same injustice when rewards and honors were apportioned; but under the pressures of humiliation and hurt pride, they reacted as their different natures dictated and pursued diametrically opposite paths. Arnold, the supreme egoist to whom only Arnold mattered, a battlefield hero corrupted by vanity and venality, was to become a traitor; McLane, a prideful man, too, but a patriot so dedicated to an ideal that he sacrificed for it the whole of his private fortune, was to become hurt, bitter, resentful—but was to remain steadfast.

The genesis of these separate destinies lay in the duel of distrust that broke out between Arnold and McLane almost the instant that Philadelphia fell. The day after McLane entered the city, on June 19th, Arnold himself led the main body of the American forces into the repossessed capital. Instantly, he closed the shops and put the city under martial law to guard against rioting and looting; at the same time, with the instinct of a commander born to battle, he could not refrain from attempting to learn what went on over the river, where the British had retreated into the pine barrens of South Jersey. And so Arnold summoned McLane and sent him across the Delaware to follow the trail of the vanishing foe.

The cavalry captain, in a bitter note in his journal, intimates that, even this early, Arnold was anxious to be rid of him and sent him quickly out of the city with faulty information about the route and location of the British force, possibly in the hope and expectation that he wouldn't come back.

"The General wished the Capt. to cross the Delaware and ascertain the rout of the Enemy assuring the Capt. that they had marched from Haddonfield that morning," McLane wrote. "A guide was procured and the Capt. crossed into Jersey, and on his approach to Haddonfield in the night, found himself surrounded by the British encampment, and only escaped being taken [here the final, acidulous phrase has been crossed out, but is still legible] by the great judgment of the General."

McLane gave no further details about the manner in which he extricated himself. But it is obvious that he kept his wits about him and that his iron nerve helped him overcome the shock of having blundered into the heart of the entire British Army; for he walked through the British encampment in the night, slipped past the forward lines and pressed on to join Gen. Philemon Dickinson, commanding the New Jersey militia.

The information that he had gleaned helped Washington, already on the way by forced marches from Valley Forge, to chart the route of Clinton's army across New Jersey on its way to the protection of the British fleet at Sandy Hook. Washington decided to head off Clinton, and the result was a massive collision of the two armies at Monmouth Court House, near Freehold. The battle, fought on June 26th in one-hundred-degree heat, was fierce and indecisive. The Americans were left in possession of the field and claimed the victory; but the British, whose only aim had been to make good their retreat, succeeded in slipping away and continuing their march to New York.

McLane and his cavalrymen fought with Dickinson's militia and after the battle harried the rear and flanks of the retreating army. McLane noted in his journal that his troop picked up "more than 300" British stragglers at a loss of just four men killed at Monmouth.

Now came the turning point in McLane's career. Some of his greatest contributions to the cause of Independence were still to come, but they were to be made not by a man hailed as the hero of the army but by a man whose career was in virtual eclipse. Up to the moment of Monmouth, it is safe to say that McLane had established himself as Washington's favorite raider, the foremost light-cavalry captain in the army. His record showed a succession of brilliant feats that outshone the reputations of even such swashbuckling rivals as Henry (Light-Horse Harry) Lee. The future should have held only the brightest of prospects; but McLane, back in Philadelphia after the Battle of Monmouth, came into head-on conflict with the one man who, more than any other, appears to have been his personal nemesis—Benedict Arnold.

Ever a swaggerer, Arnold cut a gaudy figure as the military commander of the reclaimed capital. Almost as soon as he entered the city, he set himself up in style in the John Penn mansion that had served as the headquarters of Howe. Here Arnold reigned even as Howe had reigned, with a retinue of liveried servants and a coach-and-four. Yet Arnold was possessed of no personal fortune; his only visible and legitimate

income was derived from his salary and expense allowance as a
major general—three hundred and thirty-two dollars a month in
Continental currency, a dubious medium then worth only
about one-third its face value.

Obviously, even the hero of Saratoga could not maintain
such an extravagant scale of living unless he was soiling his
fingers with dirty money. And Arnold was.

On June 23rd, just four days after he entered the capital,
Arnold enmeshed himself in an unsavory deal. He signed a contract that made him a partner of James Mease, clothier general
of the Continental Army, and Mease's deputy, William West,
in an unconscionable scheme of war profiteering.

The situation was this: when the British evacuated the city,
they left a considerable quantity of stores of all kinds behind
them. The Continental Army and the patriots who had fled the
city and had spent a winter of privation in the hinterlands had
desperate need of all kinds of food, clothing and equipment.
With supplies abandoned by the British on hand and needs so
acute, the temptation to indulge in wholesale plundering was
tremendous, and recognizing this, Washington had ordered
Arnold to seize all the abandoned British stores and hold them
until Congress and Pennsylvania officials could decide what
to do with them. Arnold had carried out this order his first day
in the city, but the delicate question of the ultimate disposition
of the stores remained. And because it did, influential insiders
who were willing to use official position for private gain were
presented with a rare opportunity to reap a golden harvest.

The high-living Arnold certainly needed this windfall, and
so he made himself the partner of Mease and West in this
scheme: Mease, in his official position as clothier general and
using public credit, was to buy up entire lots of commodities
left by the departing British. First, he was to sell the army under
Arnold what supplies it wanted, billing it of course for the con-
signments. Then the remainder of the goods—and it is obvious

that this remainder from each individual lot could be conveniently bulky—could be sold to the needy public at high prices and for the mutual profit of Mease, West, and Arnold.

Philadelphians, watching the flow of scarce and costly commodities through the hands of this combine, became suspicious of Arnold's role, but they were handicapped at the time by the lack of positive proof. This absence of formal evidence, however, did not deter Allan McLane. He became one of Arnold's most caustic and outspoken critics. Back in Philadelphia after Monmouth, the cavalryman who had dipped heavily into his own private fortune to enlist and equip his company, whose wife had ripped up her best tablecloths for cavalry breeches, was shocked to find the gilded but impecunious Arnold living the way a good patriot should not, lording it like a monarch and associating on the friendliest terms with some of the most suspect Tory families in the capital.

One association in particular seems to have attracted the jaundiced eye of McLane. This was Arnold's courtship of blonde, willowy, eighteen-year-old Peggy Shippen, daughter of a Philadelphia jurist with Royalist leanings and one of the reigning belles of the city during the British occupation. The vivacious Peggy had been much courted by the dashing Major John André, and she and her two sisters were to have been princesses in the pageant of André's farewell Mischianza for Howe. Their attendance had been cancelled at the last moment, it is said, when their staid father discovered the scantiness of the costumes in which they had been expected to display their charms. Peggy stormily rebelled at the stern paternal decree that kept her from the Mischianza's gaieties, but her absence had its compensations. When the Americans returned to Philadelphia, the beauties who had fraternized with the enemy at the Mischianza were regarded as socially leprous; but Peggy Shippen, fortunate victim of a stern parent, was under no such interdiction and soon met and captivated Arnold. The warrior and the girl half his age came to an understanding, and on April 8, 1779, Peggy Shippen became Arnold's second wife—and, almost instantly, his partner in betrayal.

Into this tangled web of courtship and wartime profiteering, Allan McLane charged headlong, with much the same impetuosity he exhibited on the battlefield. With his intimate knowledge of Philadelphia, with the espionage contacts that had proved so invaluable to Washington in the winter of Valley Forge, he set himself the risky task of gathering all the information that he could about the suspect activities of his commanding general. Just how much specific evidence he uncovered is not clear. McLane always insisted that he had information enough at this time to expose Arnold's treachery if Washington had only listened to him; but he set down no detailed account of his knowledge, and the dividing line between the specific facts he may have gathered and the suspicions that he certainly harbored becomes a hazy one at best.

In the McLane papers in the New York Historical Society, there is a carefully preserved copy of the Arnold-Mease-West profiteering contract. As far as is known, this document was not discovered until a thorough investigation was made of Arnold's affairs following his exposure and flight to the British in 1780. McLane seems to have preserved the copy of the contract as proof of how right he had been. Across the bottom of the document, in his angular scrawl, McLane appended this personal note:

"Capt. McLane entered the city of Philadelphia before Arnold, and if Genl Washington had ever given full credit to McLane's ideas of Arnold, the traitor would not have placed the Genl in the situation he did in 1780."

This episode was the turning point in McLane's career. In gathering information about the activities of Arnold, he courted the displeasure of that powerful commander. This was risky enough for a subordinate, but the greatly daring Allan McLane did not stop there. Having assembled the available facts, he risked his entire future by denouncing Arnold to Washington.

Such a procedure has never been recommended for military subordinates. And McLane was no fool. He certainly must have realized the meaningful disparity in rank between a cavalry captain and a general of Arnold's stature; he must have been aware that, in attacking Arnold, he courted personal retribution and ruin. A more cautious man, a man more motivated by self-interest never would have committed such a strategic error. He would have kept his mouth shut and watched out for his own career while he let events take their course. Such prudence was not for Allan McLane; with the fiery dedication to ideals and the impassioned patriotism that were his personal hallmarks, he went trumpeting over the head of Arnold in the summer of 1778 and laid his charges at the feet of Washington.

He stressed what he knew of the Mease-West deal and outlined his darker suspicions of Arnold's treachery. Washington was shocked. The commander-in-chief recognized Arnold's personal foibles, but he recognized equally well Arnold's military genius. It was inconceivable to him that the man who had charged with such fury into the mouths of British cannon at Saratoga could be tainted with disloyalty. Outraged at the mere suggestion, Washington blew down his presumptuous cavalry captain with a rebuke so stinging that the memory of it rankled throughout McLane's life, as repeated references in his papers make clear.

At one point, McLane wrote: "Thus it was the Great Washington's [incredulity?] as to Arnold and other pretenders of these Days [which] favored much the Enemy's plans, bribery and corruption."

As far as one can tell today, it would seem that McLane, in his detestation of Arnold, must have been anticipating events, in 1778. British headquarters records, made available to the public only in the last twenty-five years, indicate that Arnold's first overture to sell himself came about the first of May, 1779, less than a month after his marriage to Peggy Shippen. It was then he approached Joseph Stansbury, proprietor of a glass and china shop on Front Street in Philadelphia. Stansbury, unsuspected by the Americans at the time, was actually a secret British agent; and as soon as he realized Arnold was for hire, he made a hurried trip to New York to inform André. A major mystery still is: How was Arnold aware of Stansbury's secret and traitorous connection? The answer appears to be that Peggy Shippen, who knew André well, guided her bridegroom's steps to the proper go-between.

In the circumstances, it is intriguing to find a brief and cryptic note in the McLane collection that seems to hint the cavalryman may have had some fairly accurate knowledge of Arnold's negotiations with the British and perhaps some suspicion about the intermediaries through whom the contact was established and maintained.

The note appears on an order for the purchase of horses dated January 19, 1779. One of McLane's idiosyncrasies, baffling to modern researchers, was his practice of snatching the most available piece of paper—an old order form, a letter that had been written to him by someone else, a requisition or report—and on it dashing off the thought currently uppermost in his mind. He never bothered to date these jottings, and so there is no way of knowing whether they were written weeks, months or years after the date that appears on the already once-used paper. The provocative notation on the January 19, 1779 order form, slashed down with such vehemence as to be partly indecipherable, obviously must have been penned at a considerably later date, for it refers to the marriage of Peggy Shippen and Arnold in April.

"After Arnold married Miss Shippen," McLane wrote, "he opened a correspondence with the Enemy in New York and M'Lane was suspected for having the Clue, and while Arnold commanded in Philadelphia—"

Here the writing becomes sputteringly unintelligible. There

appear to be references to a co-witness, to Tories, and to some plan by Arnold to hale McLane into court, presumably for the captain's comments about the general's profiteering. At the end, the note simmers down into legibility with this comment:

"Genl Washington protected him [McLane] or he would have been abused for doing his duty."

Such is the record of McLane's bitter clash with Arnold. Whether McLane really possessed "the Clue" or Arnold merely feared that he did probably can never be determined. Whether McLane, had Washington listened, really could have substantiated his charges and forestalled the shock of Arnold's betrayal in 1780 must remain a subject for conjecture. Only one thing seems clear. The acrimonious controversy, at the time, did far more damage to McLane than it did to Arnold, his commanding general. Prior to this, McLane had galloped a steadily ascending road to fame, one breath-taking action following close upon another; after this, though action was still his destiny, the trails all led to obscurity.

Obviously, a captain who accuses his general of profiteering and treason poses a difficult personnel problem for his superiors. While there is no definite evidence to show that McLane's eclipse stemmed directly from his feud with Arnold, the life-long bitterness that he exhibited about the affair may be an indication that he himself thought so. One thing is certain: prior to the conflict with Arnold, McLane had given conclusive evidence of his worth as an independent commander of guerilla troops; proving himself on scores of desperate missions, he had been alert and indefatigable as a scout, adept at espionage and intrigue, a never-sleeping eyes and ears of the army; afterward, he was never again to hold independent command.

In the reorganization of the army, McLane's guerilla company was re-attached on June 1, 1779 to the Delaware regiment, then stationed at Middlebrook, New Jersey. The reason officially assigned was that battle and the rigors of ceaseless campaigning had reduced the company to a mere nine commissioned and non-commissioned officers and twenty men. Valid as the excuse appeared on paper, it must be borne in mind that Washington had never hesitated to reinforce McLane by sending him detachments of a hundred troopers when it was desired to keep McLane in an independent command on the forward lines; now there were to be no more such reinforcements and, quite obviously, there was no longer the wish to give the mettlesome McLane the free-roving privileges of a guerilla leader.

Instead, Light-Horse Harry Lee acquired the freedom of action denied McLane and became McLane's commander. Lee, like McLane, had been a cavalry captain. Up to this point he had performed well though far less brilliantly than McLane; but he was one of the Virginia Lees and he had valuable political connections in Congress. The result was that he had been promoted to major by Congress in April, 1778, and had been given authority to form an independent partisan corps. It had been intimated to Lee at that time that McLane's company might be assigned to him, and this move was finally made on June 9, 1779 in an order issued by Washington. The arrangement appeared at the time, on the surface at least, to be mutually satisfactory to both men, but on the still-preserved June 9th order in the McLane papers there is another characteristic, undated McLane note, reading: "This was a death blow to McLane's military career. His pride was a separate command."

Whether this note accurately reflects the feelings of McLane at the time or is a considered post-mortem set down much later, the initial collaboration of Lee and McLane led directly to one of the most dramatic feats of arms of the entire war— the storming of Stony Point.

The British, in a thrust up the Hudson, had seized a great rocky promontory jutting out into the river from the west bank, and had proceeded to fortify it heavily. Washington, alarmed by the development, moved his army from Middle-brook up the Hudson to guard against what he feared might be a new attempt by Clinton in New York to advance up the river and split the Colonies in half. Stony Point in British hands nettled and disturbed Washington; he would have liked to re-capture it, but so strong was the position that he lamented all he could do was to "endeavor to prevent a further progress on the river, and make the advantages of what they the British have now gained as limited as possible."

It was important, however, to keep a close eye on what the British were doing at Stony Point, and Washington dispatched Lee and McLane to prowl the surrounding countryside and gather information. In regular reports to headquarters, Lee described what appeared to be the overwhelming strength of the fortification. The fort itself was triangular in shape, located on the peak of the point's rocky eminence and protected by a double line of abatis. The only approach was across a narrow neck and low-lying, marshy ground, and in the embrasures of the fort, the British were mounting twelve- and twenty-four-pounder cannon, some smaller guns, a howitzer and two mor-tars. Washington, studying the details and realizing the fortifi-cation was not yet complete, began to feel a faint stirring of hope, and on June 28th, he instructed Lee to send a spy inside the fort to get exact information on the progress of the work and the size of the garrison.

Almost inevitably, the man selected for this delicate task was none other than Allan McLane—already known after a few weeks with Lee as the "most active officer" in Lee's corps.

The drama of the event is completely lost in the laconic, routine note that McLane jotted down in his diary. It reads: "Friday the 2 July—By Genl. Washington's orders went in with a flag to conduct Mrs. Smith to see her sons."

Fortunately, Alexander Garden, in writing his *"Anecdotes of the Revolutionary War,"* obtained from McLane himself a more vivid and detailed account of all that was entailed in the use of a flag of truce to camouflage an expert piece of espionage. McLane, Garden says, dressed for a role. He donned a hunting shirt and leggings, slung a powder horn over his shoulder and carried a long rifle—the complete accoutrement of the backwoodsman. Then he slouched into the fort, enacting the role of an ignorant country bumpkin escorting a mother through the lines on a visit to her sons, employed on the fortifications.

All the time that McLane was impersonating a back-country hick, however, his alert eyes were roving about the unfinished fortification and absorbing details. A young British officer, having no suspicion of the caliber of man with whom he dealt, decided to have some sport with the visitor. This is Garden's version of the conversation:

"Well, Captain, what do you think of our fortress? Is it strong enough to keep Mister Washington out?"

"I know nothing of these matters," McLane protested. "I am but a woodsman and can only use my rifle, but I guess the General—General, mind you, not Mister—would be likely to think a bit before he would run his head against such works as these. If I was a general, sure I am that I would not attempt to take it, though I had 50,000 men."

"And if General Washington—since you insist on his being styled General—should ever have the presumption to attempt it, he will come to rue his rashness, for this post is the Gibraltar of America, and defended by British valor, must be deemed impregnable," the British officer declaimed.

"No doubt, no doubt," McLane agreed, "but trust me, we are not such dolts as to attempt impossibilities, so that as far as we are concerned, you may sleep in security."

Leaving the British officer undisturbed in his smug feeling of invincibility, McLane quitted the works with the visiting mother and his flag of truce. Rejoining Lee, he promptly reported that the entrenchments needed to connect several of the batteries with the inner fort were incomplete and the place could easily be stormed. This word was relayed to Washington, who rode to the scene and reconnoitered the works himself on July 6th, well-protected by the screening cavalry of McLane and Lee. The attack was determined upon, and a special corps was organized down river under Maj. Gen. Mad Anthony Wayne to make a surprise nighttime assault on the "Gibraltar of America." To keep any hint of the preparations from leaking to the British, Lee and McLane lay in the surrounding woods day and night, keeping a tight noose drawn about the fort. So thorough were they that every dog in the surrounding countryside was summarily executed, lest an ill-timed bark should alert the British to the approach of Wayne's force.

McLane's diary describes the climactic action in these words:

"Thursday, July 15th—This morning mustered my company at Hutchins' house—at ten o'clock rode with Majors Posey and Lee to reconnoitre the enemy's lines—Genl Waine moved down from the forest to the ground near the lines—at 8 o'clock at night moved my company close to the enemy's sentrys in order to intercept intelligence—at 30 minutes past 12 o'clock the light infantry began the attack on the lines, Genl Waine at their head—they rushed on with fixed bayonets and carried the line in 25 minutes . . ."

The British, completely surprised in their Gibraltar, aroused from sleep with the bayonets of Wayne's men almost at their throats, lost sixty-three killed, more than seventy wounded and 543 captured. The prisoners were all marshaled under McLane's guard. Among them was the British officer who had had such sport needling the backwoods bumpkin. "McLane assured me," Garden wrote, "that when recognized by the officer, it would have been impossible to give a just idea of his surprise and confusion."

This signal victory, brilliantly conceived, flawlessly executed, came at a time when the long war was dragging spirits low, and it had a tonic effect out of all proportion to the military advantage that had been gained. Wayne's bayonet charge upon British regulars in a fortified position that had been considered impregnable represented a military achievement without parallel in the fighting annals of the day. Understandably, the patriots exulted. Congress hailed the news of Stony Point with a laudatory resolution; it awarded Wayne a gold medal and handed out lesser rewards to his principal officers. Overlooked in the heroic frenzy was the man who had made it all possible, Allan McLane. Overlooked, too, was his commander, Light-Horse Harry Lee.

For the high-spirited Lee, avid for recognition and glory, this was an intolerable situation. He began to look about him for a second Stony Point—one that would make the name of Lee famous. In his scouting west of the Hudson, his attention had been attracted by a British outpost known as Paulus—or Powles—Hook, a low-lying sandy spit jutting out into the Hudson from what is now Jersey City, directly opposite the New York shore. The position, in its way, was almost as strong as Stony Point, and it had an additional dramatic advantage: it lay virtually under the noses of Clinton's garrison in New York, so close to the overwhelming thousands in the main British Army that an attack upon it would represent the supreme audacity.

The role that McLane had fulfilled for Washington at Philadelphia, for Washington and Wayne at Stony Point, he now repeated for the glory-hunting Lee. For weeks, he led his hard-riding troop up and down the countryside, traveling light, fast and incessantly; scouting the lay of the land and gathering precise data on Paulus Hook for Lee's headquarters at Paramus.

The Hook, though not as craggily impressive as Stony Point, was nevertheless a formidable outpost. It was virtually an island, connected with the mainland by wide, boggy salt marshes crossed by a single, miry road. A creek, fordable in only two places at low tide, and a deep ditch, running across the entire neck of the peninsula and spanned by a drawbridge, further isolated the garrison in its fortifications. These consisted of a circular redoubt, about one hundred fifty feet in diameter, standing on a slight elevation in the middle of the enclosure. It mounted six heavy guns. Near it to the northeast was another redoubt oblong in plan, mounting three twelve-pounders and one eighteen. The drawbridge, which provided the only entrance to the works, was protected by a solid blockhouse and breastworks, the riverside was guarded by still another blockhouse and more breastworks, and the whole was ringed with heavy abatis jutting up from the water level.

Lee believed that the Hook could be surprised and stormed, and he begged Washington to let him make the attempt. The commander-in-chief had some misgivings, but as he studied the information that McLane gathered and Lee relayed to him, he gradually weakened and finally yielded to the importunities of Lee. In doing so, however, he made one stipulation: there must be no attempt to bring off the cannon and plunder from the fort; the raiding force must hit and run in almost the same instant, before the British could organize their far superior forces and turn victory into a trap and a disaster.

The attack was set for the night of August 18–19, 1779, and as the time drew near, McLane concentrated his attention on the immediate vicinity of the fort, drawing a cavalry noose about its landward side and grabbing everyone who tried to go in or come out. His vigilance, as usual, was rewarded. He succeeded in picking up a British deserter, and from him gained precise information about the strength of the garrison, depleted at the time to something under three hundred men. With this news, he arranged a rendezvous with Lee, as he later wrote, "in order to conduct him to attack Powles Hook."

Lee's attacking force, as originally organized, consisted of one hundred Virginians on the right, two Maryland companies in the center, and one hundred Virginians and McLane's dismounted troopers on the left, where Lee himself was to command. In the van at the head of each column were to be three "forlorn hopes"—"suicide squads," we'd call them today—desperado units led by daring officers whose job was to cut through the abatis and open gaps through which the attacking files could drive to put the British garrison to the bayonet.

The forward movement began at 10:30 on the morning of August 18th when Lee left his camp in Paramus, taking a number of wagons with him as a blind to delude any Tory snoopers into the belief that he was heading a mere foraging expedition. At first, all went well. Lee arrived at his rendezvous with Mc-Lane and the Virginia contingents at the New Bridge across the Hackensack River, just fourteen miles from the Hook; and at four o'clock in the afternoon, the united force set out on what should have been a routine march that would have brought them into the attack at Wayne's favorite time, half an hour after midnight. But now, suddenly, everything went wrong.

The guide who had been engaged to direct the footsteps of the raiders, either through stupidity or treachery, got them well lost in thickly forested country, delaying the march for three hours. In addition, dissension and jealousy rent the little party. Major Jonathan Clark, commanding the one hundred men from Woodford's Virginia brigade, who were to compose the right wing, was aggrieved at being placed under the command of Lee, his junior in rank. Though he continued with Lee and personally performed well, his dissatisfaction and the dissatisfaction of some of the other officers evidently communicated itself to the troops. Perhaps because of this, or possibly out of disgust at the way the enterprise was bumbling off the trail in the dark, about half of the Virginians abandoned the line of march and faded away in the night. This left only a handful of Virginians, the Marylanders and McLane's troop to carry out the assault, and this depleted force faced further hazards from bad timing. It was 4 A.M. instead of 12:30 when they reached the edge of the salt marshes before the fort; dawn would soon break, reducing the chances of surprise; and a rising tide threatened almost momentarily to make the ditch impassable.

Undismayed in the face of the increased odds, Lee refused to abandon the enterprise on which he had set his heart and his hopes. He detached Lt. Michael Rudulph of McLane's troop to reconnoiter. Rudulph quickly reported back that the ditch was still fordable, that the garrison was still apparently asleep. Lee acted at once. He ordered his men to take off their hats and hold them against their hips to make certain that no one had a free hand to reach for a trigger; he ordered them to leave their muskets unprimed and to go in, relying solely on cold steel.

The defection of the Virginians necessitated a rearrangement of the battle plan. Instead of a simultaneous attack by three columns, Lee settled for two, with the Marylanders in the center being held as a reserve. Major Clark, with the remaining Virginians, would lead on the right; McLane and Capt. Robert Forsyth of Lee's corps would drive in from the left. The forlorn hopes to cut through the abatis would be headed by Lt. Archibald McAllister on the right, and Lt. Rudulph, of McLane's troop, on the left.

The men waded by files through the marshy land and into the breast-deep waters of the ditch. Across this they pressed toward the fangs of the abatis. The splashing that they made as they crossed finally aroused the nodding sentinels. A musket was discharged, followed by another, and then a rattle of sporadic musketry fire from the blockhouses. The shooting was wild and inaccurate; as musket balls whirred harmlessly overhead, Lieutenant McAllister and his men hacked through the abatis almost without pause and charged into the fort, seizing the nearest redoubt and striking the colors. McLane and Forsyth were only a few seconds behind him, slashing their way in from the left. In the space of a few short and bloody moments, it was all over. Of the garrison, some fifty fell to the bayonet; 158 were taken prisoner. Only the commander, Major William

Sutherland, and some forty Hessians holed up in one of the remaining blockhouses and refused to surrender. For the Americans, it was an almost bloodless coup, accomplished at the unbelievably low cost of two men killed and three wounded.

There was not time, however, to exult over the victory. Alarm guns were thundering from the New York shore; in minutes, British columns would be forming to cut off the daring raiders. There was no time to storm the remaining blockhouse, no time even to spike the captured guns. Herding his prisoners in the center of the little force, Lee concentrated on making good his precipitate retreat. Once away from the Hook he split his party into three divisions, marching by separate routes. He drove his exhausted men relentlessly and finally succeeded in eluding pursuit and bringing off all his captives, fighting a rearguard, skirmishing action with pursuing British forces.

The dashing enterprise, like Wayne's storming of Stony Point, had little actual military value, but its effect on morale was enormous. Lee had tweaked the British nose virtually on the threshold of New York, and "the country resounded with his praise." He was voted the thanks of Congress and a gold medal to match Wayne's; McAllister and Rudulph were brevetted captains; and fifteen thousand dollars in Continental currency was appropriated to be distributed among the soldiery. Unhappily, this was not the only side to the story.

The dissension in the Virginia ranks, which had nearly wrecked the adventure, led to the preferment of charges against Lee by envious fellow officers. He was court-martialed and throughly vindicated, but the necessity of defending himself in his moment of triumph left a bad taste. Even worse, Congress went out of its way virtually to slap in the face other gallant officers who had contributed materially to the success of Paulus Hook. Chief among these was McLane. To a large degree, the victory had been made possible by his ceaseless activity and intelligent scouting, and he had been one of the first men inside the fort, at the head of the attacking left wing. But a resolution which would have honored and thanked him, along with half a dozen other officers, was voted down by Congress, even though it carried no appropriation, entailed no cost for medals. Understandably, the snub rankled. To a sensitive man like McLane, who already had grounds to feel that promotion and preferment were passing him by, it was a gratuitous insult—one for which, rightly or wrongly, he appears in large measure to have blamed Lee.

McLane apparently felt that Lee was capitalizing on his own hard-riding activity on the forward lines; that Lee was snatching all the glory and, unwilling to brook a rival, was shoving him deliberately into the background. Undeniably, a major flaw in Lee's character was a strong streak of personal vanity; it was this that was to result in feuds and jealousies when he commanded the Legion in the South. In the end he was to resign from the army, almost in petulance, despite the importunities of his commander, Nathanael Greene, who pleaded his need and begged Lee to stay. Perhaps nothing shows the difference between McLane and Lee more than this—that Lee could ignore such a plea and, nursing his wounded feelings, quit and go home. Had the situation been reversed, had McLane and not Lee commanded the Legion, it is almost inconceivable that anything short of a formal order could have gotten McLane, no matter how much his feelings were injured, out of the war; as it was, rebuffed, bypassed, unjustly treated as he felt himself to be, he stayed and fought as long as there was any possible need for his services, and his bitterest gripes came when he suspected there was a conspiracy to keep him away from the fighting.

Such a suspicion arose in his mind when Lee tried to shelve him early in 1781 and keep him from participating in the war in the South. The two officers had collaborated in early 1780 in a raid on the British garrison at Sandy Hook. After this success, Lee evidently tried to assign McLane to what McLane considered menial duties. "After the affair at Sandy Hook,"

McLane later wrote, "Lee attempts to throw McLane out of his element. Active service."

Lee wanted his fiery helper to go to Delaware to recruit. McLane protested vigorously and apparently carried his fight over Lee's head in an appeal to Washington. The commander-in-chief tried to settle matters by separating the two officers, who obviously could no longer get along with each other. He detached McLane and ordered him to join Maj. Gen. Benjamin Lincoln, then preparing for the defense of Charleston, South Carolina.

Even this judicious decisioin did not smooth the troubled waters. As McLane later wrote, "Lee contrived to retard McLane's march 'till after Lincoln capitulated in May, 1780." While one might have thought that McLane owed Lee at least a grudging debt of gratitude for keeping him away from the ill-fated Lincoln and out of a British prison camp, McLane didn't think so; what galled him was that he had been deprived of an opportunity to fight.

He was kept busy for some months scouting the countryside near Portsmouth and Norfolk in Virginia, and in July he rejoined Washington's Army in New Jersey, still assigned to the command of Lee. Once more McLane and his troop galloped the Bergen County countryside, gathering information on what the British were planning in New York across the Hudson. McLane, with all his old facility, established spy contacts with patriot sympathizers inside New York, and in September he learned from these sources that "there was a grand movement in the enemies camp and at headquarters on York Island." The objective of this "grand movement" wasn't clear at the time, but it became shockingly obvious on September 23, 1780, when Major John André was captured returning from the traitorous conference at which Benedict Arnold had agreed to turn West Point over to a British expedition.

Thus McLane, who had suffered for his audacity in trying to convince Washington two years earlier that Arnold was not to be trusted, was on hand to pick up the first distant rumbles caused by Arnold's projected treachery. He commented in his journal, with evident self-satisfaction, on his "vigilance and success" in obtaining information; and he quite evidently felt that Lee was jealous of this success and was determined to brook no rival in "the augmentation of Lee's Legion." For Lee had been promoted to lieutenant colonel and was building his force into a full-scale legion to join Nathanael Greene in the South. His patience, never his strong point, was doubtless sorely tried by his difficult subordinate, and he put into operation the plan that McLane had foiled previously: he got McLane out of his sight by sending him to Maryland to recruit.

McLane's personal situation was certainly not an enviable one. The promotion to major, which he would seem to have earned by his activities in the winter of Valley Forge, still was not his. Younger and less tried officers were being promoted over his head, and he noted with a jaundiced eye that Congress, eager to please our French allies, gave foreign officers promotions and commands that it denied to patriots like McLane who had proved their worth on many a hard-won field.

Furious at the prospect of being relegated to the backwash of the war, he wrote Lee a bitter protest. Lee, without comment, forwarded the letter to Washington. The commander-in-chief, whose tact and understanding were constantly and infinitely tested in ruling over his testy brood of officers, especially with the additional handicaps imposed by a bumbling Congress, attempted to soothe McLane with a letter commending him for his services, agreeing that he merited promotion—but pointing out that many others in the service did, too. This soft answer did not appease McLane. He saw the war passing him by, and he was incensed at the injustice of it all—especially so when he discovered that Lee had marched into the Carolinas without him, having reorganized the Legion "by leaving M'Lane out of the arrangement on half-pay for life."

A hatred of Lee that was to be second only to his hatred of Benedict Arnold now welled up in McLane. For the rest of his life, irate notations reveal the depth of his venom. One of the first and most furious of his denunciations is scrawled on the back of an order for the impressment of vessels for the public service. The order was dated July 17, 1780, and on it McLane wrote: "Henry Lee is a monster and Washington is deceived by him."

In another impassioned and almost indecipherable note, McLane summed up the whole of his grievance. The comment is dashed across the bottom of a brief letter from Lee, dated January 20, 1781, and was apparently written while McLane was recruiting in Annapolis, Maryland. While one has to guess at some words from the tenor of the rest, the sentiment is unmistakably clear. The note, with this essential deciphering, reads:

"Lee continues to slap at me. I must purchase horses and not serve Gen. Greene. Monster. Monster. O Washington, I deserve better treatment. I have served my country faithfully on the field of battle and found myself before Lee was known as a soldier. He plucked the laurels from my brow at Stony Point at Paulus Hook at Sandy Hook at Portsmouth in Virginia and now an opportunity for exert(ion) in the Carolinas. I am detached to recruit and the Legion—Gracious heaven that I had fallen in battle."

The fury at Lee that seethes in these lines was never to simmer much below the boiling point. Years afterwards, when Lee wrote his memoirs, McLane read them and noted with scorn that Lee had described the manner in which he spent a frigid winter night pacing the Palisades above the Hudson waiting for word from a spy in New York. McLane commented acidly that Lee never kept the forward lines in such weather; Lee, he said, much preferred "wine and whist" to such rigorous duty.

A man filled with such burning resentment obviously could not have been the easiest subordinate in the world to control. If the case rested on McLane's word alone, one might be justified in thinking that McLane was probably more to blame than Lee. But there are some pretty solid indications that McLane, testy though he may have been, retained the unwavering respect of his fellow officers and of Washington. One of those fellow officers, Alexander Garden of Lee's Legion, was to write of him forty years after the Revolution in these glowing terms: "I know of no individual, of his rank in the army, who engaged in such a variety of perilous adventures, or who so invariably brought them to a happy issue, as Allan McLane." Washington, quite evidently, held McLane in similar esteem, for he went out of his way to rescue the chafing cavalryman from the shelf on which Lee had put him and, in so doing, to entrust him with his most important mission of the war.

The preliminary step was the final and belated severing of the relationship between McLane and Lee. McLane noted with satisfaction that he "got out of Maj. Lee's trap by prevailing on Washington to attach him to Baron Steuben's command." Steuben was then stationed in Williamsburg, Virginia. Not only was McLane liberated for active service and sent to join Steuben, but now, years late, he finally got his much-coveted promotion to major. While he held the rank, he appears to have had no regular command, his only force the pickup kind that might be assigned to him at any particular moment. He was, in effect, a high-ranking scout or, as he put it, the commander of "a party of observation," playing his familiar role of riding the forward lines, on the prowl to gather information and guard against surprise.

Never was the McLane type of alertness more vital than at

this particular moment, when the emphasis of the entire war was shifting to a new theater in Virginia. In the winter and spring of 1781, the state was the focal point of British attacks. First, Benedict Arnold, rewarded for his treason with a generalship in the British Army, laid waste the tidewater area and sacked Richmond. In March, Maj. Gen. William Phillips superseded Arnold and brought another twenty-six hundred British regulars into the state. And finally Lord Cornwallis, frustrated in his battle with Nathanael Greene at Guilford Court House, unable either to destroy Greene or press the war in the Carolinas to a crushing conclusion, led his southern army into Virginia to join forces with Phillips.

Against this overwhelming might, the Americans could muster only a skeleton force under Steuben and twelve hundred men under Lafayette, whom Washington had sent south to see what he could do. Lafayette taunted Cornwallis and flitted precariously just out of his grasp—McLane wrote of one occasion when by quick intelligence he saved the Marquis from encirclement and entrapment just as he had at Barren Hill. Washington, far to the north, began to size up the new strategic situation that was presented to him.

For two years, the Continental Army had been virtually immobilized by the abject failure of Congress to provide it with the matériel of war. Continental currency was so worthless that during this period McLane had to pay six hundred dollars for a pair of boots, and an ordinary horse cost twenty thousand dollars. Arms, clothing, equipment of all kinds were lacking, and in spite of Washington's noble example and strenuous effort, the army almost wasted away. But now, in the spring of 1781, hope revived. The French alliance was making itself felt. France was extending the embattled Colonies money, arms and equipment; and, equally important, a powerful French Army had been landed at Newport under the command of Lt. Gen. Jean-Baptiste de Rochambeau. The force to justify the risk of

battle was now available. For the first time in more than two
years, a major stroke might be attempted.

To plan this stroke, Washington and Rochambeau met in
conference at Wethersfield, near Hartford, Connecticut, on
May 21 and 22, 1781. Washington, as his letters and diary notations make clear, had his heart set on one bold and culminat-
ing stroke—an assault by the combined French and American
forces on Clinton's army in New York. If New York, the center of British power in America, could be stormed and Clinton
crushed, the long and frustrating war that so many times had
seemed impossible to win would be won at one blow. Rochambeau, recognizing the extreme hazard of such an attack on
strong British fortifications, with the powerful British fleet in
the Hudson and East Rivers adding the weight of their mighty
broadsides to the defenses, seems from the first to have been
more attracted by the possibility of turning and striking at
Cornwallis in Virginia.

The decision reached at the two-day conference was recorded by Washington in his journal in these words: "Fixed
with Count de Rochambeau upon a plan of campaign in substance as follows: that the French Land force . . . should
march . . . to the North River and there in conjunction with
the American Army commence operations against New York
. . . the doing which would enfeeble their Southern operations and in either case be productive of Capital advantages, or
to extend our Views to the Southward as circumstances and a
naval superiority might render more necessary and eligible."

The last phrases in Washington's notation contained the
crux of the problem. For anything of moment to be accomplished, either at New York or in Virginia, the French fleet
would have to be brought to the American coast. Only if the
British were deprived of free use of the sea could Clinton's
army in New York or Cornwallis' in Virginia be isolated and
captured. Yet the powerful French fleet under Count de

Grasse was far away in the West Indies. It had sailed there directly from France with the intent of striking a blow at the British-held West Indian islands, and unless its plans could be changed, little could be accomplished. This situation led directly to Allan McLane's most important, most secret and most forgotten mission.

Washington's correspondence makes it absolutely clear that his own hopes were centered on being able to strike a blow at New York. He scouted and tested the approaches to New York with almost daily persistence; he appeared so absorbed in his plans for the grand assault upon the city that the British were completely deceived at the time and most historians have been since. Benson J. Lossing wrote that de Grasse had notified Washington he planned to campaign in the West Indies, but later changed his mind and sailed for the Chesapeake. Christopher Ward, the modern historian, says that the campaign of 1781 was bogging down in indecision when a letter came from de Grasse to Rochambeau—"a clear, concise and definite letter that cleared the air, resolved all doubts, and determined the course of the war."

There are teasing questions here: Why would de Grasse in the West Indies, intending to attack the British there, suddenly change all his plans? Why, if he were coming to the American coast, wouldn't he sail for Newport, where the French Army and a small fleet were stationed? Why would he, out of the blue as it were, decide on the Chesapeake? There must have been a reason for de Grasse to make the decision that he did. The answer to the riddle is to be found in the McLane papers, which reveal that the all-important seed of decision was planted by Allan McLane, acting as a special courier for Washington.

What happened was this: Washington, while he cherished the all-out blow at New York, was flexible enough to envision the possibility of the brilliant alternative in the South. Therefore, after his conference with Rochambeau, he decided to acquaint de Grasse with the full details of the strategic situation in the Colonies, urging him to come to the American coast. His selection of Allan McLane, fresh from riding the lines in front of Cornwallis in Virginia as his emissary may have meant that while he could present the advantages of a New York strike adequately himself, he wanted de Grasse to have the full benefit of talking to an officer who could present the Virginia alternative in as cogent terms. In any event, he entrusted McLane with private dispatches to be delivered to the French admiral, and the cavalryman set out on a sea voyage, enrolled as a captain of Marines on the powerful twenty-four-gun privateer *Congress*.

The *Congress* was skippered by Capt. George Geddis, of Philadelphia, and she sailed from Philadelphia for the West Indies in the early part of June. She encountered a French frigate at sea, learned the location of de Grasse's fleet and made a quick passage. In his journal, McLane later recorded the success of his vital mission with maddening brevity in these lines: ". . . Visited Cap François in July, was examined by Count de Grasse in Council of War aboard the Ville de Paris, gave it as his [McLane's] considered opinion that Count de Grasse could make it easy for Genl Washington to reduce the British Army in the South if he proceeded with his fleet and Army to the Chesapeake."

According to Alexander Garden, who had a few additional details from McLane, the *Congress* arrived at Cap François (now Cap Haitien) just as de Grasse was about to hold a council of war to map plans for an assault on Jamaica. After reading the dispatches from Washington, the admiral called McLane before the council and questioned him personally about the prospects for a quick and striking success on the American coast. McLane, according to Garden, "gave such satisfactory answers that he was informed by the Count, as soon as the Council broke up, that he would immediately proceed to America . . ."

This secret mission, though lost in history, does not rest on McLane's unsupported word. In April, 1820, when he was contemplating writing his memoirs—a project for which, unfortunately, he never found the time—McLane obtained a corroborating affidavit from Richard O'Brien, who had been a lieutenant on the *Congress* during the historic voyage to de Grasse. This document, still preserved in the McLane papers, substantiates in formal legal language the details of McLane's voyage except for some minor confusion about the identity of the French flagship.

O'Brien deposed "that as soon as possible after arrival [at Haitien] the said Allan McLane was conveyed by me in one of the ship's boats under my command on board the Ville de Finisterre, as I was then informed the Count de Grasse was holding a council of war to determine the course of their future operation. That the question before them was whether the force under the Count's Command be Employed against one of the British Islands in the West Indies—or sail for the Coast of the United States, There to cooperate with the American and French Armies.

"That the said Col. Allan McLane having produced his credentials was admitted to an audience before the said Council. . . . I was on the quarter-deck of the Ville de Paris and after a considerable time had Elapsed one of the French officers—the Captain of a 74, one of the Council of War—with great Expression . . . informed me that in Consequence of the dispatches delivered to the Council of War by Col. Allan McLane, his clear and explicit statements in persuasive representations and rational views of the probable consequences, it was then determined to abandon the Expedition against the West India Islands and to sail with all Expedition for the Coast of the United States."

It would appear that McLane had done a good job of salesmanship and had personally convinced de Grasse of the wisdom of sailing for the Chesapeake, the decision that was to make Yorktown possible. If the French admiral had any doubts about his choice, they were probably banished by the arrival of dispatches from Rochambeau, who had forwarded his version of the conference with Washington by the French frigate *Concorde* which sailed from Newport just about the same time the *Congress* left Philadelphia.

In any event, de Grasse began to assemble his fleet of twenty-nine warships, headed by huge and powerful ships of the line. He took aboard his fleet 3,200 troops with all their accoutrements, munitions, and supplies, and he sent the *Concorde* sailing back to Rochambeau with the word that he would leave Cap François on August 3rd, sail directly for the Chesapeake and stay six weeks. With de Grasse so specific, Washington and Rochambeau could plan with some confidence for Yorktown.

The decisive plans that he had helped initiate were building while Allan McLane was sailing for home on the *Congress*, impatient to get back to the war. But before he landed, such was the destiny of the man, he was again in the thick of action, embroiled in one of the fiercest sea battles of the Revolution. McLane underplays the event in one laconic sentence in his journal in which he notes that the *Congress* fell in with the British sloop-of-war *Savage* off the Charleston bar—and took her.

Actually, the action was a desperate one. The two ships sighted each other early on the morning of September 6, 1781. The *Congress*, a much more powerful ship, mounting twenty-four guns to the *Savage*'s sixteen, gave chase and opened fire with her bow chasers at 10:30 A.M. At 11 A.M., she drew up close on the *Savage*'s quarter, and the two ships coasted over a glassy sea, no more than thirty yards apart, hammering at each other with their heavy broadsides, the sharpshooters in their tops spraying the decks with musket fire.

McLane, in charge of the *Congress'* Marines, directed the small-arms fusillade from the American privateer. Throughout the long hours of the battle, he and his men maintained a hot and accurate fire that became a major factor in the victory. At one point the ships drifted slightly apart, and the great guns, as if by mutual consent, were silent while the crews busied themselves repairing the ravages of battle. Even then, the British captain noted in his official report, the "musquetry and pistols still did execution."

Despite the superiority of the *Congress*, the victory was a notable one. Privateers weren't supposed to be able to stand up to the trained seamen and gun crews of the Royal Navy, and usually they did not, usually they ran or meekly surrendered.

The day before this fierce single-ship action, a sea battle of far greater magnitude had taken place up the coast, a short distance to the north. De Grasse, true to his time schedule, had arrived off the Capes of the Chesapeake at the very end of August. He had promptly landed his thirty-two hundred troops, who had joined Lafayette before Cornwallis' entrenchments at Yorktown. Then de Grasse had established a watch off the Capes, and on the morning of September 5th he had sallied out to meet a powerful British fleet that had come down from New York to attempt to force a passage into the bay. The battle itself was one of those ponderous, drawn affairs with neither side achieving a smashing victory; but its results were as momentous as Trafalgar. The British ships of the line were badly battered, some left in sinking condition, and the British drew off in the night and headed back to New York. De Grasse re-entered the Chesapeake, sea superiority temporarily his; and Cornwallis, in effect, was doomed.

By now, Washington and Rochambeau were pressing southward on the long and arduous march from their posts upon the Hudson above New York. The forward elements of the allied army, leaving a baffled Clinton twiddling useless thumbs behind his heavy ramparts in New York, marched into Williamsburg on September 14th. A week was spent in bringing up the rear, consolidating and organizing for battle; and on the morning of September 22nd, Rochambeau and Washington sent their divisions down the long, straight road to Yorktown. By this time, Allan McLane was back in the war. He had landed from the *Congress* and joined the army under Washington.

The commander-in-chief made instant use of his talents. From the start, the siege of Yorktown was a race against time. De Grasse wanted to leave the coast before winter storms set in, menacing his fleet; and even while he stayed, he was in constant anxiety about what the British in New York might be doing. The day after his September 5th victory off the Capes, word had arrived that a new British squadron had sailed into New York. With these reinforcements, it was inevitable that as soon as they had repaired their battered warships, the British would sally forth again—this time probably in overwhelming force—and attempt to smash de Grasse and relieve Cornwallis. It was vital to Washington and Rochambeau and de Grasse that they get immediate warning of such a move; and so Washington hurried Allan McLane quickly to the north in his long-familiar role as a master of reconnaissance, his mission to get and bring word of the British preparations.

McLane, who knew the area intimately from the days of the raids on Paulus Hook and Sandy Hook, quickly picked up his old contacts. Whaleboat privateersmen ferried him across the harbor to the base of Sandy Hook outside the British lines, an observation post from which he had a clear view of shipping using the harbor. In the night, he crossed to the Long Island shore and there got in touch with American agents funneling information from spies in New York. It took several days to get the data he needed, but the patriotic spy ring produced. McLane learned the nature of Clinton's dispositions in considerable detail—even, as he later told Garden, the private recognition signals for the British fleet.

Once more he crossed from Long Island to Sandy Hook,

where he obtained a fast-sailing pilot vessel. Putting to sea in this, he raced to the Virginia Capes and delivered the data he had gathered to Washington and de Grasse. His report made it clear that there was still time. Clinton had not sailed yet, and Cornwallis' defenses were crumbling. The French and American artillery had subjected him to merciless shelling; parallels had been advanced ever closer to his lines; some of his redoubts had been stormed in desperate fighting. Cornwallis, cut off from help, beleaguered by land and by sea, recognized the inevitable, and on October 19th surrendered with all his army.

It had been a near thing. On the same day that Cornwallis yielded, Clinton sailed from New York to his aid. The British commander-in-chief had packed seven thousand troops aboard a fleet of forty-four vessels, headed by twenty-five ships of the line and eight frigates. With this powerful armada, he arrived off the Chesapeake on October 27th, just eight days too late.

With Yorktown won and independence virtually assured, Allan McLane's service in the Continental Army was almost at an end. He brought up the rear on the triumphal march northward and captured some pestiferous refugee boats that had been harassing patriots in the Chesapeake Bay area. Back once more in Philadelphia, reunited with his family, he found himself a poor man, with a wife actually in want.

The estate his father had left him, which had looked so ample, had been sacrificed for the cause, and now even food was a problem. McLane was so disturbed that, in recording the crisis, he lapsed from his customary third-person treatment of himself part way through the recital. He wrote:

"McLane received the thanks of Genl Washington and the Count de Grasse, which was very gratifying, but on his arrival in Philadelphia in December 1781 he found his wife and children suffering for want of the comforts of life. Continental money had fallen. It took a month's pay for a Major to pur-

chase provisions for his family for a week. His Patrimony had
been exhausted and his wife had sent near all her furniture to
vender to raise money to purchase Barrel Flr. Oh Heavens
thinks the Major I have brought myself to a bad market. I
must return to a family surrounded with penury and want."

His discharge from the army was dated December 31, 1781,
and was signed by Washington who noted that "from the time
of his joining the army, I can testify that he distinguished himself highly as a brave and enterprising party." The commander-
in-chief devoted a special paragraph to McLane's contributions
to the victory at Yorktown, writing: "During the Siege of
York, he was intrusted by the Board of War with the delivery
of dispatches of great importance to his Excellency the Count
de Grasse, which commission he executed with great celerity,
and was afterwards very serviceable in reconnoitering and
bringing intelligence of the Strength and disposition of the
British fleet off the Chesapeake."

With these encomiums, McLane returned to private life and
the task of making a living. He went into a mercantile venture
with Robert Morris, wealthy trader and financier, and battled
refugee boats on the Delaware as he transported shipments of
wheat up the river in small craft to mills on the Brandywine.
He became a colonel in the local militia, and as late as March,
1783, with five armed neighbors, he attacked the lair of "the
notorious refugee Captain Brooks," drove Brooks and his men
into the swamps, and recaptured two shallops laden with
wheat that Brooks had seized. Making note of this last skirmish, McLane commented with obvious satisfaction: "Thus
the Col. ended the war as he began it, fighting and finding himself."

In the postwar era, McLane had a long and distinguished
career. In 1789, he was appointed a Marshal of Delaware, and
in 1797, he resigned this job to accept the more lucrative post
of Collector of the Port of Wilmington. He was a member of

the Delaware House of Representatives from 1785 to 1791, when he was chosen Speaker. He was a member of the Privy Council in 1788 and a Justice of the Peace in 1793. An ardent Federalist, he nearly lost his port collector's post when Thomas Jefferson came to power in 1801, but friends interceded for him so successfully that he retained the job until he died in May, 1829, at the age of eighty-two.

His immediate descendants were noteworthy men of affairs. His son, Louis McLane, a disciple of Andrew Jackson, served in Congress, became Minister to England, Secretary of the Treasury, Secretary of State, and president of the Baltimore and Ohio Railroad. Louis' son, Robert Milligan McLane, was a graduate of West Point, a member of Congress, Commissioner to China, Minister to Mexico, Governor of Maryland and Minister to France, dying in Paris.

Of such heirs, Allan McLane, could well be proud. But nothing—not pride, nor years, nor honors, nor burdens—ever quenched the fires of his spirit. They flamed to the end. In 1814 when the British captured Washington, for example, McLane was on the scene as a military observer. Though sixty-eight and unequal to the derring-do of that winter of Valley Forge, he was still as fierce, as unconquerable—and as critical —as ever. In a sulphurous memorandum, the old warhorse passed this judgment on the capital's inept defenders:

"All was confusion—nothing like spirit—nothing like subordination—universal complaint for want of food, the Militia going off in every direction to seek it. Men, badly armed, being in many instances without flints in their muskets, and so completely without discipline as to exhibit a far greater resemblance to an armed mob than an organized army. I most religiously believe, that if I had been at the head of 300 men, such as I led in the attack on Paulus Hook, or such as I had under my command during the War of our Independence, I should have defeated Genl Ross, when he pressed Genl Winder over the Eastern Branch. Confident I am, that the enemy would never have reached Washington and America been spared the disgrace of beholding the British triumphantly possessing the Capital."

The words of an old fighter to whom the past is even more glorious in recollection than it was in deed? One cannot know, but can be sure that to Allan McLane all things were possible.

Unique among the fighters of the Revolution was the rifleman. He was a breed apart from the other soldiers of the Continental Line. His contributions were vital—and no other figure has attracted such a cluster of incompatible misconceptions. On one hand, for example, there is the common tendency to think of all the embattled patriots as riflemen; on the other, there is the kind of mental fixation that pictures the rifleman as the exclusive product of Kentucky. Both ideas are incorrect.

Only a small percentage of the men in the Continental Army were riflemen. And Kentucky was not the only frontier. In fact, there was another frontier just as bloody as Kentucky and no farther west than northern Pennsylvania and east-central New York. Actually, Albany was almost in the wilderness; less than fifty miles to the west, Indians raided, scalped, burned and pillaged.

The result was that the riflemen of the Revolution fought two wars. They were a relatively small but potent contingent in most of the major battles of Washington's Army. They played a pivotal role at Saratoga. And after the main armies had battled to a stale-

*mate in the north, the riflemen fought another war of their own
on the exposed frontiers of Pennsylvania and New York.*

*The scenes of this second war were laid in the Wyoming
Valley of Pennsylvania and in the Mohawk and Schoharie Valleys
of New York. It was war in its most grim and elemental form.*

*West of Albany, the thin thread of settlement extended only
a short distance into the interior of New York. Dutch pioneers
had pressed inland along the winding course of the Mohawk and
had filtered south of the Mohawk into the valley of Schoharie.
They had been followed by the Germans and the English. Small
towns had sprung up like Schenectady, a true frontier village.
Beyond the towns were hamlets and beyond the hamlets individual farms, sometimes grouped in little clusters, sometimes standing starkly and dangerously alone.*

*Beyond this precarious perimeter of farm and hamlet lay the
heartland of New York State, still the preserve of the Indian. The
Finger Lake section stretching up to the Great Lakes and the
Canadian border was the home of the Iroquois, the Six Nations,
loyal to the British crown, equipped and supplied and incited from
Canada, reinforced by Tories who were often more savage than
the Indians in the warfare they loosed on their former friends
and neighbors.*

*The weakness of the settlements, their closeness to the strong-
hold of the powerful Iroquois—this was a fateful combination.
Exposure invited attack, and life was lived in an atmosphere of
daily menace. A raiding party of a dozen braves might descend
suddenly upon isolated cabins; a veritable army of more than a
thousand British regulars, Tories and Indians might debouch
suddenly from the wilderness and scourge the entire frontier.*

*Before such savage blasts, the Colonists huddled together for
protection. A stone church or the stone mansion of one of the few
large landowners would be ringed with a rough wooden palisade
and become a fort. The settlers flocked to such islands of refuge,
abandoning homes and cattle and hard-won harvests to the raiders.
Sometimes the blow from the encircling forest fell so suddenly
that there was no warning, no time to run to the nearest palisade.
Then there was a massacre.*

In these perilous days, the rifleman became the bulwark of the frontier. He was the trained woodsman, the sharpshooter, the Indian scout. On him the settlements depended for warning; to him, they looked for leadership in fighting, in succor and pursuit after the blow had fallen. Such abnormal pressures produced some remarkable men. Greatest of all the scouts was Timothy Murphy, the hero of Schoharie, the sharpshooter of Saratoga, the double-barreled rifleman of the Revolution.

CHAPTER III

★

★   ★   ★

★

Timothy Murphy

TIMOTHY MURPHY, the one man in American history who could have claimed with some justice to have decided a war with one rifle shot, was working on his Schoharie County farm in upstate New York one day at the close of the Revolution when a tall Indian came out of the woods, trailing a rifle, a large blanket over his shoulder, tomahawk and scalping knife in his belt.

Murphy, the greatest scout on the New York frontier, a man who possessed a strong, uncomplicated hatred for Indians and had expressed it by scalping more than forty of them, was caught momentarily without his double-barreled long rifle, the novel weapon that had helped to make him famous. Murphy decided he had better talk to this Indian.

"Where are you going?" he asked in tones of polite curiosity.

"Don't know," grunted the savage.

"Where do you live?"

"There," said the Indian, jerking a thumb in the general direction of Canada. "Where do you live?"

"Down here," said Murphy, uncommunicatively.

"Do you know old Murphy?" the Indian asked.

Tim thought hard and acknowledged that he had heard of the man. The Indian promptly asked if he knew where Murphy lived, and Tim gestured off into the distance, then inquired, like a man mildly curious, what business the Indian could have with Tim Murphy.

"He kill my brother," said the Indian. "He kill Indian. He scalp Indian. They say he witch—he shoot without loadin'. Indian no hit him—he kill good many Indian. But he no kill me—I kill him!"

As far as Tim was concerned, that was just like an Indian, always wanting to kill people, and his Irish temper began to rise. Not having his double-barreled long rifle handy, he performed a feat that was more difficult for him than killing an Indian; he concealed his thoughts and even agreed that the elimination of Tim Murphy, "a wicked old devil," would be a boon to mankind. Of course, he remarked, the man who did the deed would have to be a crack shot and the owner of a fine rifle.

"You've got a very good rifle there," Tim remarked conversationally.

The Indian was delighted with the praise and agreed with the verdict.

"Do you ever shoot at a mark?" Tim wondered.

"Yes," said the Indian. "Do you shoot at mark?"

"Sometimes," said Tim. "Suppose we try."

This was a most agreeable Indian, even if he did have murder on his mind. The suggestion of a shooting match appealed to him as a game does to a little boy, and he trotted off and set up a mark against a stump a long shot away. Coming back to where Murphy stood, he politely proffered his rifle.

"You shoot first," he said.

"Oh, no, no, you go first," Tim told him, with equal politeness.

The Indian whipped up the rifle, fired and put his ball smack in the center of the mark. Even Tim Murphy shivered at the sight. Pleased with himself, the Indian reloaded the rifle and presented it to Murphy to try his luck. Tim grabbed the weapon, leaped backwards, leveled it and shouted: "I *am* Murphy!"

The Indian, too late, realized that he had been duped. Startled, he fell back a pace, then whipped out his scalping knife and with a blood-curdling war whoop, leaped at Tim. It was suicide. Tim Murphy, the deadliest sharpshooter between Albany and Canada, shot him through the heart with a ball from the Indian's own rifle.

This tale of Tim Murphy's encounter with the Indian seeking his scalp was recounted by William Sigsby of Middleburgh, New York, in 1839. Sigsby, who talked to Tim Murphy's descendants and to old residents of the countryside, gathered all the varied and sometimes incredible elements of the Tim Murphy legend. He warned that he could not vouch for the literal truth of the story of Tim Murphy's encounter with the Indian; but the anecdote was a part of the Murphy legend that was told and retold—and widely believed—among the people who had known the great scout best. And that, of course, is what really matters—that Tim Murphy was such a man; that such a feat was expected of him.

Famed as perhaps the best shot of the Revolution, Timothy Murphy was a rough-hewn product of the frontier. He was relatively short of stature, estimates placing his height at between five-feet-six and five-feet-nine; but he was solidly built, with great muscular strength and fleetness of foot. His naturally dark complexion, tanned by constant exposure, became almost as bronzed as an Indian's. His hair was black, and he had piercing dark eyes in a square-set, determined face. He never learned to read or write, and he has been described as "passionate and often rough-tongued, but with a warm heart." This "warm heart" did not keep him from nursing two burning hatreds—Tories and Indians—and it was a tossup which he hated the more.

Murphy was born on the frontier, reared on the frontier, schooled by the frontier. Its freedom was so necessary to him that he remained a common soldier and scout throughout the Revolution mainly because rank of any kind would have confined him for long stretches to a border fort—and he much preferred to roam.

The parents of the crack frontiersman, Thomas Murphy and Mary Lundy, were married in Ireland and emigrated to America when quite young. They settled first in Minisink, New Jersey, then a wild region in northern Sussex County where the boundaries of New York, Pennsylvania and New Jersey converge in the vicinity of the Delaware Water Gap. Here Timothy Murphy was born in 1751. About 1759, his parents moved further west into Pennsylvania, settling in an area then known as Shamokin Flats, now the town of Sunbury.

The available evidence indicates that Murphy, following a custom of the time, was indentured or apprenticed to the wealthier Van Campen family and that he moved with them to Wyoming, Pennsylvania. This was virtually the heart of the wilderness then, an area exposed to frequent Indian raids, scalpings and burnings; and hatred of the savages who committed such outrages was bred in the bones of frontiersmen. Bred too, by grim necessity, was a knowledge of the woods and of Indian ways, an almost instinctive wiliness. Tim Murphy learned the lessons of his environment well.

In June, 1775, when the word of Lexington and Concord reached the frontier, he enlisted in a company of Northumberland County riflemen headed by Capt. John Lowdon. Almost instantly, the riflemen set out on the long and dusty march to Boston, where the British garrison was being beleaguered. Tim Murphy was twenty-four then and the possessor of a weapon so distinctive and so unusual that, ever after, when his name was mentioned, a reference to his gun went with it. He became "the double-barreled rifleman" of the Revolution.

The double-barreled long rifle made Tim a unique figure in a rifle corps that was in itself unique. To contradict that popular misconception again, the American soldiers of the Revolution were not all riflemen. Indeed, very few of them were. The farmers who shot at the British from behind the stone fences on the road to Lexington and Concord used muskets, not rifles; and far from being sharpshooters, they sprayed an enormous amount of lead about the countryside for the damage that they inflicted. The long rifle was distinctly the weapon of the frontier, and the marksmen who used it with such deadly effect came primarily from the Pennsylvania and Virginia borders. They were a breed apart, and diaries of the day show that when Tim Murphy and his companions in Thompson's battalion of Pennsylvania riflemen marched into the American encampment in the environs of Boston they were as great a novelty to the musket-bearing New Englanders as they were to the musket-bearing British regulars.

The long rifle that became the trademark of these fighters was the creation of German gunsmiths on the Pennsylvania frontier. Rifles varied in length and design and weight. They ranged from about four feet ten inches long to five feet four inches, and weighed from nine to eleven pounds. Their great advantage lay in their range and deadly accuracy. The British Tower musket, standard gun of the Revolution, could fire a ball about 125 yards; but at that distance the shot was spent, it could only bruise, not kill. The musket was a deadly weapon only at close range, sixty-five to seventy yards; but the long rifle, in the hands of a sharp-eyed frontiersman, could be fired with almost pinpoint accuracy and telling effect at distances up to three hundred yards—and sometimes more.

There had been other double-barreled long rifles before Tim Murphy banged his name into history with some fantastic sharpshooting. Some are still preserved in museums. But the evidence indicates that without exception these had been showpieces, freaks and curiosities that had gained no acceptance in the rugged business of frontier life. Tim Murphy's gun was different; it was fashioned for just one purpose—to kill twice as effectively as a single-barreled rifle.

The exact origin of Murphy's novel weapon is a detail not preserved in history. Probably it was the product of two things; the exigencies of Indian war and Murphy's own character. Indians often fought in pairs, and a favorite tactic was for one to draw the fire of a frontiersman so that the second could spring upon him with knife and tomahawk before he could reload. Tim Murphy was a roisterer and hell-raiser; definitely a strong non-conformist, he never hesitated to break a convention or to tackle a problem wrong-way-to if that approach seemed to make sense. Given the two things, the nature of frontier war and the nature of the man, it is not surprising that Tim Murphy should have arrived at the conclusion that the double-barreled rifle, properly made, was an ideal weapon, fulfilling a very practical need. The result was the gun that he carried throughout the Revolution, a masterpiece of the gunmaker's art, fashioned for him by one of the best-known gunsmiths of the day, James Golcher, of Easton, Pennsylvania.

Tim Murphy and his brother, John, were two of the Northumberland County riflemen who were mustered into service on June 29, 1775. Aaron Wright, a companion of theirs in Lowdon's company, kept a diary in which he recorded their adventures. On the day of the muster, Wright noted, the men elected their own officers, but a few days later, when orders came to march, "our first lieutenant came and told us he would be glad if we would excuse him from going, which we refused. But on consideration we concluded it was better to consent, after which he said he would go; but we said, 'You shall not command us, for he whose mind can change in an hour is not fit to command in the field where liberty is contended for.' In the evening we chose a private in his place."

The independence expressed in that exchange was a foretaste of things to come. On the march north, the Northumberland riflemen took a variety of matters into their own hands. In New York City, they "sarched" the goods of a Tory; in Litchfield, Connecticut, they "took a girl out of jail and tarred and feathered another Tory near Hartford, who said when they marched by that he was sorry to see so many men going to fight the king." Within an hour after they reached the camp of the Continental Army, they were battling the "redcoated Philistines," as Wright described them, in a skirmish that took place about the base of Bunker Hill, almost on the site of the historic June battleground.

Such were Tim Murphy and his comrades. As soon as they arrived in the lines before Boston, they made their presence felt in more ways than one. An unruly lot, they caused almost as much trouble for their commanding officers as they did for the British. They rebelled at the normal chores of the camp like digging trenches or working on fortifications—"farmer's work," they called it; idle, they drank, fought and wenched; and when one of them was confined to a guardhouse for such offenses, the others simply tore the guardhouse apart and liberated the prisoner. Their principal pleasure aside from these strictly male indulgences was derived from sneaking Indian-fashion close to the British lines and taking deadly potshots at every head that appeared above a parapet.

The impact that these Pennsylvania riflemen made upon the farmer-soldiers of New England was recorded by Dr. James Thacher in an entry he made in August, 1775, in his Military Journal. "They are remarkably stout and hardy men, many of them exceeding six feet in height," Dr. Thacher wrote. "They are dressed in white frocks or rifle shirts and round hats. These men are remarkable for the accuracy of their aim, striking a mark with great certainty at 200 yards distance. At a review, a company of them while on quick advance fired their bullets into objects of seven inches in diameter, at a distance of 250 yards. They are now stationed in our lines and their shots have frequently proved fatal to British officers and soldiers who exposed themselves to view, even at more than double the distance of a common musket-shot."

In one such instance, a rifleman killed a British soldier at two hundred and fifty yards, though only half his head was visible. By August 13, 1775, though the riflemen had been in camp only a short time, Capt. James Chambers of Thompson's battalion wrote that they had been credited with forty-two killed and thirty-eight prisoners taken.

Tim Murphy was in the thick of the action around Boston, as a member of Lowdon's company, but there is no record of his individual performances. He had not yet achieved the fame that was to make him a marked man, and so the diary writers, whose major interest was focused on their own activities, made no mention of him.

Just one exhibition of phenomenal shooting in this period has been attributed—it is probable but not provable—to Tim. In September, 1775, a party of British soldiers pushed out in a flat-bottomed scow on a harbor-reconnoitering and buoy-planting expedition. The scow was anchored planting buoys almost half a mile out from the American-held shore, and the British soldiers worked at their task secure in the safety the distance gave them. Up on a steep hillside overlooking the scene, however, was a rifleman who figured that if he took advantage of the extreme elevation of the hill he might just be able to plant his bullets in the scow. Taking careful aim, he began to shoot.

The shots came fast, and despite the distance winged unerringly to their mark. First one British soldier crumpled to the bottom of the scow, then another. The survivors raised the anchor and tried desperately to row out of range, but in their

panic they pulled the oars every which way and the tide swept
them closer to the shore and the vantage point of the deadly
marksman. Tim Murphy, if Tim it really was, took full advantage of the beautiful opportunity for target practice. He shot
until the last grains of powder had been cleaned from his
powder horn, and when at last he loped off along the wooded
hillside, he left behind him a boatload of victims. The scow
was filled with dead and wounded, hardly a man aboard untouched; and when it finally reached the safety of British-held
Boston, stretcher-bearers had to be summoned to carry away
its crew. This was the first of the super-exploits that were to
install Tim Murphy in a special niche as *the* rifleman among
riflemen.

After the British were driven from Boston, Tim shared the
fortunes of Washington's Army. He fought in the Battle of
Long Island, in the disastrous retreat across Jersey. He was in
the ragged force that crossed the ice-choked Delaware and
achieved the stunning surprise at Trenton. He fought at
Princeton and survived the first bitter winter of privation at
Morristown. Then, in the summer of 1777, he was in the
picked contingent of 500 riflemen whom Washington dispatched to the north under Daniel Morgan, that giant who had
been a wagoner in the British Army, to attempt to block the
southward thrust of Gentleman Johnny Burgoyne, who was
driving down from Canada in an effort to split the Colonies
in half.

The Continental forces at Saratoga had been placed under
the command of Maj. Gen. Horatio Gates, a pompous blunderer and conniver who was to achieve the great victory
that marked the turning point of the Revolution despite his
own lack of talent, solely through the genius of the men and
officers who served under him. The first clash with Burgoyne's
army came on September 19, 1777 when the British general
crossed to the west bank of the Hudson and launched an attack on American entrenchments that had been erected there

to block his way. Daniel Morgan's riflemen were in the forefront of what became known as the First Battle of Freeman's Farm. They were the first in the firing lines, the last to break off the action; and their deadly shooting, as Burgoyne later admitted, cost him half the men who fell in the attack.

Repulsed in this first attempt to pierce the American lines, the British drew back, regrouped their forces and studied the situation. For almost three weeks, there was a lull, and in this lull, the riflemen found plenty of opportunity to employ their special talents as skirmishers and sharpshooters. Tim Murphy and his inseparable companion, David Elerson, formed a team that now began to distinguish itself by repeated feats of daring. On two occasions, they cut off British foraging parties, shot or drove off the guard, and brought the much-needed supplies into the American lines. Another time, they crept at night so close to the British front that they surprised and captured a sentinel. From him, they learned the password, and to Tim it seemed a shame not to use it.

Leaving Elerson to take the captured sentinel in, Tim marched boldly into the enemy camp. The pickets challenged him, but Tim gave the proper countersign with just the right touch of casualness and walked on. He roamed the camp until his curiosity was aroused by a lighted tent—with the silhouette of a British officer plainly visible against the canvas. Circling to the rear of the tent and peering cautiously under, Tim saw that the officer was alone, seated at a camp desk and writing a letter. Tim had drawn a bead on many a British officer by this time, but had yet to bring in one alive, a captive, and it must have occurred to him that he would never have a better opportunity. Wriggling under the tent, noiseless as a snake, Tim drew his knife and padded stealthily up behind the preoccupied officer.

"Don't make a sound or I'll butcher you." He whispered the threat almost at the officer's ear, the point of his knife pricking the back of the man's neck.

The startled officer was helpless. With that menacing knife constantly prodding at him he was forced to rise and to accompany Tim Murphy on a stroll out of camp. The pickets challenged, Tim gave the proper countersign, and the pair walked on like friends enjoying the night—out of the British camp, down through the dip of low-lying ground between the lines and up the slopes of Bemis Heights to the American entrenchments. There Tim turned his companion over to superior officers, and Morgan himself came to question the prisoner. This kind of calculated recklessness set Tim Murphy apart from his fellow soldiers and excited the curiosity of the camp about him; but his date with destiny was to come in the great battle of October 7, 1777.

Burgoyne, cut off and isolated in the wilderness, began belatedly to appreciate the desperate alternatives confronting him. Retreat to Canada, an agonizing trek for an army this late in the season, was virtually impossible. He had to smash his way through the American lines blocking his path and join forces with British troops advancing northward up the Hudson or he had to surrender. Burgoyne chose to fight, and the result was the Second Battle of Freeman's Farm, the dramatic conflict on which hinged the outcome at Saratoga.

The desperate assault on the American lines was spearheaded by two thousand troops comprising the right wing under Gen. Simon Fraser, a dynamic field leader. So great was his skill and his personal courage that he was known as "the darling of the army," and where he led, British troops followed, fired by a fervent belief in their own invincibility.

The drama of Saratoga lay in the fact that the battle was shaped by the personal fate of two such inspired leaders—General Fraser on the British side and Benedict Arnold, then an American hero, who had been deprived of command by Gates but who, in defiance of Gates, leaped to horse and galloped toward the sound of the guns.

Fraser opened the action by setting his troops in motion

southward in a stab aimed at the American lines. Morgan, who held the heights opposite Fraser, did not wait for the blow to fall. Instead, he led his riflemen on a circuitous march that brought them, through dense woods, down on the flank of the British column. Here they opened fire, and their deadly shooting, plus a frontal attack by Continental light infantry, halted the British advance.

At this junction, with the tide of battle swaying precariously in the balance, Arnold swept upon the field, a human thunderbolt whom no force could stay or deny. He came at a tearing, headlong gallop, and the American troops, fired by his presence, cheered him and tried to match his pace. Boldly assuming command of every detachment he encountered, Arnold gathered up regiments of New England infantry, wheeled and hurled them in a headlong charge at the British center. Hessian troops comprising the center wavered before the fury of the onslaught, but stood their ground. Arnold and the Americans were repulsed.

Behind the staggered British front, Fraser raced back and forth on a huge gray gelding. Shouting to his troops, his sword flashing in the sunlight, he stiffened the spine of the entire army, wrought a miracle of order out of chaos, and welded a new battle formation that he prepared to launch at Arnold's temporarily disorganized forces.

A vivid picture of Fraser in action and a striking estimate of all that depended on him was given by Benson J. Lossing in his *Pictorial Field-Book of the Revolution*. Lossing described this juncture of the battle in these terms:

"The gallant Fraser was the directing soul of the British troops in action. His skill and courage were everywhere conspicuous. When the lines gave way, he brought order out of confusion; when regiments began to waver, he infused courage into them by voice and example. He was mounted on a splendid iron-gray gelding, and dressed in the full uniform of a field general, he was a conspicuous object for the Americans

. . . It was evident that the fate of the battle rested upon him . . ."

This, Benedict Arnold was quick to perceive. Rallying and reorganizing his troops, whipping them up for another wild charge on the British lines, he needed time; and time, with Fraser in action against him, he might not have. Wheeling his horse, Arnold galloped furiously up to Morgan, pointed to Fraser and shouted:

"That man on the gray horse is a host in himself and must be disposed of."

Morgan acknowledged the order and called his ace sharpshooters around him. Lossing gilds the ruthless instructions that Morgan gave with words it is doubtful that Morgan ever spoke. According to Lossing, Morgan pointed out the dashing, commanding figure of Fraser to Tim Murphy and his other ace marksmen and told them:

"That gallant officer is General Fraser. I admire and honor him, but it is necessary that he should die; victory for the enemy depends upon him. Take your station in that clump of bushes and do your duty."

The riflemen scattered to carry out his orders. Most of them went into the bushes that Morgan had designated, but Tim Murphy took a cool and calculating look around him. A medium-sized tree reared itself out of the bushes, and Tim decided to climb it. In the upper branches, he paused, settled himself in a fork and looked out over the battlefield. Fraser was shouting and calling to his men, cajoling them into line, dashing up and down along their front on his rearing, curvetting horse. The range was long, about three hundred yards, and Tim Murphy raised his double-barreled rifle and began to sight.

From the bushes below, the other riflemen were trying to bring down the general. One shot cut Fraser's bridle rein near his fingers; another passed between him and an officer beside him, and killed a man behind. The near-misses alarmed Fraser's

aides. His subaltern implored him not to risk his life, to move
back to a place of safety out of range of the deadly long
rifles. Fraser was perfectly aware of his danger. He had seen
the rifles flash; he even, so it was later said, saw the figure of a
rifleman, gun extended, wedged into the crotch of a tree above
the battlefield. But Fraser would not have been the inspiring
leader that he was if caution had been one of his guiding prin-
ciples; he inspired because he led, disdaining danger and death.
He disdained them now, waving his officers away, keeping his
lonely tryst with duty.

In his treetop some three hundred yards away, Tim Murphy's piercing black eyes narrowed with the intensity of his
concentration. He waited, judging wind and distance and the
prancing movements of Fraser's horse. Then he carefully
squeezed the trigger.

The bullet struck Fraser full in the abdomen and knocked
him from the saddle into the trampled dust of the battlefield.
He lay there, mortally wounded.

Hardly had he fallen when Sir Francis Clarke, Burgoyne's
chief aide-de-camp, came galloping up with what Burgoyne
himself later described as "a most important order to Colonel
Kingston in regard to the disposition of the artillery." Tim
Murphy, squinting along the second barrel of his deadly Golcher, took careful aim at this obviously important courier and
fired again. At the crack of his rifle, Clarke pitched from the
saddle, dying almost before he struck the ground.

These two unerring shots did more than anything else to
shatter the morale of the British and to turn the tide of the
most important battle of the Revolution. According to Lossing: "As soon as Fraser fell, a panic spread among the British
lines. It was increased by the appearance of 3,000 New York
troops under General Tenbroeck. Burgoyne, who now took
command in person, could not keep up the sinking courage of
his men. The whole line gave way and fled precipitately within
the entrenchments of the camp."

Arnold, the fury of the battlefield, gathered up ever larger contingents of troops and flung them headlong at the shaken British. Circling the entire British right and rear at the close of of this bloody day, he led Morgan's riflemen and other Continental troops in a furious charge on the Breymann redoubt, anchor of the British line. The Americans swept all before them until Arnold, charging through a sally port in the redoubt, had his horse shot under him and was himself grievously wounded by a musket ball that coursed up his leg and shattered his thigh bone.

With Arnold's fall, the American tide ebbed, though the whole rear of the British army was exposed to assault had there been a field genius there to organize it. But enough had been done already. Burgoyne had lost in this one afternoon of fighting six hundred killed, wounded and captured, and all ten artillery pieces that had been brought into action. He was doomed and knew it. Just ten days later, he surrendered with all his army at Saratoga—an unprecedented event that was to lead to the French alliance and to Yorktown. As Charles Winthrop Sawyer put it, in his *Firearms in American History*, "Success at Saratoga was therefore the hinge upon which the Revolution swung, and the bearing point in that hinge was Timothy Murphy's rifle bullet."

A monument on the Saratoga battlefield today marks the approximate spot from which Timothy Murphy fired the shot that killed General Fraser. Few individual feats of marksmanship in any war have been so important.

Few common soldiers have made such an impact on history. In later years, there was much discussion about the number of times Tim had fired at Fraser. He was sometimes asked if he had been responsible for the errant shots that clipped the general's bridle rein and killed a man behind him. "Sure-Shot Tim," as he was called by one of his commanding officers, always took umbrage at such questions as if they were an insult to his marksmanship; he had fired at Fraser only once, of course, he said, as if it were ridiculous to suppose a second shot, for him, could ever have been necessary. He always maintained, however, that Arnold was the true hero of Saratoga; that Arnold would never have betrayed his country if he had received the honors and recognition he so richly deserved at that point.

After Saratoga, Tim lived through the winter of Valley Forge with Washington's army. In the following spring, he and David Elerson were with Morgan's riflemen in the pursuit of Clinton's army across New Jersey. The riflemen were stationed some miles from the battlefield of Monmouth and missed the action. But the following day, after Clinton had drawn off toward Sandy Hook, Morgan picked four of his aces—John Wilbur, Zachariah Tufts, Elerson, and Murphy—to scout the rear of the British army and see what they could accomplish. The riflemen tracked the retreating British virtually to the water's edge and succeeded in capturing an elaborate coach belonging to one of the British generals. The marksmen returned to camp riding in style.

From the New York area, Tim Murphy's battleground shifted to the frontiers, aflame with the most vicious warfare of the Revolution. Heavy detachments of Tories and Indians were descending on the isolated settlements west of Albany. Fighters were needed who were familiar with wilderness warfare, and Washington met the emergency by dispatching three companies of Morgan's riflemen to the area. In this force were David Elerson and Timothy Murphy.

The scene of their new activity was the Schoharie Valley, some twenty-five miles west of Albany. To the south of the Schoharie are the beautiful peaks of the Catskills, and to the north the Mohawk River twists through a green countryside until it passes Schenectady, twenty miles to the northeast. Stretching beyond Schoharie to the southwest is Delaware County, which extends clear to the northern Pennsylvania frontier and the headwaters of the Susquehanna River. To the west, when Tim Murphy came to Schoharie, an almost trackless forest reached to the Finger Lake section of Western New York. This wilderness was the home of warlike Indian tribes and spawning ground of marauding war parties that swept the frontier settlements. The valley of Schoharie was like a funnel open at both ends, inviting invasion by painted braves sweeping along the Mohawk River to the north or swinging up from the south along the route of the Susquehanna.

The Schoharie had been settled by stolid Dutch farmers, and to protect it they had built a chain of three forts stretching from northeast to southwest, spaced five miles apart. The northernmost bastion in the chain, known oddly enough as the Lower Fort, was a stout stone structure in what is now the village of Schoharie. Next came Weiser's Dorf, or the Middle Fort, now Middleburgh, and beyond to the southwest was the Upper Fort, located at what is now Fultonham.

When transferred to the Schoharie, Murphy was a sergeant in the rifle company headed by Capt. Gabriel Long. Long's detachment, including Elerson and Murphy, was stationed first at Middleburgh, and it wasn't long before Tim's fleetness of foot, his woodcraft and the double death that spouted from his twin-barreled rifle began the legend that was passed on for generations in the Schoharie Valley.

One of the first assignments that the new riflemen drew was to capture a man named Christopher Service, one of the noted Tories of the neighborhood. Service, who lived in a home overlooking the Charlotte River, had been accused of arming and supplying the Tories who had raided Cobleskill in May; he had been arrested and confined for a time, but had escaped and returned home. The patriots of the region were convinced that he had returned, too, to his former practice of conniving with the enemy.

Long's instructions were to "bring in Service, dead or alive." Carrying out the orders, he started for the Charlotte River, an upper tributary of the Susquehanna south of Schoharie. Tim Murphy ranged the forest well in advance of the main body of riflemen, guarding against surprise. Not far from Service's home, Tim intercepted a runner carrying a message to Service from a Tory captain by the name of Smith.

From the message, it was apparent that Smith had enlisted a company of Tories in the neighborhood of Catskill and was on his way to join Sir John Johnson in Niagara. Sir John was the son of Sir William Johnson, who had been the Indian agent for the Crown in the years just prior to the Revolution, and from his headquarters just across the border in Canada, he directed the activities of Tory and Indian bands raiding the frontier. Smith, needing supplies for his men on the long march, had sent the note to Service to notify the Tory sympathizer of his approach.

Murphy's capture of the letter-bearing runner exposed the plan. Acting on the information, Captain Long turned off the route to Service's home and led his men farther to the south, placing them in ambush across the trail the Tories were following. When Smith emerged from a thicket at the head of his men, Long and Elerson fired, killing him instantly. The other riflemen opened up on Smith's followers. Several were killed or wounded; the rest fled.

With the Tory band dispersed, Long and his riflemen turned back to their original objective—the capture of Service. The ambush of the Tories had taken place at too great a distance from Service's home for him to hear the shots, and he had no suspicion of his danger.

Swiftly and silently, the riflemen surrounded his house, and when the ring had been drawn tight, Elerson and Murphy led the rush. They burst into the house and made Service a prisoner. Told he would have to accompany the riflemen to Schoharie, the Tory appeared docile enough, but as they were going out the door, he suddenly whirled, seized an ax standing there and aimed a stroke at Murphy's head. Unexpected though the blow was, Tim was alert. He leaped nimbly out of

the way, and the ax cleaved only air. Before Service could raise
it to strike again, Elerson's rifle went off almost in his face,
and the Tory fell dead across his own threshold.

A subsequent search of the house disclosed a considerable
quantity of provisions cached there, evidently for the use of the
Tory party the riflemen already had dispersed. On Service's
body also, the riflemen found a letter signed by him and ad-
dressed to Joseph Brant, the Indian chief, containing plans
for the raising of a number of Tories to attack both Cherry
Valley and the Schoharie. This first mission of the riflemen in
Schoharie—the dispersal of Smith's band and the killing of Service—had far-reaching effects, making other Tory sympathizers think twice about collaboration.

A period of almost constant border warfare began that fall,
raid provoking counterraid and counterraid leading to fresh
atrocities. It began on September 12, 1778 when Joseph Brant
led a party of three hundred Tories and one hundred and fifty
Indians against the settlement of German Flats, now the town
of Herkimer, located in the most beautiful and fertile section
of the Mohawk Valley. The inhabitants, who had sent out
scouts, had warning of the impending raid and took refuge in
the local fort, but the entire village consisting of some seventy
houses with their barns and several grist mills was put to the
torch.

The raid had been launched by Brant from the Indian
town of Unadilla about fifty miles southwest of German Flats.
In revenge, Tim Murphy and the riflemen of Schoharie were
marshaled in a striking force to attack Brant's base. Unadilla
was not just a savage town of huts and wigwams, but a well-
built village of stone and frame houses, with brick chimneys
and glazed windows. On October 8, 1778, the riflemen surprised the village, seized the large quantities of supplies the Indians had gathered from a bountiful harvest, set the torch to all
and left behind them a mass of ashes and smoking rubble.

As German Flats had led to Unadilla, so Unadilla led directly to one of the worst atrocities of the war—the sack of Cherry Valley, a town in Tryon County about fifty miles west of Albany. The much-hated Tory, Capt. Walter Butler, gathered a force of two hundred Tory Rangers near Tioga in late October and set out on a one-hundred-and-fifty-mile march to Cherry Valley. He was joined by Joseph Brant and five hundred Indians, and together, early in the morning of November 11, 1778, the two forces descended on Cherry Valley.

The town had been garrisoned by two hundred and fifty men of the Seventh Massachusetts Regiment, headed by Col. Ichabod Allen. Unfortunately, neither commander nor men had any knowledge of Indian warfare. They were billeted in exposed houses scattered throughout the village instead of being concentrated in the fort, and when the blow fell, Colonel Allen and sixteen members of his headquarters company, slumbering in one of the houses, were promptly tomahawked and scalped. More than thirty residents of the village were murdered, their cattle and provisions seized, their homes razed.

After the sack of Cherry Valley, Tim Murphy and the Schoharie riflemen were sent in pursuit of the raiders, but they arrived too late to do more than bury the dead and rescue some of the fugitives who had taken to the woods. Tim then led a detachment of riflemen on a scouting expedition along the Mohawk River between Schenectady and Utica. In the neighborhood of German Flats, he encountered a band of roving Indians. The riflemen killed three of the Indians, dispersed the rest. One of the Indians slain was a young chief, a great favorite with his tribe, and a war party was quickly organized to pursue the riflemen and avenge him. Tim and his scouts were cut off by superior numbers of Indians. They fought a brief, fierce battle, killing several warriors, then split up and fled. Tim ran for miles, outstripping his nearest pursuers and finally eluding them in dense forest and approaching night.

By this time, Murphy's double-barreled rifle struck terror to the Indians, who had never heard of such a weapon and who sometimes believed, when the second shot followed so closely upon the first, that Tim could continue firing indefinitely without reloading. The magic gun and Tim's skill in wood-craft became the cornerstones of a growing reputation. He frequently commanded scouting parties ranging deep into Indian territory, and he sometimes painted his face and dressed like an Indian, walking into their camps to learn their plans. Once, coming back from such a mission, he was mistaken by one of his comrades for an Indian and fired upon before he could identify himself.

Back in Schoharie after these adventures, Tim Murphy drew the awed glance that is accorded the hero who thrives on incredible odds and seems to wear an invisible charm against enemy bullets. Tim himself paid scant heed to the talk and the stories about himself. He had other things on his mind. He had discovered an interest that any man with half an eye could clearly see was more intriguing than the pallid excitement of hunting Indians.

She was Peggy Feeck, the prettiest girl in all Schoharie. Peggy was the daughter of Johannes Feeck, a Dutch farmer and one of the wealthiest landowners in the region. Only seventeen, she was tall and slim, a trifle taller, in fact, than Tim himself. A catalogue of her attractions, as compiled by Jeptha R. Simms, a local historian who methodically gathered the details from those who knew her, makes it obvious why Peggy Feeck stopped the redoubtable Tim Murphy in his tracks as effectively as if he had run into an Indian ambush.

Peggy, says Simms, had "a full bust and pretty features." Her hair was a rich auburn; her eyes, dark hazel. She had beautiful eyelashes and even, pearly teeth. Her nose, Simms confesses, was just a trifle too long for perfect beauty, but her lips were ruby, her cheeks peach-colored, her skin clear and white, and she had "a neatly turned ankle."

In addition to all this, the historian vows, Peggy possessed "an amiable disposition" and "knew housekeeping better than school."

Tim Murphy was scouting past the Upper Fort, where Peggy lived with her parents, when the sight of this girl with the "full bust," the "amiable disposition," and the "neatly turned ankle" abruptly took his mind off Indians. Peggy, in a plain dress, a white kerchief over her glowing hair, was on her way to the barn with a milk pail on her arm when she looked up and saw the black-haired Indian fighter giving her the eye. The evidence would seem to indicate that Peggy Feeck forgot about the cows as rapidly as Tim Murphy forgot about Indians.

Shortly after this first chance encounter, Tim Murphy's companions noticed that, almost invariably when he set out on a scout, he went in one direction—past the Upper Fort. They asked Tim about it, and he remarked, with perfect truth, that "the scenery was more beautiful in that direction." It was some time before anyone realized just what kind of scenery he meant.

Unfortunately, one of the first on whom the truth dawned was Peggy's father, Johannes Feeck. Peggy was his only child, beautiful and bright, the sunshine in his life. She was, as a result of her father's holdings, a veritable heiress, the best catch in all Schoharie. And what, precisely, was Tim Murphy?

He was useful when the Indians were on the warpath, it was true, but this hardly compensated in a father's eyes for his lack of other qualities. Peggy Feeck may have perceived the "warm heart" of Tim Murphy, but Johannes, her father, saw only the "rough exterior." He saw a man who couldn't read or write, a rough woodsman whose fondness for roaming was such that he rarely stayed inside a stockade. He saw a man who was known to like his liquor too much on occasion and to use his fists too freely. He saw a suitor who had only the hunting shirt on his back and his double-barreled rifle; a suitor who hadn't a cent or a prospect to his name.

Johannes Feeck's reaction was inevitable under the circumstances. He weighed Tim Murphy in the balance and found
him definitely wanting. Then, with the sternness of a Dutch
parent, he made his decision known to his daughter. She was
to send the rough woodsman packing. She was not to see him
any more. If she dared, if she defied her father's edict, he
would lock her up in her room and make certain that she didn't
see Tim Murphy or anyone else.

The next time Tim just happened to set out past the Upper
Fort to view "the scenery" there, he got the full budget of bad
news from Peggy. Now Tim Murphy wasn't the kind of man
to take such autocratic banishment meekly. He was a believer
in direct action, and his first impulse doubtless was to settle
matters with Johannes Feeck with his own two fists. But obviously no one, not even Tim Murphy, could reach an understanding with the father of one's girl in such a fashion; even
Tim recognized that the situation called not for direct action,
but for strategy.

Fortunately, there was in the Feeck household a half-breed
servant girl, Maria Teabout, who was devoted to Peggy. She
agreed to meet Tim secretly and to carry messages back and
forth between the lovers. Meeting Maria Teabout wasn't as
satisfactory as meeting Peggy Feeck, but for the moment it
was the best substitute that could be arranged.

Tim Murphy's romantic affairs were in this unsatisfactory
state when spring brought the Indians again upon the warpath.
One of the first raiding parties descended upon the countryside around the Upper Fort, burned some outlying cabins and
carried off a pretty young girl. Soldiers in the fort could hear
the girl's screams, but they didn't dare go to her rescue, not
knowing how large the raiding party might be.

Holding back was not for Tim Murphy. With characteristic
fearlessness, he dropped silently to the ground outside the palisade and headed for the nearby river to watch for the retreating Indians. Hidden in the underbrush, he finally spotted four

braves dragging the nearly unconscious girl between them. They got into a canoe and paddled away. Tim took one of the garrison's hidden canoes and followed.

All night, he trailed the raiders and their prisoner. By the time dawn broke, the Indians had traveled so far they fancied themselves safe from all possible pursuit. They halted in a small clearing in the woods and started a fire to cook some food. Their captive lay bound on the ground beside them. Tim Murphy, reconnoitering the scene with absolute stealth, decided that the time had come to act. Hiding himself securely behind a tree at the edge of the glade, he leveled his double-barreled rifle at the little group around the campfire.

At the crack of his rifle shot, one brave pitched forward, his scalp lock almost in the fire. The other three leaped to their feet. Tim fired the second barrel of his rifle at the closest of these fine targets, and a second Indian fell dead. The remaining pair, thinking they had been jumped by a whole party of irate frontiersmen, scurried for the shelter of the trees. Their flight gave Tim a chance to reload his rifle. Then the cautious, deadly stalking began.

The odds of two to one were still formidable, but in such circumstances Tim Murphy always figured that his double-barreled rifle was a true equalizer. He and the two Indians played a deadly game of hide-and-seek, each trying to lure the other into the momentary exposure that could mean death. Finally, one of the braves, thinking he saw an opportunity, raised his arm and hurled his tomahawk at Tim's head. Tim ducked and the whirling ax buried itself in a tree, inches from his scalp. In the same split-second, Tim fired. The tomahawk-thrower had exposed himself to the snap shot—a fatal error, for Tim's bullet caught him full in the chest, killing him almost instantly.

The last of the Indians bolted from his shelter and fled. He had taken only a few steps when the second barrel of Tim's

rifle spoke, the ball striking the fleeing savage squarely between the shoulder blades and felling him.

Four shots, four Indians dead and a white girl rescued—it
was a good morning's work, even for Tim Murphy.

Shortly after this rescue, Tim entered upon one of the most
perilous periods of his peril-studded life. The Wyoming and
Cherry Valley massacres the previous year had touched off a
wave of indignation throughout the Colonies, and Congress
had authorized Washington to organize a major expedition to
root out the Iroquois, or the Six Nations, from their fastnesses
in western New York State. The heart of the Indian country
lay in the area bounded on the north by Lake Ontario, on the
south by the Susquehanna River in Pennsylvania, on the east
by the Catskills and on the west by Lake Erie. To penetrate
this wilderness, usually frequented only by Indians, Tories,
and a few daring frontiersmen, two forces were organized.
The main body under Maj. Gen. John Sullivan gathered at
Easton, Pennsylvania, and struck off to the north through
Wyoming to join the second force, headed by Brig. Gen.
James Clinton, which was advancing west to Tioga by Otsego
Lake and the Susquehanna. From Tioga, the united army was
to thrust directly to the north, laying waste the heartland of
the Six Nations.

Such a bold thrust into wild and almost impenetrable enemy
country obviously would flirt with disaster almost every step
of the way. The Tories and Indians who were to be hunted
down in their own private lair had all the advantage of knowing the terrain perfectly; hence the opportunities for ambush
would be innumerable. Only constantly alert and daring
scouts, ranging far in advance of the main American force,
could avert surprise and entrapment; and for this service, none
could match Morgan's riflemen from Schoharie. And none in
this matchless contingent was quite the equal of Timothy
Murphy. When Clinton's force set out from Canajoharie in

June, 1779, Tim Murphy regularly roamed the dark and
menacing forest far in advance of the main body.

The hazards of such solitary scouting are illustrated by an
adventure of Murphy's side-kick, David Elerson, while the
army was encamped at Otsego Lake. Elerson left the encampment at the head of the lake and made his way alone to an old
clearing about a mile away to gather pulse for dinner. He had
filled his knapsack and was about to return to camp when his
sensitive ears detected a rustling in the coarse herbage around
him. Looking sharply, Elerson saw about a dozen Indians
sneaking up on him, evidently in the hope of capturing him
alive.

Grabbing his rifle, Elerson bounded from the field in flight.
A shower of tomahawks winged after him. One almost severed
the middle finger from one hand; the others missed. Elerson
plunged into a thicket of tall weeds and bushes, scaled an old
brushwood fence, and darted into the thick woods. The Indians
fired their rifles at him, but the shots all missed his dodging,
fleetly running figure. Cut off from camp, Elerson had no hope
except to outrun his pursuers. He ran and ran, dodged, turned
and used every woodland device to shake off pursuit; but the
Indians, as wily as he, clung doggedly to his trail. From 11
A.M. to 3 P.M. the chase lasted, and Elerson, winded, staggering
from exhaustion, paused for a moment to get his breath and
recuperate.

He thought that he had distanced the pack enough to be able
to take the risk, but hardly had he paused when an Indian
popped up out of the bushes in front of him. Elerson threw up
his rifle to shoot, but as he did a rifle cracked behind him and a
bullet creased his side. The Indian in front had ducked out of
sight when Elerson leveled his rifle, and the scout, his side
bleeding, leaped forward again.

Once more he ran until he was ready to drop from fatigue.
Crossing a little ridge, he came down a slope to a swift-running

brook, and here he flopped face down, gasping as he drank the cold and refreshing water. He had taken only a few swallows when his watchful eyes saw the head of one of his pursuers pop over the crest of the hill. Elerson reached once more for his rifle, but found that he was so exhausted, his hands were shaking so, that he could not steady it. In desperation, he quickly braced the barrel of the rifle against the notch of a nearby tree, sighted and pulled the trigger. The bullet sped true to its mark, and the warrior tumbled headlong down the slope of the hill.

Hastily, Elerson reloaded his rifle and staggered away to shelter behind the trunk of a huge hemlock. He was barely out of sight when the rest of his pursuers, rushing to the sound of the shot, swept over the hill and down to the spot where the fallen brave lay. Seeing their comrade dead, they set up a loud keening, and while they were preoccupied with their grief, Elerson, unable to run further, burrowed deep into a thicket of hemlocks where he finally found the hollowed-out trunk of a tree. Into this he crept.

Motionless as a corpse in its coffin, he lay in the hollow trunk for two days without food or water or dressing for his wounds. When he backed out of his hiding place at last, he could barely stand, and when he looked about him, he did not know for a time where he was. He started off through the forest, finally picked up a familiar sign and came out into a clearing near Cobleskill, more than twenty-five miles from the spot where the chase had started.

Such hairbreadth escapes were to become almost commonplace to Tim Murphy and Dave Elerson before Sullivan's great campaign against the Indians was finished.

From Otsego, where Elerson's famous chase started, Clinton moved his division to Tioga and the rendezvous with the sluggish Sullivan. The two forces were united on August 22nd, and Sullivan began a push up the Chemung River into the heart of the Indian country. Thirty miles in advance of the main body went Timothy Murphy at the head of a scouting party.

He and his men were proceeding cautiously along the Chemung when they spied a rival party of three Indians reconnoitering down the stream. Two of the Indians were walking along the shore of the river, pulling their canoe over a rapids. The third Indian was standing erect in the canoe, pole in hand, fending the thin-skinned craft away from the rocks.

Tim Murphy studied the scene. The three Indians were all but safe, at fantastically long range, but that erect brave in the canoe made a fine and enticing mark.

"I've a notion to try the one in the canoe," Tim whispered to his companions.

Experienced woodsmen, they looked at him, studied the range, and shook their heads skeptically. Casually, almost as if it were a routine shot, Tim raised his double-barreled rifle, aimed, fired. At the crack of his shot, the Indian in the canoe suddenly threw up his hands, reeled backwards and splashed into the water. The other two Indians dropped their tow lines and fled.

Such exemplary markmanship, demonstrated repeatedly during this campaign, made Tim Murphy the most famous scout with Sullivan's army and led Maj. Moses Van Campen, who often observed Tim in action, to write in his memoirs that the great scout was one who "never missed his aim."

As Murphy's clash with the Indian scouts on the Chemung River showed, the advance of the combined American Army, numbering some thirty-seven hundred men, had not gone unobserved. So far, the Indians had abandoned their villages and fled before the invaders; but on August 29th, near the Indian village of Newtown, about six miles southeast of the present city of Elmira, they decided to make a stand.

An elaborate ambuscade was prepared for the approaching Americans on the left bank of the Chemung River. A height ran parallel to the river and not far back from its edge. Along this, the Tories, British and Iroquois had erected a long breast-work of logs, artfully concealed by planting green bushes in its front. From this breastwork, a sudden and murderous fire could be poured down the slope on the flanks of the advancing American column, and once this had been done, the entire force might be routed by fierce attacks in front and rear. All that was needed was for the Americans to stick their heads in the noose.

But this, thanks to Tim Murphy and other keen-eyed scouts under the command of Maj. James Parr, of Morgan's riflemen, was precisely what the Americans did not do. The skilled scouts spotted the phony foliage concealing the breastworks, the alarm was flashed, and Sullivan halted and made plans for battle. Artillery was set up to bombard the breastworks, a circling movement menaced the enemy's rear and a bayonet charge disconcerted the Indians. The entire enemy force—some five hundred Indians under Joseph Brant, some two hun-dred Tories and two battalions of Rangers and a small detach-ment of the British Eighth Regiment under the notorious Cap-tain Butler—was routed at the slim loss to the Americans of three killed and thirty-nine wounded. In the flush of victory, the Americans were not above taking some strange and bloody mementos. Lt. William Barton, of the First New Jersey Regi-ment, recorded in his journal that the bodies of two dead In-dians were "skinned . . . from their hips down for bootlegs; one pair for the Major, the other for myself."

After the battle of Newtown, the riflemen pursued the flee-ing, disorganized enemy, caught up with them again near what is now the town of Horseheads and bloodied them in another battle. Settling themselves in the heart of the conquered coun-tryside, Sullivan's force now began the systematic destruction of everything of value in the entire area. Town after town was burned. Huge fields of corn, beans, potatoes, pumpkins and watermelons were laid waste. Orchards were destroyed. To the lurking Indians and Tories, the ruthless leveling of their homes and crops brought the specter of winter hardship and starvation, and passions mounted as they watched and waited for a chance for a counter blow.

They got their opportunity on September 13, 1779, when Sullivan's army reached the Genesee River opposite what is now the town of Cuylerville. Sullivan ordered Lt. Thomas Boyd to take three or four riflemen, a guide and the Oneida chief, Hanyerry, to reconnoiter the Indian town across the river and report to headquarters the next morning. Boyd, evidently one of those officers to whom a little rank gave a pompous idea of importance, promptly magnified these orders beyond anything that had been intended. Instead of a small scouting party of five or six men, he rounded up a detachment of twenty-eight—a force too large to proceed through the woods on a silent and unobserved reconnaissance and at the same time a force too small to withstand the battle that, by its very presence, it invited.

In Boyd's party were men who knew better—Tim Murphy and Dave Elerson among them—but who were without authority to avert the imminent tragedy. Boyd led his men across the river and approached the town of Canaseraga (now Groveland), where Tim Murphy, directing the forward scouts, encountered a party of Indians on a hillside. The Indians, led by a rash young brave, attacked the scouts, but Murphy shot the young chief, scalped him and took his moccasins. The rest fled.

Boyd now deployed his men in the woods ringing the town, and with Murphy crept toward the village. Two Indians were lurking in the woods on the outskirts. Murphy brought one of them down with a shot from his rifle, but the second dodged behind trees and escaped. The escaping warrior and the loud gunfire in the heart of a hostile countryside were almost guaranteed to bring Indians in overwhelming numbers. Even Boyd must have recognized that his position, isolated from the main body of the army, was extremely precarious, for now, too late, he ordered a retreat.

The courageous Oneida, Chief Hanyerry, and Murphy led the way. Had they been alone they could easily have flitted through the forest and escaped, but Boyd's column of twenty-eight men could not travel so swiftly. It filed along cautiously, slowly, until within two miles of the American camp and safety. Then, Hanyerry and Murphy spotted a large force of Tories and Indians hidden in a ravine that crossed the trail.

The Americans were cut off from Sullivan's camp, and within a few seconds, they were completely encircled by the savage horde, directed by Joseph Brant himself. Boyd saw that his only hope was to attack, to try to cut through the menacing circle. Putting himself at the head of his men, he led a desperate charge. Several of the Indians were killed, but their numbers were too great. The Americans were beaten back and forced to take cover on a wooded knoll.

The rifle fire came hot and heavy. The sharpshooters in Boyd's company picked off more of the Indians, but their position was untenable. If they stayed and fought, in the end they must be overwhelmed. Recognizing this, Boyd led a second charge. Again he was driven back. A third time, he tried, and a third time, he failed.

The desperate rushes had cost him heavily. The firing was sometimes so hot and close that powder grains from the rifles were driven into the flesh along with the pellets that killed. Hanyerry, a special target, a special object of hate to Brant's Indians because he was one of their own kind fighting against them, was overwhelmed by numbers and literally hacked to pieces. Eighteen of the original twenty-eight in Boyd's scouting force lay dead.

The survivors now had the strength for only one more attempt. If they did not break through on the fourth try, they would all be killed. Recognizing this, realizing how desperate were the odds, Tim Murphy still had no intention of dying. He determined to lead the final charge himself.

Boyd, in his attempted break-throughs, had sought to pierce the Indian line in the direction of the American camp. Brant, to prevent this, had massed the bulk of his Indians at that precise spot. Tim Murphy realized that the only hope lay in making the final break to the rear, away from the American camp, away from obvious safety.

Yelling to Elerson and the others to follow him, he led the rush. One huge warrior leaped from behind a tree and tried to block his path, but Tim, lowering his shoulders, catapulted into him like a charging fullback, bowling the brave to earth and trampling right over him. The sight of the powerful warrior sprawled on the ground under the feet of the much smaller Tim Murphy was so ludicrous that it created a momentary diversion. The other braves, survivors said later, broke into laughter, and while they were enjoying their mirth, Tim Murphy led Elerson and six others through the gap. Boyd and Michael Parker, another rifleman, tried to follow them, but they were too late and too slow. Both were captured.

Even with the break-through, Murphy and his comrades were by no means safe. The Indians, recovering from their surprise, set out at once in pursuit. The fleeing riflemen split up, each seeking his own way to safety. This divided the pursuers, but not enough to help Tim. A large pack stuck on his trail.

He could not easily make for the American lines nearby, since the escape route had headed him in the wrong direction; he would have to make a long circuit through the woods to get back to camp. Tim's fleetness of foot earned him a good lead but he realized that the Indians, sprinting by turns in a relay-like system, would eventually run him down. Somehow he would have to outwit the warriors pounding so relentlessly through the forest behind him.

And so, as he fled, Tim's keen black eyes kept studying the trail on either side, hoping to discover some hiding place, some unusual feature of the terrain that would help him to shake off pursuit. He had sprinted so fast and had kept the pace so long that he was beginning to feel exhausted when, at last, he found what he sought. A huge tree, felled by a winter storm, had crashed across the trail. The reason for its fall was obvious—a core that was rotten and hollow. Quickly, Tim ducked beneath the trunk and wormed his way into the hollow, replacing a cobweb that he had disturbed in his passage. Then he lay rigid and quiet while the pursuing Indians, unsuspecting, leaped across the trunk directly above his head.

Some hours later, when the hunt seemed to have spent itself, Tim crept cautiously from his refuge in the hollow trunk and started once more on his way back to camp. The forest was still, he saw no one, and he was just beginning to exult over his escape when he heard a bush crackle. In the woods, directly in front of him, was an Indian.

The two saw each other at almost the same instant, and both molded themselves against the protective trunks of the nearest trees. There followed an intent and deadly game, each trying to lure the other into momentary, rash exposure.

Time was in the Indian's favor. The longer the stalking lasted, the greater the chance that other Indians might come upon the scene. Then Tim Murphy would be doomed. Realizing this, Tim determined to force the issue by resorting to a ruse that had worked before.

He took off his hunting cap, placed it on the ramrod of his gun, and poked it cautiously just beyond the curvature of the tree that sheltered him. The Indian fired at once. His ball pierced the cap and hurled it violently from the ramrod. With an exultant whoop, the brave leaped from the safety of his tree, tomahawk flashing as he bounded forward after the white man's scalp. A most obliging Indian. Tim didn't even have to sight. He just flipped up his rifle and fired.

Back in Sullivan's camp, Tim rejoined Dave Elerson and the other riflemen who had escaped with him. A few days later, the army pressed on to the Indian village of Little Beardstown, and here Tim and the other survivors of Boyd's party discovered convincing and gruesome evidence of the extent of their good fortune. The evidence was the mutilated, hideously tortured body of Lieutenant Boyd. William L. Stone, in his *Border Wars of the American Revolution*, gives this description of Boyd's death:

"Having been denuded, Boyd was tied to a sapling, where the Indians first practiced upon the steadiness of his nerves by hurling their tomahawks apparently at his head, but so as to strike the trunk of the sapling as near to his head as possible without hitting it; groups of Indians, in the meantime, brandishing their knives, and dancing around him with the most frantic demonstrations of joy. His nails were plucked out, his nose cut off, and one of his eyes plucked out. His tongue was also cut out, and he was stabbed in various places. After amusing themselves sufficiently in this way, a small incision was made in his abdomen, and the end of one of his intestines taken out and fastened to the tree. The victim was then unbound, and driven round the tree by brute force, until his intestines had all been literally drawn from his body and wound round its trunk. His sufferings were terminated by striking his head from his body. It was then raised upon a pole in triumph."

Such savagery inevitably inspired counter-savagery. It explains the feeling of Tim Murphy and other frontiersmen that the Indian was a beast to be killed on sight; it explains the Indian-skin leggings.

The record of Sullivan's expedition is replete with such brutality and ruthlessness. When the army disbanded at Easton, Pennsylvania, on October 15, 1779, it had laid waste the entire Iroquois country. Forty towns and innumerable scattered cabins had been reduced to ashes. Some 160,000 bushels of corn, orchards, vast quantities of vegetables had been destroyed. Only one town some eighty miles from Genesee had escaped the torch, and in the whole broad area, the Indians had been left to face the frigid upstate New York winter without shelter, without provisions.

Yet the expedition had not accomplished its purpose. It had driven the Indians and Tories in flight before it, but it had not killed or captured large numbers of them. It had not destroyed them as a fighting force. Instead, it had sent them reeling back on the British post at Niagara, there to be sheltered and fed through the bitter winter, there to be wedded even more firmly to the British cause—and there to be organized for vengeance in the spring.

In anticipation of this vengeance, Tim Murphy returned to Schoharie. His enlistment in Morgan's rifle corps had expired, so he promptly enrolled as a private under Capt. Jacob Hager in the Fifteenth Regiment of Albany County Militia, commanded by Col. Peter Vrooman. His presence was a tonic to the frontier. His reputation as an incomparable Indian fighter had been enhanced by his exploits with Sullivan, and all Schoharie rejoiced that he had come back to lend his talents to the defense of the valley. "When Murphy returned to Schoharie," Sigsby later wrote, "he was greeted with joy and exultation by every patriot in the County."

By every patriot, Sigsby should have said, except one—the one who really mattered. It did not make any difference to Johannes Feeck how big a hero Timothy Murphy was. Johannes Feeck's door was still firmly closed to Timothy Murphy and Peggy Feeck's sprightly presence was still denied him.

In the circumstances, Peggy and Tim had recourse to their old system. Tim sent love messages to the girl by Maria Teabout, and once in a long while, if he was lucky, he caught glimpses of Peggy as she went about her work on her father's farm. But that was all. Johannes Feeck was a stubborn Dutchman who had made up his mind. The winter of 1779–80 was a frustrating period for Tim Murphy, relieved only by potations in the taverns. And when spring came, as had been expected, the Indians returned, wild to avenge Sullivan's desolation of their homeland.

It was this renewed and savage warfare that brought Tim Murphy's career to a climax—that brought him closest to death and bestowed upon him his greatest good fortune. It was the paradox of the man that, the worse things were, the better he thrived, and it was now, when no sane person would have given a Continental for his life, that he swept the board with his winnings.

As soon as the winter eased, Tim began ranging the forest, watching for Indian signs. He frequently traveled far to the south and west, roaming into the wilds of Delaware County, home of scattered Indian bands and an area where the first trouble might be expected. Alexander Harper, a militia captain, often accompanied him on these scouting expeditions, and on one such mission, deep in the Delaware County forest, the two of them were surprised and captured by an Indian war party. (Jay Gould described the encounter in a history of Delaware County that he wrote before he concentrated his energies upon railroad finance and the amassing of millions.)

The war party, consisting of eleven braves, jumped Harper and Murphy so suddenly that they had no chance to defend themselves. In seconds, they were disarmed, their hands trussed behind them. The warriors recognized Tim, of course —he was the most hated white man on the Schoharie frontier because he had killed so many Indians. With grim satisfaction, no doubt, at the prospect of the tortures they would devise for him, they started marching the two prisoners briskly back to their camp at Oquago, now the town of Deposit, about sixty miles away.

All day they traveled at a fast pace, hustling their captives along in the center of their marching file. When night came, they made camp, fatigued by travel. Knowing themselves safe from all pursuit, they built a fire, ate, and then began to sample a few bottles of the white man's firewater that they had secured during their raid before they captured Harper and Murphy. The liquor stimulated the braves and soon they were prancing about their captives, waving their tomahawks menacingly, sometimes almost shaving the scalps of Harper and Murphy, and obviously restraining themselves only because they envisioned greater pleasures when they reached Oquago and brought the hated Tim Murphy to the stake.

The liquor, the celebration, the day's rigorous march—all combined at last to wear the Indians out, and they collapsed in sleep about the campfire, their two captives securely bound in the middle of the sleeping circle. Murphy and Harper knew that this was their last chance. Inching along the ground, careful not to bump into the sleeping braves, they wormed their way toward each other. Then, lying back to back, they began to tug at each other's thongs.

The stubborn knots yielded slowly—but they yielded. Bit by bit, they loosened under the clawing fingers until at last Harper and Murphy freed their hands. Quickly, they cast off the rest of their bonds, rubbed circulation back into their numbed wrists and ankles and rose with catlike stealth to their feet. Now they had to make a choice. They could either tiptoe out of camp and flee at once, trusting that the Indians would sleep until they were so far away that pursuit would be useless; or they could stay and fight to insure their safety—two men against eleven.

For Tim Murphy, the choice was simple. For him, the bold way was always the best way, and besides he hated Indians. Gesturing to Harper, he began to collect the rifles of the sleeping warriors. The two men moved swiftly and quietly about the camp, stashing the rifles out of sight in the underbrush. Then, armed with tomahawks and knives, they returned to the dying campfire and the bloody finale of their choice.

Clamping hands over the mouths of the sleepers to prevent outcry, they drove their knives deep under their victims' ribs. Time and again the knives rose and fell, in deadly silence. Suddenly, one of the sleepers awoke and emitted a strangled yell; he fell in a moment, tomahawk splitting his skull. But the outcry had been enough to arouse the camp.

The other warriors came to their feet, hands clutching at tomahawks and knives. But Harper and Murphy, the need for silence gone, were raging furies. They swept through the clearing, knives flashing, tomahawks rising and falling in skull-splitting strokes. In little more than seconds, it was over. Ten Indians lay dead. Just one had escaped.

Knowing that the survivor would carry word to Oquago and bring back a wolf-pack seeking vengeance, Murphy and Harper headed for the nearest settlement. They traveled in the bed of a small stream until daybreak, then took to a ridge to avoid surprise by Indians. Near nightfall, they reached a settlement ten miles from Schoharie. They were greeted joyfully; the settlers had feared that their failure to return from their scout meant that it had ended fatally.

The jubilation in the settlement, however, was short-lived. The adventure of Harper and Murphy clearly demonstrated that the Indians again were on the warpath. Obviously, a considerable force of them must be amassing at Oquago, and it would be only a matter of days before their fury was loosed once more on the frontier settlements. Reinforcements would be needed badly. Captain Harper mounted a horse to carry the word to Albany, and Tim Murphy pressed on to Schoharie to alert the troops there.

When Colonel Vrooman received the report of his ace scout, he acted with dispatch. He rushed a rifle company to the Delaware County frontier, and Tim Murphy went with them to lead the way. Near Harpersfield, the riflemen encountered a large force of Indians. Tim and five other scouts, well out in advance of the main body, made the first contact. They discovered three Indans, similarly scouting, and Tim promptly shot one. Almost with the crack of his rifle, a pitched battle developed.

Jay Gould subsequently described it in these words:

"Murphy took his station behind a large pine tree, within twelve rods of the Indians who lay in a ravine directly before him, and for a few moments the Indians directed their fire to that point and pierced the tree with more than 50 balls, many of which I later cut out when I was old enough to use an ax."

Tim and his sharpshooting comrades routed the Indians, who lost thirty of their warriors. Just four of the Schoharie riflemen were killed.

This first battle of Harpersfield accurately forecast summerlong flames on the border. In April, 1780, Brant and his warriors returned to Harpersfield, surprised and captured the town and took Captain Harper prisoner. They had intended to raid Schoharie, but finding it too heavily garrisoned with riflemen for their current strength, they drifted away down the Delaware to Oquago.

Other Indian bands raided the outskirts of the settlements all through Delaware County and along the Mohawk River valley to the north. On one occasion, Tim Murphy entered a town on the Mohawk where he was little known just after four Indians had raided an outlying cabin and carried off a young girl. Tim picked up the trail and shadowed the band until they made camp for the night.

The Indians, after eating, stretched out and went to sleep, first having trussed the girl securely and stretched her on the ground in the center of the camp. Tim Murphy, approaching stealthily, signaled her to silence. Then he crept noiselessly into the camp, cut the girl's bonds and led her to safety. He whispered to her to flee and leave him to attend to his unfinished business, but the girl shook her head and stoutly refused, determined to stay with her rescuer.

Tim cat-footed back into the camp, quietly removed the Indians' guns and brought them out to the spot where the girl stood. Then he stole back once more and went to work on the sleeping braves with his knife. He had killed three before the deadly struggle aroused the fourth and last brave. The warrior grabbed a tomahawk and raised it to strike, but at this point the spunky girl Tim had rescued snatched up one of the captured rifles and shot the Indian.

During a momentary lull in the border warfare, Tim slipped back to Schoharie. On the very day he arrived, a roving band of eight warriors seized two men at work in a cornfield and made off with them. Tim gathered together a party of riflemen and set out in pursuit. He caught up with the Indians in the nick of time. The two captives had been bound to a tree, faggots had been piled around them, and the Indians had begun a war dance, working themselves up to a pitch to enjoy the torture that was to follow. Tim, stationing his riflemen around the clearing, interrupted the celebration with a fusillade of rifle shots. Six of the Indians were killed, the remaining two fled, and Tim Murphy and his men brought the rescued and much-shaken farmers back to Schoharie.

This desperate sequence of battles and escapes brought a change in Tim's personal fortunes. Ever misfortune's darling, Tim had won more by these last games of tag with death then by all his earlier heroism on the frontier: Peggy Feeck, having all but lost her lover in the perils of this disastrous summer, apparently determined to have her love before it could be snatched from her; she agreed to elope with Tim.

Her consent posed problems. The first lay in the difficulty of arranging for the legality of the union. In those days, before a couple could be married it was necessary that the banns, signifying their intent, should be read for three consecutive Sundays before a religious congregation. Such a public pro-

nouncement, as Peggy and Tim realized, would be clear warning to stern Johannes Feeck, who would promptly lock his
beautiful daughter securely away, a prisoner in her room.

Tim's first problem, then, was to have the banns read pub-
licly—but in secret. Solving this paradox was easy for Tim
Murphy, who had spent most of his life turning impossibilities into possibilities. He scouted around Schoharie until he
found just the man to fit his need—John Van Dyck, a deacon at
the Middle Fort and a kindly man whose heart was attuned to
the appeal of young romance. For three Sundays, Van Dyck
read the banns at "a conference meeting," and it must have been
a select gathering indeed for not a word of the performance
reached the ears of the large Feeck clan in the valley.

With a signed document from the deacon attesting that this
formality had been complied with, Tim next sought out Maria
Teabout and asked her to tell her mistress to meet him by the
bank of the Schoharie River at nightfall October 1, 1780. Maria whispered the word to Peggy who, according to local tradition, replied promptly:

"Tell him I will meet him near the river at the time he says."

Peggy realized that it would not be easy for her to keep
the rendezvous. Tim Murphy's mere presence in Schoharie
had been enough to increase her family's watchfulness. Her
father had established a veritable family guard over her, and
she was never allowed out of the house unless she was accompanied by a relative. Even at milking time, another girl,
a cousin, always went with Peggy while she performed her
chore among the cows. But if Tim Murphy was a wily strategist, so was Peggy Feeck.

On the evening set for her elopement, Peggy took her milk
pail and went out to the barn with her cousin just as usual,
just as if her heart were not pounding so loudly that she was
afraid the vigilant cousin could hear it, too. She milked her
cows just as usual, and just as usual she walked back to her
home with her cousin. The cousin left Peggy standing on her

own doorstep, said good-by and went off to her own home. And the instant she disappeared, Peggy Feeck departed from the routine of the usual.

She tipped her pail, spilling a lot of milk upon the ground. Then she walked into the house. Her mother noticed at once that the pail was only part full.

"What is the matter?" she wanted to know, with a Dutch housewife's thrifty concern. "You only bring back part of a pail of milk?"

"There was one cow I couldn't find," Peggy said. "She must have wandered off."

"Then you must go after her," Peggy's mother snapped severely. "That cow must be milked."

"Yes, mother," said Peggy, the demure and dutiful daughter.

She picked up the pail and left the house, alone at last. At the end of the lane by the cow yard, she hung the pail on a stake, lifted up her skirts and ran to meet Tim Murphy by the river.

Her plan had gone so smoothly that its very success now almost sent it awry. Peggy Feeck was early, and Tim Murphy was not there. Afraid to wait on the river bank lest she be discovered, Peggy forded the river and set out to walk along the opposite bank to Middleburgh. Tim, riding to the rendezvous with three companions and not finding her, feared that their plan had miscarried. He rode on, and the lovers very nearly missed each other. But Tim, coming back to the appointed spot to search the river bank, heard Peggy calling to him, spurred his horse through the stream, and soon clasped in his arms a wet, shivering, distraught girl.

Lifting her to the saddle before him and cradling her there, he set out with his companions at a gallop for the Middle Fort. This they reached at eight o'clock that night.

Back at the Feeck household, in the meantime, discovery had disrupted supper. Johannes Feeck, sitting down to the evening meal, noted the absence of his daughter.

"Where is Peggy?" he asked his wife.

"She went out to look for a missing cow," his frau informed him.

"There is no cow missing," Feeck exclaimed. "They were all in the barn when I came in to supper."

He sprang up in alarm. There were two possibilities, both dire: either the Indians had kidnapped Peggy or Tim Murphy had.

A quick check with the cousin who was Peggy's escort on her nightly milking chores exposed the ruse by which Peggy had given them all the slip. Johannes Feeck realized at once that his daughter must be in the hands of that barbarian Timothy Murphy, and he flew into a fine rage.

With Joachim Follock, a relative of the family and a soldier at the Upper Fort, he set out at once for Middleburgh. He traveled fast, arriving at the fort before Peggy and Tim had a chance to depart on their wedding journey; but the garrison, joining with zest in the romantic plot, had barred the gate of the palisade and had posted a sentry to watch for the irate father. When the sentry challenged, Feeck bellowed:

"It's me, Johannes Feeck. I'm come in search of my daughter. Let me in."

"Give the password," the sentry ordered.

"I don't know the password," Feeck sputtered.

"Then if you come one step further, I'll shoot," the sentry told him.

Feeck shouted for Peggy; he roared threats at the sentry. A titter of merriment swept along the palisade as the imperturbable sentry kept repeating his litany: no password, no entrance. Furious, vowing vengeance on the stupid soldier who had kept him from finding his daughter, Feeck finally gave up and stormed away into the night.

As soon as he had left, Peggy and Tim, with a few of their friends, drove away in a wagon. On the ride to Duanesburg, near Schenectady, Tim Murphy let his fiancée in on a little secret. He produced a purse containing five hundred dollars in gold, a sizable sum in those days of depreciated Continental currency; an aunt, he said, had just died and left him the money. Whether this was truly the source of the windfall, Tim Murphy was obviously determined to show Johannes Feeck he knew how to do things right. When the wedding party reached Duanesburg, he purchased silk for a bridal gown, put several dressmakers of the town to work fitting the cloth to Peggy's pretty form, and finally, when his bride was glowingly arrayed, got the Rev. William Johnston, a Presbyterian clergyman, to perform the wedding ceremony.

Immediately after the wedding, Peggy and Tim returned to the Middle Fort at Middleburgh. Johannes Feeck appeared once more upon the scene, found that matters had proceeded much too far for a father's opposition to matter, and stormed off in high dudgeon to his home at the Upper Fort. Unyielding still, he vowed to his wife that if Margaret ever wanted to return home she would be welcome, but never, never, said he, "can she bring that thieving Irishman over the threshold."

At the moment, the "thieving Irishman" was too happy to worry very much about a father-in-law's black mood; but now, in the very moment of the honeymoon, a dark shadow descended—the shadow of the worst Indian threat that had been posed to the Valley of Schoharie in the entire war.

The first rumble of the approaching storm came to Middleburgh immediately after the marriage of Peggy and Tim. On the evening of October 3, 1780, the garrison of the fort staged a party and dance in honor of the newlyweds. Only a few figures had been danced, however, when a scout came in with a rumor that a large force of Tories and Indians had massed along the Susquehanna and were about to descend upon the Schoharie settlements. Hearing the news, Tim Murphy quickly kissed his bride, picked up his double-barreled rifle and slipped out into the hostile night, heading a scouting party to learn the strength and intentions of the enemy.

He soon discovered that the first alarming rumor had been no exaggeration. In September, Sir John Johnson had assembled three companies of his own Tory troops at Lachine, near Montreal. To these, he added a company of British regulars, a company of Hessian jagers and two hundred of Butler's Rangers. A large number of Indians under Brant and a famous Seneca chief, Cornplanter, had joined this invading army on the Susquehanna, and now the entire combined force, some one thousand five hundred Tories and Indians, was about to sweep through that open funnel at the southern end of the valley and against the Schoharie settlements.

The disparity in strength between invaders and defenders was enough to shock the stoutest heart. The Middle Fort, strongest of the three stockades in Schoharie, was manned by just 204 militia and Continental troops under Maj. Melanchthon Woolsey—204 against 1,500.

But one of this tiny garrison was Timothy Murphy—a man who was sometimes worth almost an army to his own side and a man who, sometimes fortunately, was too much of a handful for his own officers to handle.

On the night of October 16th, Johnson's army poured silently through the defiles of the southern hills near the Upper Fort, intent on surprise. They were discovered, however, by the garrison that had been anticipating the blow for nearly two weeks. Alarm guns boomed—the warning to the residents of the valley that the much-dreaded raid had started at last.

Johnson, realizing from the signal guns that his planned surprise had failed, took the leash off his Indian allies. War whoops rent the air as the savages fanned out in all diections. Soon such huge columns of smoke rose into the morning sky that the rising sun filtered through the overshadowing pall and came to earth tinged an ugly bronze red. By midday, an ancient Dutch church and more than three hundred farm-houses and barns had been put to the torch, and so many columns of smoke arose that it seemed as if the entire valley had become an active volcano.

In such a furnace, Tim Murphy began branding the hides of the marauding enemy with his rifle.

He led out a party of twenty riflemen in the pre-dawn, fire-lit grayness. Stationed behind a fence, the riflemen poured in several accurate volleys as the columns of Tories and Indians filed down the valley toward the Middle Fort. It was, of course, only the briefest of holding actions. Outflanked, in imminent danger of being overwhelmed by the mass of Johnson's army, the little party of sharpshooters had to leave the fence and drop back toward the fort—all, that is, except Tim Murphy. He lingered, waiting for another shot; got it, bagged his Indian, and then, at the last possible second, sprinted after his comrades.

At the gate of the fort, instead of going quickly inside, he ducked into a ditch and waited, with rifle reprimed, for the arrival of his incautious pursuers. They obliged him, and Tim gratified himself by knocking another Indian kicking. Then even he decided it was time to go. As he rose from the ditch, a bullet smacked against the logs of the palisade inches from his head. Whirling around, Tim spotted the Indian who had fired the shot, let him have the bullet in the second barrel of the Golcher, and then, finally, slipped himself inside the gate.

There he was greeted by a worried bride who, with Angelica Vrooman, daughter of the Colonel and her bridesmaid of two weeks ago, was already hard at work molding bullets to be fired at the Indians.

Outside, the floodtide of savagery lapped almost to the walls of the palisade. For four hours, the Tories and Indians ringing the embattled fort kept up a steady barrage of rifle fire from the shelter of the woods. Riflemen fired back from their blockhouse loopholes. Fire arrows, soaring from the crest of a ridge, started fires inside the palisade, but the flames were quickly quenched by Peggy and the other women, passing water buckets from hand to hand.

This desperate defense was maintained despite the drawback of craven example. Maj. Melanchthon Woolsey, in the exigency that confronted his garrison, was an unnerved and twittering wreck of a man. When the first rifle fire broke out, he had been found cowering among the women and children. Compelled by the jeers of his troops to show himself, he crept about the parapets on hands and knees, an abject figure, his fat body quaking at every rifle-crack. In every crisis of the day, he showed the white feather, and yet, with the perversity of the weak in exalted position, he retained the arrogance of command.

Tim Murphy and Dave Elerson watched this display, first with contempt, then with concern. In early afternoon, when a blare of trumpets sounded from the edge of the woods and a British officer emerged carrying a white flag, the two riflemen became genuinely worried. This, they knew, would be a demand for surrender. And their gallant commander, they strongly suspected, would be just the man to accept it.

Their fears were quickly confirmed. Major Woolsey, rising from all fours at the sight of the white flag, promptly began to throw his weight around as a commander.

"Prepare to admit the party with the flag!" he ordered with a flourish.

A growl of protest ran along the ranks of the riflemen. Tim Murphy and Dave Elerson held a whispered consultation. Any fool knew that no bargain made with the Tories and Indians would be kept. Once the surrender had been accomplished, the massacre would begin. And Tim Murphy and Dave Elerson had both seen the horribly mutilated body of Lieutenant Boyd; they knew exactly what to expect.

Tim looked over the parapet at the slowly advancing British officer. He had a personal tally of more than forty Indians killed; he knew it and the Indians knew it. They knew it so well that they had even offered special incentives to their braves to bring in his scalp and the scalp of Dave Elerson. And then there was Peggy. If Woolsey surrendered the fort, as he was almost certain to do, it wasn't hard to imagine what would happen to the women at the hands of the Tories and Indians. Tim's lips tightened, and black anger swept over him. His mind made up, he turned to Elerson.

"I'm goin' to stop that flag, commander or no commander," he muttered. "And just you remember—if anything happens to me, shoot him."

He nodded his head at Maj. Melanchthon Woolsey.

Then he turned, flipped up his rifle and touched off a casual shot that whizzed just above the head of Capt. Andrew Thompson, of Butler's Rangers, who was bearing the flag of truce. The bullet passed so close that Thompson felt its deadly wind, and he promptly ducked and ran back to the shelter of the woods.

Major Woolsey was almost as startled as Thompson at the crack of the unauthorized shot. In a towering rage, he stalked up and down the bastion of the fort.

"Who fired that shot?" he demanded. "Who dared disobey my orders?"

The riflemen just stared at him blandly, shrugging their shoulders. Their attitude said as plainly as words that none of them, impossible as it was, had seen a thing.

This silent opposition only infuriated the Major. He raged and stormed, and as he did, there came a new outbreak of firing from the forest. It lasted for several minutes, then subsided. And the white flag appeared again.

Once more Tim Murphy flipped up his rifle and touched off a shot that sent the truce-bearer scurrying back into the forest.

But this time Major Woolsey had kept his eyes on the riflemen. He knew just who had fired, and he rushed up to Tim, pointing and screaming with fury.

"There's the man!" he shouted to his officers. "Arrest him! Arrest him!"

A couple of the Continental officers moved forward, but the sight of the grim-faced riflemen, standing shoulder-to-shoulder in silent solidarity, stopped them in their tracks. The officers decided to try to reason with the riflemen. One of them pointed out that it wasn't honorable to fire on a flag of truce. Tim Murphy snorted.

"Honor be damned!" said he. "It's our scalps we've got to worry about. Once you let them inside that gate and they see how weak we are, we're all dead men."

Woolsey drew his sword and waved it at Murphy.

"If you fire a shot at that flag of truce again, I'll kill you," he threatened.

He whirled on his officers, especially the regulars in whom discipline was so ingrained that they would obey orders, even if the orders were to surrender. He argued that the garrison and all the residents of the countryside who had sought shelter in the fort would be massacred if they didn't surrender, and he finally ordered: "Pull down the colors."

Tim Murphy swung a purposeful rifle barrel on the group of officers.

"I'll kill the first man who tries it," he warned grimly.

No one moved to lower the flag.

In the midst of the impasse, Sir John Johnson tried again, sending out his flag of truce for the third time. And for the third time, Tim Murphy chased the standard-bearer back with a rifle bullet.

The instant he had fired, Murphy swung the business-end of his double-barreled Golcher directly at the quivering Major Woolsey.

"I still have a shot left," he reminded his commander. "And sooner than see that flag enter this fort, I'll put a bullet through your heart."

It was mutiny of the rankest sort, of course, but never was there a more patriotic mutiny than this. The method might have been wrong, but it was a situation in which no other method could possibly have served. And Tim Murphy was never the man to embrace convention at the expense of common sense.

Major Woolsey, balked by the firm stand of Tim Murphy and the riflemen, was led away by his officers. A few minutes later, he abdicated command of the fort in favor of Colonel Vrooman, who may have been only a militia officer but who certainly had the one quality the situation demanded—a stout heart.

The troops greeted the change of command with an outburst of cheers—a sound that carried clearly to the ears of the enemy in the surrounding forest, though they of course could not know its cause. The spirit those cheers expressed and the resolute defense convinced Johnson that he would never be able to storm the stronghold. And so, toward nightfall, unaware how close he had come to succeeding, having no inkling of the actual weakness of the garrison, he drew off his powerful forces and retreated down the valley past the Upper Fort.

Behind him, he left scorched earth and more than one hundred settlers dead. The only holdings that had been spared were those of Tory sympathizers, and Johnson might just as well have razed them as to stigmatize them by his leniency. As soon as he had departed, Tim Murphy led an irate band of frontiersmen from the fort, and the spared houses of the Tories were put to the torch by the patriots snapping at the heels of Johnson's retreating army. The raid, marked by the usual individual atrocities, had been horrible and devastating; but it had failed in its purpose to wipe out the Schoharie settlements. The three forts still stood and most of the settlers still lived, ready to begin the task of rebuilding—thanks, in large measure, to the wrongheaded, mutinous but sublimely courageous stand of Timothy Murphy.

The war still had nearly three years to run, and Timothy Murphy wouldn't have been true to form if he hadn't gone on playing a part in it. Since there was a lull on the frontier for some months after Johnson's raid on Schoharie, early in 1781 Tim enlisted again as a private in the Continental Army, serving in the Pennsylvania regulars under Mad Anthony Wayne in the campaign in Virginia that led to Yorktown. He was present at the surrender of Cornwallis, and then, early in 1782, he came back to Schoharie.

He was so much the hero that even Johannes Feeck had to capitulate. A family reconciliation was effected, and Peggy's stubborn father began to take a normal pride in the arrival of his grandchildren. There were still sporadic Indian raids, and Tim Murphy, until peace came in 1783, still took to the trail in pursuit of the marauders. But his great work had been done—at Saratoga, in Sullivan's campaign, in the defense of Schoharie in 1780—and he became more and more a farmer and a substantial man of affairs.

He and Peggy became the parents of five sons and four daughters. He acquired a number of farms and a grist mill. In the years following the Revolution, he even took to the stump and became a local political power. After Peggy died in 1807, he married Mary Robertson, by whom he had four more sons. Throughout his life, until his death from cancer of the neck in 1818 at the age of 67, he was a celebrity—a man to whom other men pointed in awe as they recounted his deeds, as they wondered how many of his country's enemies he had actually killed in battle, as they marveled that despite the hazards of his career, his innumerable flirtations with death, he had never received even the slightest wound in battle. It was no wonder he became a legend.

Even age did not dim the eagle sharpness of the eyes that had felled Fraser at Saratoga. Twenty years after the Revolution, some veterans were holding a shoot on the lawn by the local tavern. The mark was a round scrap of paper fastened by a nail to a board at a distance of one hundred yards. Tim Murphy was the last to shoot. Lying prone on the ground, he remarked: "Boys, I can see the head of the nail."

Then he fired one barrel of his famous Golcher, and the paper fluttered to earth. His bullet, it was found, had hit the nail squarely on the head and driven it clear through the board!

The wartime ordeal of the Valley of the Schoharie, where Timothy Murphy and his double-barreled rifle became the talk of the countryside, was surpassed both in number of atrocities and degree of desperation in the Mohawk Valley to the north. The Mohawk River crosses the breadth of New York State, and in the days of the Revolution, it offered an ideal watery highway for invasion.

The river rises almost at the break of the watershed that separates streams flowing from west to east into the Hudson from those that run from east to west into Lake Ontario. From staging grounds on islands in the St. Lawrence and from their major base at Oswego, the British sent out a succession of Tory and Indian war parties. The raiders could ascend Wood Creek, make a short portage and hit the upper waters of the Mohawk, or they could travel from Oswego to the end of Oneida Lake, cross through the forest and come out on the Mohawk farther to the east.

Set at the apex of this strategic triangle, a watchdog over both the northern route along Wood Creek and the southern route from Oneida Lake, was one isolated bastion in the wilderness—Fort Stanwix. It had been built originally by the British during *the French and Indian War, and it guarded a bend of the Mohawk some ninety miles west of Albany. As long as it stood, war parties had to skirt it to accomplish complete surprise in their raids against the more settled countryside some forty miles to the east.*

Inevitably, one of the great frontier dramas of the war revolved about Fort Stanwix and the Mohawk Valley. Raid piled upon raid and massacre upon massacre until, along the entire length of the valley, little was left except blackened ruins and the isolated nuclei of towns, clustered behind their wooden palisades in a deserted countryside.

In this savage and relentless warfare, two figures came to dominate all others. One was the detested Capt. Walter Butler, commander of companies of Tories known as Butler's Rangers and the organizer of such murderous forays as the sacking of Cherry Valley. To the settlers of the Mohawk, Butler became known as a fiend and a sadist, possessed of a viciousness and savagery that dwarfed the worst Indian instincts.

Butler's rival and nemesis was a tall, powerfully-built New Yorker with a flair for command and an intuitive skill in wilderness fighting. He was Marinus Willett, one of the leading patriots of New York City in the days before the Revolution. After he took over command along the Mohawk, in the valley's darkest and most hopeless hour, the fate of the frontier depended upon the outcome of the duel between two men—Walter Butler, who had hundreds of well-equipped Tories and Indians at his back, and Marinus Willett, who had inherited a devastated countryside and a handful of dispirited troops lacking both the means and, almost, the will to fight.

CHAPTER IV

★

★　★　★

★

Marinus Willett

THE BRITISH GARRISON WAS evacuating New York. The news
of Lexington and Concord had rung the tocsin of rebellion
throughout the Thirteen Colonies, and on the island of Manhattan, the regulars were leaving, about to board ship to join
their beleaguered comrades in Boston. It was a fine spring
morning, brilliant sunshine dappling the waters of the harbor
with dancing diamonds, and the Lobsterbacks stepped out
briskly through the city streets to the East River, where the
transports waited. In their train, along Broad Street, five
wagons trundled, heavily loaded with extra muskets, arms and
ammunition.

A crowd gathered to watch the peaceable departure of a
garrison that had been a canker on the heart of a town whip-
sawed between the passions of opposing factions. Predominant
sentiment favored the patriot cause, and there were many in
the watching throng who were heartily glad to see the backs
of the departing troops. But they were less pleased to see the
British taking those five wagonloads of arms with them. Weapons were the crucial need of the patriots, and here were weap-

ons being trundled out of the city under their very noses. But it looked as if nothing could be done about it.

The apathetic silence of the crowd was broken by a sudden commotion—the thunder of a horse's hooves, hard-ridden. From a lane opening into Broad Street, a lone rider charged upon the scene. He was a tall, powerfully built man, and he galloped directly for the munitions caravan, seized the bridle of the lead horse and forced the animal back upon its haunches. The following wagons came to a stop in the blocked road. A British major bustled up, demanding to know what was going on. The tall horseman looked down at him, almost in contempt, then swung out of the saddle and leaped onto the foremost cart. He began to harangue the crowd.

Marinus Willett was in his element. He was known to all New Yorkers as one of the most fiery of those sizzling firebrands known as the Sons of Liberty, and he was at his impassioned best now. He reminded his listeners that an agreement had been reached concerning the evacuation of the city—an agreement the British troops were in the act of violating. He proposed not to let them break their word.

His biting sarcasm, his daring appealed to the temper of the crowd. He stood there ringed by British soldiers, an isolated target high up on his improvised soapbox, yet he seemed disdainful of danger, unaware that death was just one easy musket shot away.

At this juncture, some of the city's most distinguished citizens attempted to intervene. The interventionists were led by David Matthews, the much-hated Tory Mayor of New York.

"I am surprised that you would hazard the peace and endanger the lives of our citizens when you know that the Committee have directed the troops shall be permitted to depart unmolested," the Mayor told Willett.

"My Mayor, the Committee has not authorized the troops to carry off any spare arms," Willett retorted. "You seem to forget, Sir, that there has been bloody business in Massachusetts recently. The Sons of Liberty are bound together by ties of honor as well as interest. We are detaining these arms for the use of our country."

This audacious statement of intent touched off a vigorous debate. The wealthy Gouverneur Morris, a gallant of the drawing rooms and a conservative adherent of the patriot cause, sided with Mayor Matthews; but the sentiment of the crowd was overwhelmingly with Willett. Sensing this, the wagon-top orator boldly switched the theme of his talk. He appealed directly to the British soldiers, urging them to desert the cause of the King and to join their American brethren in battle for the rights of man.

"Enjoy the air of freedom," he pleaded passionately.

Discipline was so ingrained in the regulars that, with one exception, they listened stolid and unmoved. The exception was an Irishman who broke from the ranks and joined the patriots in the crowd.

With this lone recruit to his credit, Willett hopped down from his exposed perch, took the foremost horse by the head and turned away from the line of march. The other wagons, flanked by a cheering and excited throng, followed Willett's lead, coming to a stop finally in a vacant lot near a back alley off John Street. It was a fantastic coup. A single man, by supreme daring, had outfaced the entire Royal garrison, backed by the Tory Mayor of New York, and had snatched in the very presence of an armed soldiery five wagonloads of arms—guns that were to be used to equip the first soldiers raised in the state to fight against the King.

The action was typical of Marinus Willett. A soldier in the French and Indian War when he was little more than a boy, he was a fiery individualist, one of that special breed the Revolution seemed to produce in such abundance—men who recognized no odds as too daunting and who dared, alone and unaided, to take risks from which even the most elementary grain of prudence would have restrained them. Willett's single-handed seizure of the Royal munitions carts was an action in harmony with the spirit of his day. It was also a clear indication of the caliber of the man who was to be hailed at the war's end as the hero of the Mohawk Valley and the savior of the New York frontier.

This patriot who was to play such a pivotal role in the fierce border warfare of the Revolution was a descendant of one of America's oldest families and the son of a devout Loyalist sympathizer. An ancestor, Thomas Willett, had come to Plymouth on the *Lion* in 1632. Marinus himself was born on July 31, 1740, near Jamaica, Long Island. When he was nine, his father, Edward, moved to New York. There he eventually became proprietor of the Province Arms, the most important hostelry of its day and the site of the city's most notable social functions. Naturally enough, Willett Sr. absorbed and shared the viewpoint and the loyalties of the wealthy and conservative class to whom he catered.

Not so his son. Marinus Willett grew into a tall, strong, ruggedly handsome man. He seems to have been endowed with three strong instincts: he loved action, splendid martial attire and pretty women. As an old man, writing a narrative of his life, he recalled with nostalgic affection the splendor of his first uniform. He wore it in 1758 when, not yet eighteen, he raised a company of his Long Island neighbors to fight in the French and Indian War. Commissioned a second lieutenant, he marched off in a uniform consisting of a "green coat trimmed with silver twist; white under clothes and black gaiters, a cocked hat with black cockade of silk ribbon, with silver button and loop."

Young Marinus received his indoctrination in the very area and the very type of warfare that were to bring him fame in the Revolution. He was in the army massed under the command of the blundering Lord Abercrombie for an attack on French-held Fort Ticonderoga, strategically located to command the bottleneck between Lake George and Lake Champlain. The campaign swiftly degenerated into a bloody fiasco, with the indecisive Abercrombie, guarded by two regiments, huddled under a huge tree trying to determine what to do, what orders to issue, while all the time the exposed ranks of his men were being swept by a withering hail of lead from the embrasures of the fort. Finally, having settled on no plan, having launched no real attack, Abercrombie withdrew, leaving some two thousand casualties on the field behind him.

The necessity of salvaging something from this abortive campaign led Abercrombie to send one section of his army to the west to lay siege to the French fort at Oswego. Willett went with this new expedition as a volunteer. Three days of fierce fighting reduced the defenses of the fort, and the French surrendered. The victory was an important one, for Oswego had been a key base for French and Indian war parties raiding the New York frontier; but the after-price was heavy.

The British and Colonial troops participating in the Oswego campaign suffered from all the rigors of wilderness warfare—long and exhausting marches, inadequate food and water, constant exposure. The health of entire regiments had been undermined, and disease became epidemic. Near Rome, New York, on the return march, some five hundred of the ailing soldiers collapsed and died. They were buried where they fell, and the emaciated, ailing survivors pressed on, struggling step by step through the wilderness to avoid a similar fate. Finally, on September 10, 1758, the remnants of the victorious army straggled into Fort Stanwix, a new outpost built during the year on the upper reaches of the Mohawk River.

Stanwix, which was to bulk large in the later career of Willett, was considered to be among the most formidable border forts of its day. It had been built at a cost of $266,000, then a tremendous sum. It consisted of a high, sharpened palisade surrounding blockhouses and breastworks. The palisade was circled by a deep, wide ditch from which protruded the sharp spikes of abatis. It was here at Fort Stanwix that even Willett's

rugged constitution buckled under the twin assault of privation and disease. He lay seriously ill for more than two months,
and when he recovered in November sufficiently to travel, he
was little more than a skeleton of his former self. He made
his way slowly by boat down the Mohawk to Schenectady,
traveled overland to Albany, and then took a boat down the
Hudson to New York. At home, he slowly recuperated, but
the war for him was ended.

Willett, faced with the necessity of making a living, went to
work in the shop of a cabinet maker. It wasn't long before the
tall, strapping youth caught the eye of his employer's daughter, Mary Pease, and in April, 1760, they were wed in Trinity
Church. About the same time, Willett's Loyalist father gave
up tavern-keeping and returned to his Jamaica farm. With the
tensions of the years, the split between father and son became
more pronounced, for Willett became increasingly active as a
leader of the radical element opposing the policies of the British Crown.

So ardent a patriot did he become that he gave up his pew in
Trinity Church because the prayers included a wish for the
health and welfare of the King. He joined the Sons of Liberty,
helped make placards attacking the Stamp Act, and helped
erect a gallows to hang Lt. Gov. Cadwallader Colden in
effigy. On January 18, 1770, he became involved in a riot over
the dispatch of supplies from New York to British troops in
Boston; in 1775, he was one of the leaders of a band of the Sons
who boarded a sloop bound for Boston and stripped it of its
cargo; and finally when Isaac Sears, the foremost leader of
the New York Sons of Liberty, was arrested and flung into jail,
Willett helped raise a band of volunteers to rescue him.

His leadership in these tumultuous activities naturally entailed great personal risk and involved personal retribution.
Willett was in business with his father-in-law at the Sign of
the Clothes Press and had developed a sideline as a public auc-
tioneer; but his patriotic activities alienated some clients and

hurt business. They also strained his relationship with his aging father, Edward Willett, who told him sadly when he left to join the Continental Army: "My son, I never expect to see you again, for you will either be killed in battle or hung."

Shrugging aside this gloomy prophecy with its equally un-palatable alternatives, Marinus Willett became the second Cap-tain in the First New York Regiment, commanded by Col. Alexander McDougall. His commission was dated June 28, 1775, and on August 8th, his company left on a sloop for Al-bany, armed with the very muskets Willett had snatched from the departing British troops by his impetuous, single-handed action in Broad Street.

The northern theater to which Willett had been assigned was preoccupied at the time with grandiose plans for the inva-sion of Canada. An army was being slowly assembled under Maj. Gen. Richard Montgomery for a drive up Lake George and Lake Champlain. In early September, Willett and his com-pany were in a force of five hundred men dispatched by Mont-gomery to seize the British stronghold of St. Johns at the northern end of the lake.

The command of this advance detachment had been given to Lt. Col. Rudolphus Ritzema, an officer who moved with all the speed of a sloth and who failed for days to cut off supplies flowing into the fort from the surrounding countryside. By the time he finally drew the lines tight, St. Johns was well supplied to withstand a siege. This it did for fifty days. Not until Wil-lett finally placed batteries of Lamb's New York Artillery on a hill commanding the fort did the five hundred British and one hundred Canadian troops inside at last surrender. It was the kind of belated victory that insures defeat. The garrison of St. Johns had delayed the American invasion of Canada for nearly two months; the time lost could not be recovered; and Montgomery pressed on to a mid-winter invasion and to disaster and death before the walls of Quebec.

Willett seems to have been the only officer who came out of

the protracted St. Johns siege with credit. His handling of the artillery had impressed his superiors, and he was given command of the troops escorting the captured garrison back down the lake to Fort Ticonderoga. Later he was placed in command of St. Johns itself. In the spring, he was detailed to accompany some of the captured British officers and their families downriver, and on March 5, 1776, he was back in New York.

A promotion to Major followed in April. Willett joined Col. John Lasher's company of militia and helped in the construction of the Bayard Hill redoubt west of the Bowery, one of the forts on which the patriots relied to blunt the imminent British attack on New York. While he was working on the defenses, the need arose to lead a foray against the Tories.

A strong Tory band had been organized in Willett's native Jamaica. A hill near the town had been seized and fortified by the construction of a palisade. The tiny stronghold was a challenge and an irritant to New York patriots, who naturally became more incensed, as war drew closer to them personally, at what they considered the treasonable activities of their neighbors. And so Willett was dispatched with a mounted troop to wipe out the Jamaica nest.

On the way, he passed his father's house. It was closed and shuttered. Not knowing whether this meant that the aging Edward Willett had sought refuge elsewhere or had gone to join the Tories on the hill, the son pressed on, determined to attack even if one of those whom he had to fight might turn out to be his own father.

Arriving before the Tory fort, Willett dismounted his men and deployed them in a circle around the base of the hill. He instructed them to take cover behind stumps and trees, Indian fashion, and to wait until he gave the signal to fire. The Tories inside the palisade opened up with a heavy musket fire, but Willett's men waited for his signal before replying. Then, in a sharp fusillade, they killed one of the Tories and wounded several others. The rest surrendered, and Willett sent eighteen back as prisoners to New York. To Willett's heartfelt relief, his own father had not been among the defenders.

Victory in this skirmish raised Willett's stock even higher with fellow patriots, but it was no cure for the low state of Willett's personal fortunes that coincided with it. His private business had been ruined; from the army, he had received no pay. He needed income to support his wife Mary and his son Marinus, a gay young blade who had been studying medicine at Kings College and had earned a bad conduct report by stealing wine from the garret of the college president. Casting about for a means of livelihood, Willett decided to go into partnership with a friend, setting up furnaces to extract salt from sea water. He asked Congress for a loan of one thousand pounds to help finance the project, but before the loan could be acted upon, he plunged ahead with construction. The location of the salt works was Long Island. They became almost the first installations destroyed when the British stormed ashore.

With the invasion of Long Island, Mary Willett left New York and went to live with relatives in Danbury, Connecticut. Young Marinus joined his father, fought in the battle along Brooklyn Heights and stayed in the army as a surgeon's mate. Willett aided Colonel McDougall in ferrying Washington's troops across the East River and also occupied himself supplying the army, bringing in provisions and ammunition by boat from Long Island and Connecticut and by wagon overland through White Plains.

In November, Willett was commissioned a lieutenant colonel in Col. Peter Gansevoort's Third New York Regiment, and he spent the winter of 1776–77 at Fishkill on the Hudson, recruiting, drilling and equipping his men. In the spring, he was given command of Fort Constitution on the river opposite West Point. The British made a tentative thrust up the river at this time, and McDougall, who commanded in the highlands, called on Willett for help.

The express rider carrying McDougall's message reached Willett on March 23rd, a Sunday, while his troops were parading for a field review. Willett promptly set out on the march to Peekskill, where he took up position on heights commanding the countryside. He noticed that a detachment of one hundred men had become separated from the main body of the enemy, and he moved swiftly in an effort to cut them off. Leading his men by a circuitous route, he crossed fences and rough terrain and at dusk reached the river. The British, however, had seen him coming and fled precipitately to the refuge of their warships, leaving behind cloaks, blankets and baggage. One blue camlet cloak was to become an item of special significance for Willett. From it was to be cut the blue field for the flag he flew over Fort Stanwix during the later crises of this desperate year.

Willett's transfer to Stanwix, the bastion on the upper Mohawk in which he had been so critically ill during the French and Indian War, came on May 18, 1777. The fort, when Willett had seen it last, had been new and strong, a formidable outpost in the wilderness; now, on his return to the scene of his boyhood soldiering, Willett found a veritable ruin.

The ditch had filled up. The embankments had crumbled away. The pickets of the palisades had rotted. The barracks and the magazines were tumbling down. An engineer who had been sent to the fort to supervise repairs had constructed new barracks in the most novel and impossible of positions—outside the fort, perfectly exposed to Indian attack. He had done almost nothing to strengthen the fort itself. Willett, surveying the scene, erupted in wrath. He denounced the engineer as a traitor. Colonel Gansevoort, apparently of more placid temperament, was inclined to view the man only as an incompetent blunderer; but Willett, outraged and seething, wrote a letter denouncing the offending expert to Maj. Gen. Philip Schuyler commanding the northern department in Albany. The engineer was cashiered from the service, another was sent to replace him and repairs were rushed to strengthen the fort for the blow that was about to fall.

The British grand design for the campaign of 1777 had envisioned a three-pronged attack to slice up New York State. Burgoyne led the major force directly south down the chain of lakes from Canada. He was supposed to be supported—but was not, when the chips were down—by British troops thrusting up the Hudson from New York. The third invading arm was to thrust directly east from Oswego on Lake Ontario, strike at Fort Stanwix and sweep on down the Mohawk Valley to a junction with Burgoyne at Albany.

This third striking force was under the command of Barry St. Leger, a British lieutenant colonel holding the temporary rank and performing the functions of a brigadier. Gathered under St. Leger were all the major raiders who were to become so hated on the New York frontier. Sir John Johnson was there, commanding his Royal Greens. Col. John Butler, whose brutal son, Capt. Walter Butler, was to become the most detested of all Tories, led a company of Butler's Rangers. And finally there was Joseph Brant, also known as Thayendanegea, the war chief of the Mohawks—a man whose sister had been the acknowledged wife of Sir John Johnson's father, William; a man who had been educated in Connecticut, who had been entertained by James Boswell in London and had had his picture painted by Romney. He led a veritable army of about one thousand Indian braves. The entire force—Indians, Tories and British and Hessian regulars—numbered about eighteen hundred men; and only Stanwix, recently and imperfectly rescued from ruin, and Stanwix's tiny garrison of seven hundred and fifty men stood in their way.

St. Leger's horde descended upon the fort on August 2, 1777. Some two hundred men and a train of supplies, brought up-river in five bateaux, slipped into the fort little more than minutes in advance of the invaders. Indeed, it was such a near thing that one of the bateau-men was killed and two wounded by Brant's Indians. Without the reinforcements and supplies, defense of the fort would have been almost impossible; even with it, the garrison was outnumbered more than two to one, they had provisions for only six weeks, and there was little powder. Willett and Gansevoort estimated that the only way the powder could be made to last as long as the provisions was to limit the firing to nine cannon shots a day.

One of the first acts of Brant's Indians was to burn the barracks that had been constructed outside the fort. The next day, August 3rd, St. Leger arrived with the bulk of his army. His first act was to stage a full-dress review, intended to intimidate the defenders by the display of overwhelming numbers. Actually, Brant's one thousand Indians produced the opposite effect. The sight of so many warriors, to men who knew their savage methods well, aroused not fear but desperate determination to hold out. St. Leger followed up his demonstration of power by sending the defenders a pompous declaration demanding surrender. They ignored it. And the siege began.

St. Leger was faced with the necessity of hacking a road through the forest to bring up his artillery and supplies. While his axmen went to work, Brant's Indians squirmed close to the fort and sniped at defenders as they worked piling clods upon the embankments. Several of the patriots were wounded, and for two days a brisk, intermittent firing was maintained. Then, on the morning of August 6th, the defenders of Stanwix noted a change.

The sniping of the Indians fell off. Many seemed to be slipping away into the forest. The besieging troops, too, seemed greatly reduced in numbers. While the Americans were trying to figure out the meaning of this change in tactics, two scouts slipped through the encircling lines with an explanation. Nicholas Herkimer, son of a German immigrant and a brigadier general commanding the Tryon County militia, was on his way up the Mohawk at the head of a relief force. St. Leger was drawing off the bulk of his strength to meet Herkimer, laying the ambush that was to lead to one of the bloodiest frontier battles of the war at Oriskany.

Herkimer had asked for a sortie from the fort to aid his own attack. Colonel Gansevoort summoned Willett and gave him command. The garrison was drawn up, and Willett asked for volunteers.

"Soldiers," he said, "you have heard that General Herkimer is on the march to our relief. The commanding officer feels satisfied that the Tories and Queen's Rangers have stolen off in the night, with Brant and his Mohawks, to meet him. The camp of Sir John Johnson is therefore weakened. As many of you as feel willing to follow me in an attack upon it, and are not afraid to die for liberty, will shoulder your arms and step one pace in front."

The men responded almost in a body, and an attacking force of two hundred was quickly organized. They were given one of the fort's tiny three-pounder cannon for a field piece, and another fifty men were formed into a special guard entrusted with making certain that, if the attack went awry, the cannon should not fall into enemy hands.

While these preparations were being made, rain started to fall. As soon as it stopped, Willett led his men from the fort and launched them, in one lightning-swift stab, straight at the heart of the enemy camp where Sir John Johnson, protected by his Royal Greens, had set up his headquarters.

Willett drove the attack home with such force that the thin screen of guards before Johnson's headquarters was quickly shattered. Sir John, not even pausing to put on his coat, rushed from his tent and tried to rally his troops; but Willett's men smashed through the camp, cutting down all who opposed them. The Tories, demoralized by the suddenness of the blow, scattered and fled in all directions. Sir John himself and some of his men crossed the Mohawk to St. Leger's camp on the opposite side of the stream, and Willett concentrated on the swift, methodical looting of the captured camp site.

His men loaded twenty-one wagons with the spoils of victory—clothing, blankets, stores, camp equipage, five British standards, Sir John's baggage and all of his official papers, together with the property and correspondence of other officers. From across the river, St. Leger's forces opened up on Willett's men with two field pieces, but a hot return fire quickly flushed them from the thicket in which the guns had been concealed. Willett then returned to Stanwix with his booty. The captured standards were raised over the fort beside the crude American flag fashioned in part from the cloth coat Willett had seized at Peekskill, and the garrison celebrated their victory with three loud cheers. Willett had achieved the triumph, for which he was later presented with a sword by Congress, without the loss of a man.

Brilliant as the stroke had been, it did not greatly alter the situation at the fort. Stanwix was still under siege, and soon it was more isolated than ever. Herkimer, ambushed and surrounded at Oriskany, fought his way out of the bloody trap in a stubborn, drawn battle. The general himself was mortally wounded, and his army had to fall back. St. Leger, freed from the threat to his rear, concentrated all his efforts on the reduction of Stanwix.

He drew the siege lines so tight that no messengers could slip into the fort. The patriots, completely cut off, had no knowledge of the outcome at Oriskany and could only assume the worst from Herkimer's failure to smash through to their relief. St. Leger had suffered so severely in the battle that it was almost as much a defeat as a victory for him. His invading force had been weakened, its power blunted; but he realized that the defenders of Stanwix could not know the truth and promptly decided to take advantage of their ignorance. He would represent Oriskany as an overwhelming triumph, he would picture Burgoyne as sweeping all before him, he would convince the defenders of the fort that they had no alternative except surrender.

Under the white flag of truce, Col. John Butler and two other officers were sent out from the British lines. Colonel Gansevoort made careful preparations to receive them. He ordered the visitors blindfolded before they were admitted, an essential precaution to keep them from observing the poor state of the fort's defenses and the inadequacy of its garrison. Eyes swathed in heavy bandages, St. Leger's delegation was let inside the gate and led directly to Gansevoort's dining room. The windows of the room had been tightly shuttered so that the British officers could not see out when their blinkers were removed, and the conference took place in a dungeon-like darkness, relieved only by the wavering light of candles.

Gansevoort had assembled the officers of his staff to hear the ultimatum. Of the group, Willett was easily the dominant figure, overshadowing even his own commander. Tall and ruggedly built, he had a commanding presence. His forehead was high, intelligent; his eyes deep-set. He had a long, beaked nose; wide, firm-set lips; and a jaw that seemed to have been chiseled from granite. His was a craggy profile, expressive of a determined personality; and as the British officers delivered their message, the cragginess became more pronounced, the features more tightly and grimly set.

Major Ancron, the most fluent of St. Leger's aides, delivered the British message. He dwelt upon St. Leger's humane desire to avoid bloodshed; he pictured the Indians as being restrained from atrocity only with the utmost difficulty. The only solution, he said, was for the garrison to surrender the fort and all its stores immediately. Otherwise, there would be a massacre. But if the surrender was agreed to, the officers and soldiers of the garrison would be allowed to retain their personal baggage and their safety would be guaranteed. In any event, what choice did the Americans have? Burgoyne, Major Ancron told them, lying boldly, already "had possession of Albany"; they were isolated, abandoned, lost to all hope; and if they did not accept St. Leger's terms now, the offer could not be repeated because the Indians would be completely out of hand.

Willett listened to this concoction in coldly mounting fury. He was a man who hardened under threats. When Major Ancron had finished speaking, he started forward impulsively, then looked at Colonel Gansevoort. The Colonel, knowing well the temper of his chief aide and his reputation as a speaker possessed of a rough, blunt eloquence, nodded his permission; and Willett promptly delivered the American answer. In scathing terms, he harangued the British officers and ridiculed their position.

"Do I understand you, sir?" he asked Major Ancron. "I think you say you came from a British colonel, who is commander of the army that invests this fort; and, by your uniform, you appear to be an officer in the British service. You have made a long speech on the occasion of your visit, which, stripped of all its superfluities, amounts to this—that you come from a British colonel to the commander of this garrison, to tell him that, if he does not deliver up the garrison into the hands of your Colonel, he will send the Indians to murder our women and children.

"You will please to reflect, sir, that their blood will be upon your heads, not upon ours. We are doing our duty; this garrison is committed to our charge, and we will take care of it. After you get out of it, you may turn round and look at its outside, but never expect to come in again, unless you come a prisoner.

"I consider the message you have brought a degrading one for a British officer to send, and by no means reputable for a British officer to carry. For my own part, I declare, before I would consent to deliver this garrison to such a murdering set as your army, by your own account, consists of, I would suffer my body to be filled with splinters and set on fire, as you know has at times been practiced by such hordes of women-and-children killers as belong to your army."

The British officers flushed under the lash of Willett's tongue and departed in a haughty silence, blindfolded as they had come. The contemptuous rejection of the demand for surrender compelled St. Leger to redouble his efforts to reduce the fort. Indian marksmen renewed their sniping; redoubts were built closer to the fort, field guns were set up in the embrasures. Cannon balls began to pepper the walls, but St. Leger's artillery was too light to penetrate the sod embankments. Unable to smash a gap in the defenses with artillery, the British general began digging ditches, regular approaches by parallels, inching ever closer to the walls in the hope of ultimately being able to undermine and breach them.

Despite Willett's bold answer, the situation of the garrison was daily becoming more desperate. If the British ever made a breach in the walls, the defenders of Stanwix would hardly be able to cope with their overwhelming numbers. It became imperative to get a message through the British lines acquainting the American command of their plight. Yet the imperative seemed impossible. So tightly had St. Leger invested the fort that even before Oriskany, Herkimer's scouts had had to wait for days, had had to wait until St. Leger had drawn off most of his force, before they could venture through the hostile lines. Those lines were even tighter now. Trying to slip through them was virtually a suicide mission.

It was a mission for which Willett volunteered.

In most armies, a high-ranking officer hardly would have been employed in so hazardous a task. Willett was a lieutenant colonel, the second in command of a garrison, many ranks removed from a woodland scout; but in the Revolution, among the amateur soldiers who were in rebellion against their King, these distinctions counted for less than they would in a veteran army with an ingrained military caste system. Officers, at the outset at least, were often elected by their own men; they were close to the rank-and-file, shared the sufferings and the hazards of the rank-and-file, to a far greater degree than would have been the case in a professional military machine. They led by example, and because they did, suicide missions were not beneath them. In this case, obviously, Willett believed that he knew the terrain, the way out of the fort, the way through the enemies' lines, better than anybody; and he determined to carry the vital plea for help himself. Another officer, Lieutenant Stockwell, volunteered to go with him.

The night the two men picked for their mission was an inclement one. Severe thunderstorms swept across the countryside. Lightning crackled, wind blew and rain came down in blinding torrents. Willett and Stockwell, each armed with a spear, slipped out of a sally-port at 10 P.M. They dropped flat on the ground and wriggled on hands and knees along a morass to the river. Enveloped in the storm, they crossed the stream on a log and felt their way past the line of huddled, drenched, miserable sentinels. They pressed on into thick and tangled woods; in the darkness of the night and the blinding storm, they quickly became lost. Trying to put distance between themselves and the enemy encampment, they blundered on. Then they heard a dog barking. They knew that they must have gone in the wrong direction, that they must be near an Indian camp.

Willett and Stockwell halted. They stood unmoving, as rigid as the trees that surrounded them. They knew that, if they made a sound, they would arouse the dog still more; that his yapping would bring the Indians down upon them. Motionless, muting even the act of breathing, they stood and waited. Finally, the storm clouds broke, the eastern sky began to pale with the dawn. Able to pick out their proper course again, they trod softly as they crept away from the dangerous proximity of the Indian camp. They found the bed of a small stream and followed it silently, hiding their trail. For two days, through country infested with Indians, they worked their way steadily east, emerging from the forest at last at Fort Dayton, some twenty-five miles away. There they mounted horses and rode hard to the headquarters of Schuyler at Stillwater.

The American commander, alert to the danger at Stanwix, had already organized a relief force under the command of Benedict Arnold. Willett's description of the plight of the garrison spurred Arnold to hurry to the fort's relief by forced marches. Willett accompanied him. Arnold's force was only about half the size of St. Leger's, far too puny to challenge the British army in pitched battle. A stratagem was needed. And Arnold possessed the guile to devise the ruse to fit the need.

A party of Tories had been captured near Fort Dayton. They were headed by Capt. Walter Butler, and they included a half-wit country bumpkin, Hon Yost Schuyler, a nephew of General Herkimer. Willett presided as judge advocate of the court-martial at which both Butler and Hon Yost were tried. It was the first time the war had pitted against each other the two men, Butler and Willett, whose duel of wits and strength was to determine the fate of the New York frontier; but at the moment Hon Yost Schuyler was more important in the scheme of things than Butler.

Willett's court-martial board condemned both men. Instantly, Arnold was beset with pleas for clemency. Hon Yost Schuyler's mother begged him to spare her son's life; and as the general listened to her, a plan began to form in his mind— a plot that was a measure of both the deviousness and the genius of the man. Arnold agreed that he wouldn't march Hon Yost before a firing squad, but in return for this consideration, he required a service. Hon Yost was well known to the Indians, and Arnold would let him live if he would agree to enter St. Leger's camp and scare St. Leger's Indian allies with a horrifying tale of the overwhelming might of Arnold's approaching host. To insure that Hon Yost would keep his promise, Arnold proposed to hold his brother as a hostage.

Hon Yost, a dullard who was easily swayed and had no

strong convictions, wasn't so stupid that he couldn't recognize life was preferable to a firing squad. He entered into the scheme with boyish enthusiasm. Taking off his jacket, he fired several musket balls through it, and with this stage prop for his story, he set out for St. Leger's camp, accompanied by a friendly Oneida Indian. When he neared the siege lines, Hon Yost began to run, and he burst upon the Indians thoroughly winded, eyes rolling, a perfect picture of terror. The Indians, curious, gathered around him, and he babbled an almost incoherent tale about his miraculous escape from the terrible Arnold. He held up his bullet-riddled coat as evidence. Impressed, the Indians asked the inevitable question: How many men did Arnold have? Hon Yost rolled his eyes again and gestured to the leaves of the trees in graphic answer.

The Indians began to quake. St. Leger and other British officers tried to reason with them, cajoling, pleading; but the Indians heeded only their own inner panic. And just at this juncture, the Oneida who had set out with Hon Yost, came running into camp, confirming Hon Yost's tale. That did it. The Indians melted away into the forest, and St. Leger, abandoned by half his army, had to lift the siege. His, however, was no orderly retreat; the panic that had stricken the Indians communicated itself to his own troops. They threw away guns and knapsacks to flee faster, and some of the Indians, seeing white men helpless, began to scalp the soldiers who had been their brothers-in-arms.

So ended the siege of Stanwix, a battle won by bluff and play-acting rather than by muskets. Marinus Willett had emerged from the action as a frontier hero, and the stage had been set for his future struggle with Captain Walter Butler. Butler, like Hon Yost Schuyler, had won a reprieve, and he promptly misused it. Taking advantage of the compassion that had been shown him, he escaped to Canada and returned to wage vengeful war along the entire frontier.

Four years were to intervene before Butler and Willett clashed again. They were years of disaster in the Mohawk Valley, years filled with vigorous campaigning for Willett. In 1779, he commanded a detachment of six hundred troops and destroyed a dozen villages of the Onondagas before joining Sullivan's expedition in its invasion of the homeland of the Iroquois. The winter of 1779–80 saw Willett back with Washington's Army. The cold was so severe that the waters of New York harbor froze, and Willett led a force of five hundred men across the ice to Staten Island, raiding the British lines and bringing off seventeen wagons loaded with supplies. Later, during the same winter, he raided Paulus Hook in Jersey City, captured one of the redoubts and rounded up a herd of cattle belonging to the British.

With the spring of 1781, the war in the Mohawk Valley had reached the stage of crisis. Tryon County had been subjected to almost ceaseless raids and had suffered more severely than any other section of the colonies. More than three hundred women had been widowed, some two thousand children orphaned, twelve hundred farms laid waste. In May, even Fort Stanwix, which Willett had helped to save in 1777, had to be abandoned. It had been damaged by fire and flood; its garrison had been reduced to a mere handful of ragged troops, inadequate to repair and defend it. Though it was a vital bastion in the upper reaches of the valley, it was evacuated without a blow having been struck against it, and the defense perimeter shrank to the outposts of Fort Dayton and Fort Plain, only some fifty to sixty miles west of Albany. Even these so-called forts were not secure. They were garrisoned by tiny squads of disorganized, ill-equipped troops and raw militia. New invasion from the west could result only in more horrible massacres; the people of the valley recognized the hopelessness of their plight, and their spirits were all but crushed. Only a strong, centralized command, only a leader of exceptional ability familiar with the terrain and adept at wilderness warfare could save them from what seemed an inevitable tide of disaster.

In this extremity, Gov. George Clinton of New York appealed to Willett to leave the main army under Washington and take command of all the scattered forces in the Mohawk Valley. Willett was loath to accept, feeling that he was being relegated to the backwash of the war, but the appeal was one that, in final analysis, he could not turn down. And so, late in June, 1781, he returned to the Mohawk. He established his headquarters at Fort Rensselaer, now Canajoharie, some fifty miles west of Albany, and quickly took stock of the situation. He found that he had under him in the main garrison just one hundred and twenty men. There were twenty more at Fort Herkimer, an outpost some thirty miles to the west; thirty at Ballston and twenty at Catskill. In all the rest of the Mohawk area, some one hundred additional troops were scattered.

Assessing his forces, Willett found, as he wrote Governor Clinton, that he had been left with mere fragments of companies "hastily collected from the ruins of the last campaign." He added: "I confess myself not a little disappointed in having such a trifling force for such extensive business as I have now on my hands; and, also, that nothing is done to enable me to avail myself of the militia. The prospect of a suffering country hurts me. Upon my own account I am not uneasy. Everything that I can do shall be done; and more cannot be looked for. If it is, the reflection that I have done my duty must fix my tranquility."

Willett had no time to reorganize his fragmentary units before he found himself plunged into battle. On July 9, 1781, one of the section's more active Tories, Capt. John Doxstader, led a raiding party of between three hundred and four hundred Indians against the settlement of Currytown, some seven miles east and slightly south of Canajoharie. There were only a dozen houses in the hamlet. One, a Cape Cod-style structure, had been fenced around with a palisade and served as a fort. The settlers were all at work in the fields around their cabins when, about noon, the Indians burst out of the forest upon them.

Dropping their hoes, the farmers tried to flee into the fort. One of them, Jacob Dievendorff, outraced the Indians, but his son, Frederic, was caught outside the palisade and scalped before the father's eyes. Another son, Jacob, then eleven, was taken prisoner. Captured with him were seven other residents and a girl of ten.

The surprise had been complete, and Doxstader's Tories and Indians, resistance crushed, plundered the settlers' cabins and put them to the torch. Content with their prisoners and booty, they made no attempt to attack the puny fort, but set off in the direction of a strong Tory settlement called New Dorlach, now the town of Sharon Springs, some ten miles south of Canajoharie.

Willett at the time was in Fort Plain, four miles west of Canajoharie. Early on the morning of the attack, he had sent out a party of thirty-five men under the command of Captain Gross to reconnoiter the countryside around Sharon Springs. Even as the smoke from the sacking of Currytown started to rise into the summer sky, Gross came upon the trail of the Tory and Indian war party. It led for more than a mile into the center of a dense cedar swamp some two miles east of Sharon Springs. Gross sent a couple of scouts along the trail and found that the packs of the raiders were still at the campsite in the swamp and that a few braves were cooking about the campfires. Obviously, the war party expected to return to this base after the attack on Currytown. Having obtained this information, Gross led his patrol to one side, hid his men securely in the forest and sent a messenger to inform Willett of his discovery.

Willett had seen the smoke of burning Currytown from Fort Plain and already had gone into action. He had dispatched

Capt. Robert McKean with sixteen men to Currytown to investigate and feel out the strength of the enemy, and had then set out himself to round up the militia. This task took most of the afternoon, and even then Willett could muster only one hundred and fifty men.

Gross' messenger arrived while Willett was rallying the militia. The news determined his course of action. He decided to unite all of his available forces for a night attack on the hideout in the Sharon Springs swamp. A messenger was sent off to notify McKean in Currytown of the plan. McKean's scouting party had arrived too late to make contact with the raiders, but had stayed to help put out the fires and bury the dead. Receiving Willett's message, McKean marched at once to join his commander.

The night was exceptionally dark and lowering. Willett's guide became lost, and it was nearly 6 A.M. before the detachments of Willett, Gross, and McKean were united. By this time, all chance of a surprise night attack had been lost. The enemy was alert and stirring. Apprised of the approach of their attackers, they had left their campsite and taken up a strong position. Willett, outnumbered almost two men to one, paused to devise a strategy to offset the odds.

A frontal attack would be suicide, and Willett had no intention of committing such self-destruction. He decided that he would have to lure the Tories and Indians from their strong defenses, that he would have to entice them into making an attack upon him; and he made his dispositions accordingly. He drew up his forces in two parallel lines, shaped like a crescent. One he hid in a small ravine; the main line, he strung out behind it along the crest of a small ridge. Having devised the trap, Willett now pushed forward a morsel of bait in the form of a small detachment, thoroughly briefed on the role it was to play. The unit climbed out of the ravine and across the crest of a slight rise; it lanced straight forward in a thrust at the enemy's postion. Then, at the last moment, apparently discovering for the first time the overwhelming strength of the Tories and Indians in front, its members halted, turned and scattered in flight.

The prospect of easy scalping lured the Indians from their hiding places. Whooping at their fancied victory, they poured from their lines, raced over the crest of the hill and plunged down into the ravine—and straight into Willett's cleverly conceived ambush.

The riflemen hidden in the ravine opened up with a withering fire. Willett, leading one hundred men, charged upon the stunned and reeling warriors. McKean, commanding a squad at the outer tip of the crescent on the ridge, saw the chance to smash down upon the Indians' flank—and took it. The twin blows rocked the Tories and Indians, but they fought desperately, stubbornly. Fading back, they turned each sheltering tree trunk into an individual fort, and for two hours the Battle of Sharon seesawed from tree to tree through the forest. Then the Tories and Indians, pressed relentlessly, broke and fled.

"Come on, boys, the day is ours," Willett shouted. "I can catch in my hat all the bullets the rascals can send."

Cheering, his men followed his lead and scattered the raiders of Currytown in utter rout. Their baggage, camp equipment and plunder were all left behind. Only for the prisoners taken in Currytown was Willett's victory a disaster, and for them, it was a virtual death sentence.

When the battle started, the Indians had placed the prisoners on horses stolen in the Currytown raid. Each was well guarded. When the rout began, the Indians abandoned all their loot except the one, most precious thing—scalps. Even in the act of fleeing, they took time to murder and scalp their captives. One of these, young Jacob Dievendorff, seeing what was happening, leaped from his horse and ran into the woods, attempting to escape. A brave pursued him, overtook him, felled him with one blow from behind—and ripped off his scalp.

Hours later, Willett's men, having abandoned the pursuit, returned to the battlefield to bury the dead. One of the soldiers saw a blood-covered body struggling and thrashing among the leaves on the ground, and assuming it was an Indian, leveled his rifle to deliver the *coup de grâce*. Just in time, one of his comrades knocked up the rifle barrel.

"That's no Indian, that's a white man," he cried.

The bloodstained, hardly human object on the ground was young Jacob Dievendorff. The boy was lifted gently and carried to Fort Plain. There he eventually recovered. He lived to become one of the wealthiest farmers in Montgomery County, dying finally at eighty-five, but throughout his long life, the scalp from which the hair had been lifted at the Battle of Sharon remained sore and tender. In 1848, when Lossing interviewed Dievendorff about the details of the battle, he reported that the victim's head still "had the tender appearance and feeling of a wound recently healed."

In their after-battle search of the field, Willett's men counted the bodies of forty fallen Indians and Tories. Their own loss was only nine killed and four wounded. Among the dead was Captain McKean, who had been mortally wounded in the action and died four days later at Fort Plain. Willett's victory in the Sharon swamp had a profound, double effect on the entire frontier. The patriots exulted at having found a commander who had the tactical genius to overcome the deficits of inadequate force and insufficient arms; the Indians and Tories, on the other hand, were shocked at the manner in which Willett had penetrated to their lair in a swamp they had considered nearly impassable, and they were stunned by the skill with which he had used ruse and ambush to nullify their superior numbers. The Indians promptly labeled Willett "the devil," but the Albany Common Council, taking the opposite view of his talents, passed complimentary resolutions and voted him the freedom of the city.

The victory brought peace to the Mohawk frontier for the rest of the summer. It was a tenuous, uncertain peace, but a most fortunate one. Willett was scarcely in shape to fight another battle. He was beset with infinite problems of morale, arms and supply. His men were unpaid; they were almost in rags. Grumbling took on a mutinous note. Four of Willett's officers, setting the poorest of examples for the men, consoled themselves by playing cards until the small hours of the morning. Willett put a stop to the practice by ordering them confined to barracks. Some of the men tried to desert; Willett had them shot.

By such stern measures, he imposed discipline and pieced together the rudiments of an effective fighting force. It was soon needed. In late October, the enemy descended once more upon the Mohawk, this time in overwhelming strength. The invading army was composed of one thousand British regulars, Tories and Indians. They had been welded together on Carleton Island in the St. Lawrence under the command of Major Ross and Captain Butler; they had crossed Lake Ontario to Oswego, had traveled by canoe to the lower end of Oneida Lake and then had set out through the forest. They were discovered on October 24, 1781 when they debouched suddenly from the wilderness near Argusville in Schoharie County. From that point, they began to cut a bloody, plundering swath across the countryside through Currytown to Warrensbush, now Florida, where the Schoharie Kill empties into the Mohawk River. The surprise had been complete, and the track of invasion was marked by corpse-studded, smoking ruins.

Willett was in Canajoharie when the smoke of burning Warrensbush, some twenty miles to the northeast, apprised him of the new emergency. He quickly marshaled his entire available force of 416 men and set out on a forced, all-night march to cut off the invaders. He reached Warrensbush in the morning and found that Ross and Butler had passed on and were then engaged in raiding and sacking Johnstown. Exhorting his men to new exertions, Willett pressed a swift pursuit and finally, about 4 P.M., he caught up with the marauders on the outskirts of Johnstown.

Again Willett's little command was outnumbered by more than two to one, and to add to his troubles, the situation made it imperative for him to attack, to drive off the invaders. Willett, assessing the problem, decided upon a pincer movement to catch the enemy both front and rear. He divided his little force, sending Col. Aaron Rowley with a strong contingent of state troops and militia on a circular, flanking march. While Rowley was getting into position, Willett diverted the enemy's attention by leading the remainder of his men in a direct, lance-like attack on the front and center.

So furiously was the thrust delivered that the far superior mass of the invading army headed by Ross and Butler was rocked back and driven from an open field into the shelter of the woods. There the enemy rallied and held, and there, in a line running along the fringe of the woods, the battle raged in seesaw fashion. The one small field piece Willett possessed changed hands several times as charge and counter-charge swirled around it. But slowly the massed weight of one thousand men pitted against Willett's handful of some two hundred-odd began to be too much; pressed back, overborne, his troops broke and fled into a stone church in Johnstown. The Indians and Tories whooped after them, but soon became disorganized by their eagerness to collect scalps and prisoners. And just then Rowley struck.

He led his men in a fierce charge on the enemy's unprotected rear. The shock and surprise of the new blow threw the invaders into confusion. They were given no chance to recover. Willett, rallying his men, led a sally from the stone church and charged the enemy fiercely in front. Caught between two fires, the forces of Ross and Butler split into struggling, disorganized groups. Until after dark, the battle swayed back and forth; then the enemy broke and fled, seeking refuge on the top of a mountain about six miles from Johnstown.

The casualties had been about even, some forty men killed and wounded on each side; but the Americans, in addition, had taken some fifty prisoners. The victory had disrupted the invaders' plans and put an end to their murderous foray. Under the circumstances, especially considering his own numerical weakness, Willett might have been well content, one would think, to rest satisfied with this achievement. But he was not. He determined to pursue Ross and Butler and to destroy them, if he could, so that never again would such savage warfare be brought to the Valley of the Mohawk.

Willett's men were worn out by the night-long, day-long marching and fighting. They rested exhausted on their arms that night, but in the morning, whipped on by their commander, they took up the chase. At Stone Arabia, Willett halted briefly and sent forward a light detachment, hoping to destroy the boats the invaders had left on Lake Oneida. This scouting party found no trace of the retreating foe, however, and reported back to Willett at German Flats, now Herkimer. Willett, in the meantime, had picked up new information indicating that Ross and Butler had struck out almost due northward, evidently planning to follow West Canada and Canada Creeks in their flight to the St. Lawrence.

The weather had turned cold, and pursuit promised untold rigors. But Willett was determined. He rallied some four hundred men and was joined by about sixty friendly Oneida Indians. In a driving snowstorm, carrying provisions for just five days, he led his men out on the track of the much-hated Walter Butler. He moved swiftly, and by the time he entered the densely wooded Royal Grant along the west side of West Canada Creek, scouts told him that the enemy was just a short distance ahead. Willett encamped in the woods and sent Jacob

Sammons forward with a scouting party to investigate. Sammons reported that the enemy was in a strong position, well-organized, well-armed; and Willett, who had been toying with the idea of a night attack, decided against it. Instead, he waited for morning, and in the dawn, as Butler resumed his retreat, Willett resumed his pursuit.

It was early afternoon when Willett's forward lines caught up with the straggling rear of Butler's column. The Americans pressed the fight, and a bloody, running skirmish began. Several Indians were killed and scalped, and the Americans, scenting victory, stepped up the pursuit. The battle became a foot race. Near evening, Willett and his men caught up with the main body of Butler's force at Jerseyfield on the northeast side of Canada Creek. Willett attacked at once, and another running fight developed.

The Indians, terrified by the fierce and relentless nature of the chase, fled across the creek at a small ford. On the opposite bank, Walter Butler tried to rally them. Bullets sped back and forth across the narrow stream, and one of Willett's Oneida Indians, spotting Butler as he exposed himself to encourage his warriors, drew a bead and fired. Butler fell, screaming in agony. The Indians and Tory followers near him panicked and fled.

The Oneida who had shot the most-hated Tory on the New York frontier bounded across the stream, brandishing his tomahawk. Butler saw him coming.

"Save me, save me," he pleaded. "Give me quarter."

"Me give you Sherry Falley quarters," the Oneida warrior cried, referring to Butler's inhuman sacking of Cherry Valley.

Suiting action to words, he scalped the screaming Tory. Willett's men crossed the creek and swept on in pursuit, leaving Butler's body where he had fallen—a place known as Butler's Ford from that day forward.

With the fall of their leader, the disruption of the enemy force became complete. They threw away blankets, packs, equipment; they dispersed into small bands and fled as swiftly as their feet could take them into the wilderness. Willett pressed the pursuit until after nightfall, then drew off and consolidated his forces. He had achieved the climactic victory of the war on the New York frontier. He had shattered a powerful invading force into fragments and had left it to the mercy of the frigid New York winter—an ally that was to claim many additional lives before the famished, frost-bitten survivors staggered from the forest seven days later and found refuge at last on Carleton Island. Their overall loss was never known. As Willett, who sometimes dabbled in poetry, wrote to Governor Clinton in almost lyric terms: "The fields of Johnstown, the brooks and rivers, the hills and mountains, the deep and gloomy marshes through which they had to pass, they only could tell; and perhaps the officers who detached them on the expedition." By contrast, Willett had lost just one man killed in that long, running pursuit.

With this triumph, the New York frontier was secured. It was a frontier in blackened ruins, but one that, with patience and labor and fortitude, could be rebuilt. This was Willett's accomplishment, one that would have seemed impossible just a few short months before; and in the flush of victory, the hero of the Mohawk became the talk of the valley, in more ways than one.

Willett's lot in the war had been a lonely one, marked by personal tragedy. His wife was still in Connecticut, and his son, Marinus, who had remained in the army as a surgeon's mate, had contracted a fever and died in Danbury, Connecticut, in July of 1778. Separated from family and home, the architect of the great victory over Butler looked about him, and it was not long before his eye lighted upon an attractive widow, a certain Mrs. Seeber, who lived in Fort Plain where Willett commanded. Willett, as considerable evidence attests, possessed a high-voltage charge of that mysterious attraction we now call sex appeal, and it was not long before he and the attractive widow were furnishing the gossips with enough spicy morsels to keep tongues clacking all winter long by the Valley's firesides. The clacking was not, as is sometimes the case, a lot of noise without substance; for in due course of time, as if to confirm the most salacious suspicions, a boy child made his appearance and was promptly named Marinus W. Seeber.

Willett made no secret of his paternity, and in later years, he provided for the boy's upkeep and education. His illegitimacy was something, however, that could not be hidden, nor could the scar that it left, in that day and age, easily be eradicated. Long years later, a grown man, Marinus W. Seeber returned to Fort Plain as a dancing master, but the long-memoried local residents virtually hissed him out of town. And when he left Fort Plain, he simply vanished, a pale and scandal-tinted shade that faded from Willett's life.

The boy and the liaison that had produced him were still titillating the old wives' circles when Washington sent Willett on one final, hazardous expedition. The project was a desperate and ill-conceived one—a midwinter attack on snowshoes across the white plains of New York against the British stronghold at Oswego. Willett, much against his better judgment, undertook the attack in February, 1783; but an Oneida guide, who was supposed to know the way, blundered badly, leading the invaders into the frozen quagmire of a swamp, where many of the men broke through the ice and were plunged into frigid ooze and water. One was frozen to death, many suffered frost-bitten legs and feet, and the attack had to be abandoned.

The postwar years were active ones for Willett. He was elected to the State Assembly, and he served for seven years as the Sheriff of New York County. In 1790, President Washington dispatched him as a personal representative to treat with the Creek Indians, then threatening war on the Georgia and Alabama frontiers. The mission lasted four months and ended in an agreement that insured peace.

In these first years after the war, Willett, who had never had much money, began to lay the foundations of a considerable personal fortune. He became a merchant, opening a store at 36 Water Street. He was the friend of powerful and influential men, and he prospered. President Washington and Governor Clinton became his partners in one land venture. In another, Willett took advantage of the fact that confiscated Tory estates were being sold at ridiculously cheap prices, and for ninety-six pounds, he purchased a tract at Corlear's Hook bounded by the East River, DeLancey, Broome and Willett Streets. Here he built an imposing two-story mansion, with wings at either end, surrounded by spacious grounds that included a garden, walks, carriageways, arbors and fruit and shade trees. He named the estate "Cedar Grove."

One of the inspirations for the construction of "Cedar Grove" was a new romance. Willett's first wife, Mary, died in 1793, and the warrior-hero soon became enamored of a beautiful widow, Susannah Vardle, the reigning toast of New York society. Willett captured the prize, but it was not long before he had reason to wonder who had captured whom. Susannah Vardle, more spitfire than beauty, quickly began to give Willett more trouble than Butler and his Indians ever had; and it was not long before she was spending most of her time tearing Willett's reputation to pieces in vicious gossiping sessions with her high-society friends. Finally, in 1797, she divorced her husband—an event for which, from all indications, Willett was devoutly thankful.

He advertised "Cedar Grove" for sale, but finding no buyers, he boarded the place up. It did not stay long shuttered, however. Willett may have been chastened by his marital vendetta with Susannah Vardle, but he was far from crushed. He soon began to take notice of the charms of Margaret Bancker, the young daughter of a close friend. The disparity in their ages—Willett was almost old enough to have been her grandfather— might have seemed to outlaw the suit, but it didn't. In 1799, when Willett was 59 and Margaret Bancker 24, they were married, and "Cedar Grove" was reopened.

By this third marriage, Willett had four children, three sons and a daughter. One of the sons became a physician, one a lawyer and the other a Methodist minister. Two lived well into their eighties. As for Willett, evidently happy in this third marriage to a much younger bride, he lived through the years as if there was no time. He was a founder of the Society of the Cincinnati, an ardent leader of Tammany, a staunch believer in grass-roots democracy and an equally staunch foe of the oligarchical theories of Alexander Hamilton and the Federalists. In one bitter gubernatorial election, Willett actually fought a duel with a misguided friend who had become a strong Federalist, but fortunately both missed their fire and, honor satisfied, composed their differences.

For one brief period, Willett served by appointment as Mayor of New York, and for years, in one position or another, he was constantly in the public eye. Even in 1814, during the gloomiest days of the War of 1812, he still possessed the fire, though nearly seventy-four at the time, to make a rousing patriotic speech at a war rally in City Hall. Even for Willett, time finally ran out. In 1830 he suffered a stroke and a few weeks later, on August 22nd, the fifty-third anniversary of the abandonment of the siege of Fort Stanwix, he died in his home at "Cedar Grove." He was ninety years old, almost a public institution, and the entire city mourned his death. More than ten thousand persons passed in review before his coffin before it was lowered to rest in the graveyard behind Trinity Church—a place of worship to which Willett had returned once the Revolution had canceled out the customary prayers for the King's good health.

The Revolution was a war of many phases. It was something like a running brush fire that, beaten out in one spot, leaps beyond into tinder grass and sparks an entirely new conflagration. The war began with the pitched battles fought by the major armies in the North; it spread to the borders in a wave of flame-lit atrocities; and even while the borders were still ablaze, the firebrand of conflict was tossed into a new and previously unscarred theater, the South.

The shifting emphasis in the battle tide underscores the fact that Great Britain did not free her rebellious colonies until she had probed every section of them in a prolonged and persistent hunt for permanent foothold. The initial effort was concentrated almost exclusively against the North, the birthplace of rebellion, and for the first three years, the destiny of the Colonies hinged on the fate of Washington's Army. But, by the end of 1778, the British had lost nearly all their northern footholds. They retained only New York. New Jersey had been overrun, but it could not be held. Philadelphia had been captured—and evacuated. Burgoyne had tried to split the Colonies in half by invasion from Canada—and had been lost with all his army. Obviously, this was *not progress. And so the British switched to a new theater, mounting an all-out blow against the South.*

The southern Colonies were more sparsely settled; Tory sympathy was strong. They were a branch, it seemed, that might be lopped easily from the tree. If they could be overpowered and isolated, the British crown might still retain a large and fertile section of the Colonies when peace was made. The prospect stirred all-out invasion. Savannah fell. So did Charleston. All of Georgia, virtually all of South and North Carolina were overrun.

The initial success of the British, the dire threat that it posed, gave the South a new priority in the planning of high strategy. The result was an almost complete turnabout in theater activity. In the North, the Battle of Monmouth Court House in 1778 marked the last large-scale collision of armies. For three years after that, Washington and Clinton watched each other from opposite sides of the fortified perimeter of New York; but in the South, where the first years had been almost peaceful, there was an unremitting succession of battle and campaign. In the South, a war was being lost—and won again.

Among the men who fought through both the losing war and the winning war in the South was one incredible private. His name was Peter Francisco. Even as Allan McLane became the symbol of the dashing cavalryman in the winter of Valley Forge, Peter Francisco epitomized the heroism of the Continental Line. He was the kind of man other men talked about around the campfires long afterwards.

CHAPTER V

★

★ ★ ★

★

Peter Francisco

"I scarcely ever met a man in Virginia who had not some miraculous tale to tell of Peter Francisco."—Alexander Garden, of Lee's Legion.

Peter Francisco was the Revolution's Paul Bunyan of the South. He was both fact and legend, and the proportions of the mixture are sometimes difficult to determine. Just when it seems that legend must predominate, one encounters the reality of hard facts. Indisputably Peter Francisco was a giant of a man. He stood six-feet-six and weighed two hundred and sixty pounds. Indisputably he possessed a giant's strength. On the disastrous field of Camden, South Carolina, he is said to have saved an eleven-hundred-pound cannon from capture by the British by lifting it on his back and walking off with it. Legend? Perhaps. But just as one is about to decide that no man could ever be *that* strong, one finds many eyewitnesses agreeing that Peter Francisco could heft a one-hundred-sixty-pound man in the palm of either hand and lift both simultaneously to the ceiling.

The man who could perform with ease such feats of strength emerges from the annals of the day larger than life, shadowed by the unreality of the superhuman. Yet Peter Francisco was undeniably real, and much tangible evidence indicates that in action the real man was as fascinating and improbable as the legend.

The massive five-foot-long broadsword that Washington had fashioned for him because conventional weapons were too puny in his hands is one of the realities; it exists, a carefully preserved historical treasure. So does the handsomely inscribed razor case that Nathanael Greene, Washington's greatest general, presented as a token of personal esteem to the man who had been his greatest private. A yellowed letter from Lafayette recounts that, long years after the war, he wept at the news of Francisco's death as if he had lost a brother. And on the historic field of Guilford Court House, a monument commemorates the supreme feat of Peter Francisco—the cavalry charge in which he clove in the heads of eleven British soldiers in a row.

The trooper who performed such deeds and registered with such impact upon the great men of the day began life as a waif.

The story, mysterious and romantic enough for the pen of a Dumas, began on a morning in early June, 1765, when a strange ship came in from the sea off City Point near what is now Hopewell, Virginia. A longboat put out from the ship, rowed to a deserted dock and deposited a boy about four years old. Then the boat crew pulled hastily back to the ship, the vessel made sail and stood away from the coast, vanishing over the horizon and leaving behind an abandoned child—and an enduring and intriguing mystery.

The boy, large for his age, was swarthy of complexion and handsome of feature, with black hair and snapping black eyes. His suit was soiled and badly worn, but the fabric and the cut, the presence of lace about collar and cuffs, indicated that it had been of good quality. Quality, too, was to be seen in the handsome silver buckles of his shoes, each fashioned to spell out the initials "P. F."

The abandoned child was discovered by two planters coming down to the wharves to check on their shipments. Sailors and dock hands crowded around. They tried to question the boy, but they soon found out that they could not understand him nor he, them. The lad spoke a foreign gibberish—a mixture of Portuguese, French and Spanish, it was later said; of English, he understood only a few words.

His plight, however, was obvious. It stirred the pity of dock workers. They fed him scraps of food from their own scanty store to keep him from starvation, and they found him a place to sleep in a shack at the landward end of the dock. So for a week the boy lived, lost and forlorn in a strange land. Then he was taken to the Prince George poorhouse, where parish authorities cared for him while trying to find him a home.

The strange story of the mysteriously abandoned boy spread through the countryside. It intrigued Judge Anthony Winston, an uncle of Patrick Henry. The judge investigated, found himself attracted by the appearance of the boy and removed him from the poorhouse, taking him to the Winston estate, "Hunting Towers," located about a mile east of New Store on the old stage road between Lynchburg and Richmond in Buckingham County. Here a Negro maid in the household cared for the waif, and here he lived and worked and grew, his status much like that of a poor family relation.

As the boy learned to speak English, he searched the vague memories of his childhood and tried to explain to Judge Winston what had happened to him. It was a strange tale, drawn from the vague images that register on a mind emerging from babyhood, and it served, if anything, only to deepen and increase the mystery.

The boy was sure of just one thing—his name, Peter Francisco. As for the rest, he had a dim memory of living in a great mansion and playing with a little sister in a lovely garden. His mother was a vague and beautiful vision in his mind. He could remember little about her except that she spoke French. His father was an even more shadowy figure. He had spoken a different language from the mother, the boy felt sure, but that was about all he could recall.

One final scene of his life at home had registered with un-forgettable vividness upon his mind. One day as guests were assembling for dinner, Peter and his sister had been sent out of the way into the garden, enticed by candy and cakes and toys. They were playing there when, suddenly, some roughly clad men burst in upon them, seized them and started to carry them away. Francisco's sister struggled and cried out; she managed to wriggle free and escaped. He was manacled, blindfolded, gagged. When he was finally released, he was on board a ship. He was on the ship a long time—until the day he was put into the longboat and rowed ashore at City Point.

Such was the mystery. What could it possibly mean? How much was truth and how much the colored fancy of a young boy's imagination? Judge Winston and his Virginia friends, who puzzled over the details, could make nothing of the story at the time, but long years later researches abroad seemed to suggest a reasonable hypothesis.

There was in Portugal in the eighteenth century a noble house of Francisco. At one time, the head of the house became entangled in some unsuccessful political machinations. The penalty for political failure in those days was usually the head of the offender, but in this instance a more diabolical punish-ment was decreed. It was ordered that the father should see his young son beheaded in expiation of his crime. Before the sen-tence could be carried out, however, the boy suddenly and mysteriously disappeared. Records that would have established his name and the names of his parents had been lost; but the dim outlines of the story suggest that Peter Francisco may well have been the once-doomed and vanished son; that his parents, to save his life, may have arranged for his kidnaping and transportation to America in the strange ship that had come up out of the sea to deposit him on a Virginia wharf.

This possible solution of the riddle was unknown at the time, and the boy grew up on Judge Winston's estate, set apart from the common run of man both by the mystery of his past and the awesome power of his rapidly developing physique. From his earliest days on the estate, the boy helped around the forge, and as he grew he developed the skill and muscles of a smith. When he was only sixteen, he had attained his full stature; he was two hundred and sixty pounds of energy and muscle. Judge Winston had come to love the young giant like a son and made plans formally to adopt him; but before this could be done, the Colonial world of America was turned upside down by Revolution.

Judge Winston represented Buckingham County in the Virginia Assembly and was one of the patriot leaders who defied Royal authority when, on May 26, 1774, Lord Dunmore exercised his prerogatives as Governor and autocratically dissolved the rebellious chamber. The delegates promptly repaired to the Raleigh Tavern in Williamsburg, then the capital, and held the first of a number of extra-legal sessions in which, in defiance of Royal decree, they continued to act and, in effect, to run the affairs of the colony.

The most momentous and most dramatic of these unauthorized legislative sessions was the Richmond Convention which opened on March 20, 1775 in St. John's Church. Judge Winston attended as a delegate from Buckingham County, and since the meeting was being held so close to home, he took with him his young charge, Peter Francisco. For the boy it was an exciting, never-to-be-forgotten experience.

The greatest men of Virginia attended the convention— Thomas Jefferson, Peyton Randolph, Patrick Henry, Richard Henry Lee. Stormy and stirring, crucial in its decisions, the session ignited in young Peter Francisco the spark of patriotic fervor. Yet the beginning was almost routine. By a unanimous

vote on March 22nd, the convention sanctioned the proceedings and resolves of the Continental Congress. The next day
came the storm. A resolution was introduced by Patrick
Henry that drew a clear line between peaceful protest and
armed revolution; it authorized action to put Virginia "into a
posture of defence" and directed the appointment of a committee to prepare a plan for raising and arming militia.

This decisive measure from which, if adopted, there could
be no retreat touched off bitter debate. While there was unanimous agreement on the necessity of stressing the Colonies'
rights and grievances against the mother country, a strong core
of conservatives opposed any step so drastic as resort to armed
force. Peter Francisco, listening to the arguments, thrilled as
Patrick Henry, his benefactor's nephew, rose to impassioned
heights in defense of his proposal. In the great peroration that
was to write his name indelibly into history, he cried out:
"Gentlemen may cry peace, peace—but there is no peace . . .
Is life so dear, or peace so sweet, as to be purchased at the price
of chains and slavery? Forbid it, Almighty God! I know not
what course others may take; but as for me . . . give me liberty, or give me death!"

It was eloquence that swept all before it. Virginia authorized
a militia. War was just a step away.

Peter Francisco, though he was only fourteen, wanted to
enlist immediately. This eagerness was in keeping with his
character. In normal times, he had much of the huge man's
placidity of temperament; but exigencies aroused in him the
strong man's pride of strength. He was always to retain something of a small boy's delight in risk and danger—and corre-
sponding pride in the display of strength and courage to meet
such tests. In later life, he delighted in the kind of parlor-game
exhibitionism that consisted of hoisting grown men in the palm
of his hand; but, when angered, he sometimes used this playful
strength with crushing force. In the young giant were all the
gamboling qualities, the curiosity and eagerness—and the men-

ace—of a great bear. He fretted for excitement and battle; but Judge Winston, more cautious and conservative, considered him too young at fourteen and made him promise to wait for a year. When the time expired, nothing could hold Peter Francisco longer at "Hunting Towers"; he enlisted in the Tenth Virginia Regiment as a private, and with this celebrated infantry outfit marched off to war.

He first saw action on the desperate field of Brandywine, the little stream south of Philadelphia along which Washington tried to block the advance of Howe's Army. The battle was fought on September 11, 1777, and Peter Francisco, only sixteen at the time, participated in some of the day's most savage fighting. Howe, with a circular flanking movement reminiscent of his tactics on Long Island, surprised the Americans, who were expecting a frontal assault. The charging British rolled up the right wing of Washington's Army in fierce "Muzzle to Muzzle" fighting and threatened for a time to scatter the entire army in rout. To prevent this, the Tenth Virginia and other fresh regiments were rushed on the field late in the day in an effort to protect the rear and halt the fierce British advance.

Peter Francisco and his comrades in the Virginia line were stationed in a place called Sandy Hollow, a narrow defile flanked by woods. British troops were pursuing the fleeing Continentals along the road that ran through the narrow pass, and the Tenth Virginia was one of the regiments given the job of blocking their path. With the Marquis de Lafayette galloping furiously back and forth across the battlefield, with Washington himself spurring up to the front to inspire his troops, the Virginians and detachments of the Pennsylvania line fought for forty-five stubborn, bloody minutes—a rock-like stand against the overwhelming might of the victory-flushed British army. They held the pass and blunted the pursuit until nightfall. Then, overborne at last, they slowly gave way; but they drew off in good order, still fighting, and the British,

spent by march and battle, abandoned the pursuit. The desperate stand in the wooded defile of Sandy Hollow had saved an
army. Washington had been beaten, but he still had a force
capable of fighting again.

Two of the fighters who had stood out in the fierce melee of
Brandywine met for the first time after the fighting was over.
One was Lafayette, who had drawn all eyes by his reckless
dashes across the fire-swept field; the other was the sixteen-
year-old giant who had towered above his fellows of the Virginia line in the defense of the Sandy Hollow pass. Both had
been wounded by British musket balls, and both were treated
at the home of a Quaker near the battlefield. Lafayette, perhaps attracted by the Homeric size and the youth of the infan-
tryman, drew Francisco into conversation, the first tentative
step in what was to become a life-long, enduring friendship.

The Brandywine wound, the first of a series Peter Francisco
was to collect on his huge person, did not keep him long from
the front. Less than a month later, on October 4, 1777, he was
in a battle again at Germantown, and he went straight from
this futile attack on Howe's entrenchments to an even more
desperate trial in defense of American forts guarding the lower
Delaware.

The Delaware forts were vital to both sides. As long as they
stood, the Americans could keep British ships from passing up
the river; and if ships could not use the river, Howe could not
be supplied. And if he could not be supplied, he could not continue to hold Philadelphia. The inevitability of this sequence
led to an all-out British effort to force a passage up the Delaware.

The main American defense line, composed of obstructions
and the channel-sweeping guns of two forts, was based upon
Fort Mercer at Red Bank on the New Jersey shore and Fort
Mifflin directly opposite on Mud Island in the middle of the
river. Peter Francisco was among the four hundred fifty men
assigned to the defense of the only partially completed Fort

Mifflin, a post that should have been garrisoned by at least one thousand.

The British first tried to storm Fort Mercer at Red Bank and were bloodily repulsed by some of the most concentrated, most deadly small-arms fire of the war. Foiled here, they turned their attention to the much more vulnerable Fort Mifflin on its exposed island in the Delaware.

Since the British held the Pennsylvania shore, they easily assembled heavy batteries of 24- and 32-pounders, together with howitzers and mortars, with which to bombard the fort from the land side. A floating battery was added to the land-based guns, and on November 10th a heavy cannonade was opened. The firing went on incessantly for days. One by one, the guns inside the fort were dismounted by direct hits; the barracks were shattered; the palisades partially destroyed. One by one, members of the garrison fell, killed or wounded, and the gaps in their ranks were filled by replacements crossing the river from the New Jersey shore under the cover of night.

Still the pounding went on. On November 15th, it even mounted in intensity as British frigates and ships-of-the-line moved up the channel and added the weight of their crashing broadsides to the shot and shell of the land-based artillery. Projectiles rained on the garrison at the awesome rate of one thousand every twenty minutes. The last two guns in the fort were dismounted, and the British warships, with perfect impunity, drew in so close to the island's shore that the Marines in their tops picked off every man who exposed himself. The defenders, their ranks grievously thinned, could only huddle in the ruins and endure. By nightfall, their palisades had all been blasted away, the blockhouses had been destroyed, the entire parapet had been leveled. Under cover of night, the survivors set fire to the ruins and escaped to the New Jersey shore. It had been one of "the most gallant and obstinate" defenses of the war; some two hundred and fifty of the defenders had been killed or wounded; and even the unharmed survivors were almost stupefied from the shelling and on the verge of collapse from lack of sleep and exposure. Among the more fortunate of the unfortunates, having come through the storm unscathed, was Peter Francisco.

His had been as harsh an indoctrination in the horrors of warfare as it is possible to conceive, but the sixteen-year-old youth was unimpressed. He evidently felt no urge to consider himself well out of the mess and to go home. No sooner had his first enlistment expired than he enlisted again, and the following June found him on the battlefield of Monmouth, where he received his second wound, a serious one, from a British musket ball. The effects of this were to bother him the rest of his life, according to his son's account; but neither the narrow escape nor the pain curbed the lusty appetite of Peter Francisco for war, hazard and adventure. A year after Monmouth, in the summer of 1779, he was back as a private in the Virginia line, ready to take part in the storming of the strong British outposts at Stony Point and Paulus Hook.

For the attack on Stony Point, a rocky and heavily fortified promontory jutting into the Hudson, some 1,350 men were quietly assembled near West Point. They were the pick of the Continental Army. The assault plan devised by Washington and Mad Anthony Wayne called for them to go in pincer-like, in two strong columns striking from the left and the right. The attacking forces would have to wade across low-lying marshes, cut through a line of abatis and charge the outer defenses of the fort. Once these were taken, they would have to cut through a second row of abatis before they reached the main bastions. Heading each column were groups of sturdy axmen whose job was to hack through the wooden fangs of the abatis. Right behind the axmen came the forlorn hopes. Each squad was headed by an officer and composed of twenty men. The squad on the left was led by Lt. James Gibbons, and among his twenty carefully selected desperadoes was Peter Francisco, wielding the huge broadsword that Washington had ordered made especially for him.

When the attack opened shortly after midnight on the morning of July 16, 1779, Peter Francisco was the second man in the forlorn hope led by Lieutenant Gibbons. The tide was higher than usual and some of the men sank in the marsh almost up to their necks. But they pressed on, helping each other, and reached the first line of abatis. The blows of the axmen rang out.

The thudding strokes alarmed the defenders, and muskets began to explode in the night along the parapet. Many of the shots went wild, but some struck home. Men began to fall. The furious-stroking axmen rained blows upon the abatis, hacked a gap, and Lieutenant Gibbons and Francisco leaped through, the sharp splintered wood tearing and slashing at their clothes. In a furious rush, they stormed the outer defenses, Peter Francisco's huge blade rising and falling in the night. The surprised, disorganized British gave way before them.

With the troops of the left-hand column pouring up behind them, the daredevils in the van of the suicide squad raced for the second row of abatis. Once more, the axmen hacked a gap; once more, Gibbons and Francisco leaped through, cleaving a passage for the men behind them. They were in the inner works now, and they swung to the right, driving for the bastion of the main fort.

This already was under attack. Wayne's column, the stronger of the two attacking prongs, had smashed through the double row of abatis with equal celerity. The leaders of its forlorn hope poured through a sally port and struck the colors. Just as they did, Lieutenant Gibbons and Francisco charged in from the left. British troops, attempting to rally to the standard, put up a brief and spirited resistance. Francisco's huge broadsword split the head of one of the defenders, and in the act Francisco received his third wound of the war—a raking, nine-inch long bayonet slash across his abdomen. In almost the same instant, the British ranks collapsed; crushed, they threw down their arms and the fort was taken.

The appearance of the victors attested to the desperate nature of the enterprise. Lieutenant Gibbons and Francisco stood caked in mud, their clothes torn to tatters on the splinters of the abatis, Francisco bleeding from his abdominal wound. Of the nineteen men who had followed them, only two were standing; the rest had been shot down, either killed or wounded.

After Stony Point, Francisco recuperated briefly at nearby Fishkilns, but only a month later, he was back in action, one of the picked band of raiders who followed Light-Horse Harry Lee and Allan McLane into the fortifications of Paulus Hook, a strong outpost on the New Jersey shore just across the Hudson River from New York. Here, in the lightning-fast sweep of steel that swept all before it, Francisco's huge sword split the skulls of two British grenadiers; and here, the legend was born. Peter Francisco, the giant wielding a giant's sword, became the invincible man of the Continental line; and in after years, veterans of the war averred that no foe ever stood up to sword and man in battle and lived to tell the tale.

With his feats at Stony Point and Paulus Hook making the giant loom as a superhuman warrior, Peter Francisco returned to Virginia. Three times wounded, only by providential good fortune still alive, the black-haired giant with the snapping black eyes had served out his second enlistment, and if he had possessed one grain of caution, he should have considered that the odds of chance were running strongly against him. Evidently, Francisco never weighed the possibility, or if he did, he ignored it, impelled partly perhaps by the almost fanatical patriotism of the times and even more powerfully by his own personality—his irresistible boyish desire for action and the flexing of Homeric muscles. And so he promptly enlisted again, this time in a militia regiment headed by Col. William Mayo of Powhatan County. With this step, Peter Francisco embarked on a new series of adventures even more startling than those that had gone before; for if he was already virtually a legend as the one-man host of the Continental line, he was now about to become the Paul Bunyan of the South—a truly fantastic fighter of whom, as Alexander Garden wrote, hardly a man in Virginia "had not some miraculous tale to tell."

The times certainly called for miracles. Never had the plight of the embattled patriots in the South been so desperate. The British had made the astute switch in strategy which had led them to invade the South in force, determined to split it apart from the rest of the Colonies. Savannah and Charleston had fallen, and just at the time Francisco re-enlisted in Colonel Mayo's militia, the Continental Congress was attempting to assemble a new army under a new commander in the hope of driving the British out. It was a desperate hope at best, but the Congress, in its ineffable wisdom, picked the one commander who could be guaranteed to insure disaster. He was the incompetent intriguer, Horatio Gates, bloated into the deceptive image of a general by the success earned for him by better men at Saratoga.

Gates, made more dangerous than ever to himself and his army by the fatuity resulting from past triumph, took command of a disorganized conglomeration of men in rags and tatters, desperate even for food. Disdainful of reality, he set out to attack the British under Lord Cornwallis. He kept insisting to his aides that he commanded an army of seven thousand men, and he refused to listen when one of the most capable officers in the South, Otho Williams, his deputy adjutant general, tried to show him that actually only 3,052 were present and fit for duty. Relying sublimely on the four thousand phantom fighters that existed only in his own deluded mind, Horatio Gates blundered south to strike Cornwallis at Camden, South Carolina. Never in the entire war did Cornwallis have so easy a task.

Instead of waiting to be struck, he struck first. The first premonition of disaster came on the sultry, moonless night of August 15–16, 1780. Banastre Tarleton, Cornwallis' effeminate-looking and almost psychopathically cruel cavalry leader, surprised Armand's Legion, Gates' advance scouting force; he smashed it and drove it in upon the First Continental Brigade. Soon all was confusion. The Americans, who had been on a night march toward the enemy, halted and huddled together; the British withdrew temporarily and prepared to launch their thunderbolt.

It exploded in the dawn. The full force of the attack fell on the American left, where the Virginia militia were stationed. There were few veterans like Peter Francisco among them. By far the greater majority had never heard a shot fired in anger; they had never seen a bayonet used except to roast a ration of beef. When Cornwallis' seasoned regulars loosed a volley and charged with gleaming steel, the Virginians quailed at the prospect, then broke, turned tail and ran. Their panic communicated itself, as panic will, to the North Carolina militia stationed next to them in the center; these troops, too, hurled aside their muskets and took to their heels. Some twenty-five hundred men, fleeing in uncontrolled terror from those evil blades pricking almost at their backs, burst upon and through and over the sturdy Continentals, throwing them into disorder; in seconds, all was confusion, panic, rout and irredeemable disaster.

Even a Washington, magnificent of presence, probably could not have stemmed such a mad and hopeless tide. And Gates was no Washington, not even a dim shadow of Washington. In the crisis of his army, he became a twittering old woman. Mounted on the fastest steed available, he won the race to the rear and paused not in his frenzied gallop until he had put sixty miles between himself and the specter of Corn-wallis' steel.

On a day when the commanding general shows the white feather so conspicuously, the man of courage who stays and fights stands larger than life-size by contrast. So loomed Peter Francisco now.

All around him were wildly running, screaming men. Their eyes rolled with horror, their tongues hung out like those of hard-run dogs, and they collided with one another in the fevered effort to flee faster. Abandoned in the melee was a small field piece, one of two that had been wheeled into line between the Virginia and North Carolina militia. Its horses had been shot, its cannoneers had fled, it waited to be seized by the enemy.

Peter Francisco saw the cannon and acted. According to the legend, he ran to the gun, stooped, strained his mighty smith's muscles until they almost cracked—then straightened and shouldered the eleven-hundred-pound cannon on his back! Bowed under more than half a ton of iron, he staggered off to the rear, found a knot of Continentals still standing firm and delivered his burden.

Even legend admits that Peter Francisco was pretty badly spent after this exertion. His own command had been scattered like dust before a tornado; there was no duty for him to perform; and so he went into the woods and lay down to rest. He had hardly regained his breath when one of Tarleton's hard-charging troopers burst through the scattered pines, surprising him. The great broadsword that was Francisco's favorite weapon dangled uselessly at his side; the musket that he carried could not save him, for the British trooper reared above him, prepared to cut him down at the first hostile gesture.

"Surrender or die!" the British trooper thundered.

"My gun—it isn't even loaded," Francisco replied, almost on a note of entreaty.

Meekly, submissively, he rose. He lifted the musket and extended it sidewise, stretching it out to the trooper in a mute gesture of surrender. The cavalryman fell for the ruse. He reached for the gun. As he did, Francisco twirled it rapidly in his hands and thrust viciously with the same motion. The bayonet speared the incautious trooper through the body and pitched him, dying, from the saddle. Francisco leaped upon the horse and rode off through the woods.

He had not gone far when he found Tarleton's men all around him. Again he was in imminent danger of being cut down or taken. Again he resorted to guile. Rising in the stirrups, he impersonated a deliriously happy Tory. "Huzzah, my brave boys," he cried out, "we've conquered the rebels!" And so, shouting and cheering like one of Tarleton's very own, he passed through the troop and up the road to safety.

Again he had not gone far when he came upon a sight that demanded action. His regimental commander, Colonel Mayo, was trudging along on foot, the prisoner of a British officer. Francisco, charging up on horseback, cut down the officer and liberated his commander. Then, alighting from the horse, he insisted that Colonel Mayo take it and ride to safety. The colonel argued, but Francisco was insistent and so it was arranged. The colonel rode from the field on the captured horse, and Francisco relied on his own giant strides to outspeed the pursuing British.

Right here the modern skeptic, trying to sift fact from fiction in the Francisco legend, comes upon one of those undeniable nuggets of fact that seem to say that all, incredible as it may seem, is true. Francisco's deed in lugging the eleven-hundred-pound cannon from the battlefield is part of the word-of-mouth legend. It was a story always told in his lifetime, widely believed, never challenged; apparently, no one who knew him ever doubted that he could indeed lift an eleven-hundred-pound cannon and carry it away upon his back. About the rest of the story, the sequence of action that led to the rescue of Colonel Mayo, it appears there can be no doubt at all.

The colonel himself never forgot Francisco's generosity in insisting that he take the captured horse and escape. Years later, after the end of the war, he presented Francisco with the small dress sword he had always worn on formal occasions, and still later, in his will, he remembered the soldier who had rescued him at Camden by bequeathing to Francisco one thousand acres of Kentucky land. The colonel's heirs protested this provision of the will, however, and Francisco, too proud to battle the case in court, never did receive the bequest. But he treasured Colonel Mayo's dress sword all his life, and the weapon is still preserved in the State Library in Richmond.

These firm links to reality provide needed reassurance in following the career of the fantastic Peter Francisco, who seemed always to be topping his last exploit with another more incredible still. Back in Virginia after the disaster of Camden, Francisco with characteristic imprudence concentrated on finding the fastest way to get back into the war. A cavalry troop was being formed under a Captain Watkins in Prince Edward County, and Francisco took his huge broadsword, equipped himself with a good horse and joined up. His troop soon left for the embattled Carolinas again, where the Americans at last had found a real commander, Maj. Gen. Nathanael Greene. Greene, like Francisco, had been a smith. When war broke out, his military knowledge consisted almost solely of what he had learned by studying tactics in books, but with experience he had become Washington's ablest general. And he was now attempting to repair the wreckage left by Gates.

Greene was parrying and fencing with Cornwallis, keeping just out of reach while he built up his army, when Watkins' cavalry troop joined Greene's light dragoons, commanded by Col. William Washington. In the interval before the major armies met in battle, the Carolinas were the scene of fierce, unremitting guerilla warfare. Brief but deadly skirmishes, lightning-fast raids were almost daily occurrences. Washington's dragoons and the Legion of Light-Horse Harry Lee joined forces during this period. Backed by bodies of Carolina militia, they harassed the British and Tory outposts. In one of these clashes, according to a petition filed with the Virginia Assembly years later, Peter Francisco performed with typically boyish daring.

The combined contingents of Washington and Lee had encountered about five hundred Tories at a place known as Scotch Lake. The enemy had established themselves some one hundred yards from the lake on the top of a hill shaped like a sugar loaf. This they had fortified.

The Americans deployed around the base of the hill, and heavy firing broke out on both sides. While the Tories were blazing away at the Americans in front of them, Francisco circled around to the rear, where the sugar-loaf crest began to drop steeply to the lakeside. It occurred to him that the odd, overhanging crown of the hill offered an ideal opportunity for reconnoitering, and leaping from his horse, he sprinted beneath its protecting shelter. Here he found himself perfectly screened from the fire of the enemy directly above him, and he roamed along under the crest until he reached the rear of the camp. The Tories were still preoccupied with firing at Washington's and Lee's men, and Francisco took advantage of their distraction. He crawled up the hill, poked his head above the summit and stealthily wormed his way into one of the adjacent marquees. Standing up, he found himself looking at the enemy's large stock of provisions.

Francisco reacted to the hoard of booty the way a small boy does to a cookie jar. He selected a large hogshead, threw it down upon its side and rolled it from the tent. At the crest of the hill, near the narrow path by which he had ascended, he dropped out of sight behind the hogshead and began to wriggle backwards toward the lake, drawing his prize after him. The Tories discovered him and began to shoot. Musket balls whizzed all around and several whacked into the hogshead; but

Francisco, keeping the stout barrel always before him like a shield, backed off until he was out of musket range, escaping unscathed with his prize. When the hogshead was opened, it was found to contain shirts, pantaloons, overalls and other clothing, items much needed by the ragged American forces.

While Francisco's comrades were arraying themselves in the purloined apparel, he decided upon an even more daring bit of thievery. He had noticed during his excursion into the enemy's camp that eight fine horses, evidently the prize property of Tory officers, had been picketed in the rear about one hundred yards from the fort. Borrowing a whip and mounting his horse, Francisco set out at a gallop. He crossed the plain between the fort and the horses, exposing himself to a barrage of musket fire. Leaning down in the saddle as he swept by, he cut the tethers, cracked his whip and stampeded all eight horses toward the American lines. Then he wheeled and rode back through the musket fire, exhilarated by the success of his lark.

This looting of the Scotch Lake camp was little more than a tepid prelude to the most sensational day of battle in the life of twenty-year-old Peter Francisco. Greene, uniting his little army, returned to North Carolina and a battle site he had picked out long before during his preliminary maneuvering with Cornwallis. His chosen field was Guilford Court House, and here, on March 15, 1781, the Americans and British collided in one of the bloodiest battles of the war, one that was virtually to determine the fate of the South.

Greene drew up his army in three lines. The third line, the heart of his position, was on a cleared crest of steeply rising ground surrounding the Court House. To attack this line, the British had to lance straight up a road that led through a wooded defile, across a clearing ringed by woods, and then through more woods up to the open slope about the Court House. The woods bordering the lone approach made ideal cover for sharpshooting riflemen, and rising ground shouldered the road on both sides. This added element of elevation meant that Americans hidden on the flanks could pour a withering fire down upon the files of the advancing enemy, and it meant that the British, to get at them, would have to breast the upward slope, marching straight into the muzzles of their guns.

In early afternoon, on a day of bright sunshine, with the air cool and crisp, Cornwallis approached through the wooded defiles to challenge Greene on Greene's chosen ground. Greene's first line, thrown across the road midway up the slope to the Court House, was composed of North Carolina militia. The second, halfway between the first and the third, consisted of Virginia militia, and the last line on the crest of the Court House was held by rugged Continentals. The flanks of the first line were covered by detachments of riflemen and light infantry spread out through the woods, bolstered by seventy-five horsemen of Lee's Legion on the extreme left; by eighty-six troopers of William Washington on the extreme right.

Greene, knowing militia could not be counted on to meet a fierce charge by regular troops, pleaded with the North Carolinians holding the first line in the center to give him just two volleys. Then they could fall back. Nervously, the untried militia waited as the British moved up the road through the woods, formed at the edge of the little clearing and then charged directly across it. The North Carolina militia delivered their two volleys with good effect, but they were up against some of the toughest, most battle-hardened veterans in the British Army. The regulars marched steadily through the hail of lead, emitted a deep-throated battle roar—and charged. The militia, terrified at the menacing sound and sight, broke and fled in utter panic, casting knapsacks, canteens, muskets and powder horns into the woods as they stampeded. Lee raged among them, threatened to turn his Legion loose upon them; but they would not halt, they would not face that menacing British steel.

Only the wings of the first line held. A portion of the British wheeled and attacked the American forces on the left, practically isolating them from the rest of the battle. On the right, Kirkwood's light infantry, Lynch's Virginia riflemen and Washington's troopers fell back through the woods, aligning themselves with the second line.

On stormed the British, grimly elated. Having broken the first line with such ease, they tore like bloodhounds for the second. The Virginians awaiting the shock were militia, too, but they were made of sterner stuff. Their commanders had stationed riflemen behind them with orders to shoot the first man who tried to flee. None did. The Virginians stood firm, battled fiercely, threw back three separate bayonet charges; then, overborne by the sheer weight of numbers, their line slowly caved. Even so, they were not routed. They swung back, as if on a hinge, leaving open the roadway up the hill; but then they stood again, stubbornly holding their ground on a slope off to the left.

The British did not pause to finish them off. They simply surged on, in a tidal wave of scarlet strength, straight up the hill to the open ground about the Court House, where Greene's Continentals waited. This was the crisis of the battle.

Kirkwood and Lynch, firing all the time, covered by Washington's cavalry, had fallen back to protect the flank of the third line on the hill. They waited until the charging British were within one hundred feet, then loosed a withering blast, a fusillade so deadly that it halted even the veteran British infantrymen in their tracks. Instantly, Marylanders from the front and Kirkwood from the flank charged with the bayonet. They broke the British ranks and drove them down the slope in great disorder.

Stunned at first, the British re-formed and came back for more. Lieutenant Colonel Stuart rallied the crack British Guards, drew off other detachments from the battle with the Virginia militia on the Americans' left, and hurled the whole force up the slope at the last American line. The Americans

had not yet completely re-formed from their victorious bayonet charge, and the brunt of the British blow fell on a new
Maryland regiment, being tested in battle for the first time.
The Marylanders broke and ran, and the British Guards, capturing two guns, poured through the gap and over the crest
of the hill, cracking the very heart of the American front.

In this moment of triumph, the Guards swept forward
shouting, the day all but won, and just as they did, off on the
right wing, William Washington and his cavalry changed all
with one mighty stroke. Ordering his bugler to sound the
charge, Washington launched his eighty-six troopers straight
down the slope in a thundering charge on the flank and rear
of Stuart's victorious British Guards. In the foremost file of
the hurtling band, a massive figure wielding his tremendous
broadsword, rode Peter Francisco.

The shock as the cavalry crashed into the exposed ranks of
the Guards resounded over the battlefield. The momentum of
the charge swept all before it. Peter Francisco's mighty broadsword cut a bloody swath. Sabers rose and fell; men went
down screaming under the plunging hooves of the horses.
Over the Guards, through the Guards, Washington's cavalry
rode roughshod; they wheeled and back they came, literally
hacking the crack British regiment to pieces.

Especially terrible in the forefront of every charge was the
gigantic figure of Peter Francisco. Man after man went down
before the overpowering strokes of his broadsword. Legend
has it that Francisco, possessed by the frenzy of battle, delivered one blow with such super-human force that it split a
Guardsman's body in half down the column of the backbone.
Eleven men in a row fell before him. Benson J. Lossing told
how one of the Guards finally "pinned Francisco's leg to his
horse with a bayonet. Forbearing to strike, he [Francisco] assisted the assailant to draw his bayonet forth, when, with terrible force, he brought his broadsword down and cleft the
poor fellow's head to his shoulders! Horrible indeed were the

events of that battle; the recital will do no good, and I forbear."

Even the leg wound, his fourth of the war, did not take Francisco out of the fight. The issue had not yet been decided; more remained to be done. The Continental infantry, plunging down the slopes of the Court House hill, rushed into the bloody breach Washington's troopers had carved, putting the stunned Guardsmen to the bayonet. Seeing this massacre, Cornwallis rushed up the road to the relief of his reeling army. He was protected only by a thin screen of troopers; William Washington, alert to the opportunity presented, shouted to Francisco and the others and led a charge on the British ranks in the hope of capturing the general.

Cornwallis quickly drew back. His troops formed a protective screen around him and repulsed the charge. Washington, foiled, drew off and led his cavalry in one final assault on the rear ranks of the shattered Guards. Veteran troops, they had recovered slightly from the first shock, they were forming in squares, and they met the new blow with stiffened resistance. In this last melee, Peter Francisco received another and almost-mortal wound.

Riding headlong upon the solidifying squares of the Guardsmen, he was impaled on one of the bayonets upthrust from the prickly hedge of steel they had formed. The bayonet entered his leg just above the knee, sliced deep almost to the bone and ripped upward, laying open the flesh along the entire upper leg almost to the hip socket. Nearly unhorsed by the shock, doubled up with pain, Francisco wheeled out of the action, clung to his mount in desperation, and then, losing consciousness, tumbled from the saddle and collapsed on the battleground.

Behind him, the fate of the day and the South was being determined. The bayonet-wielding Continentals, seizing the opportunity the cavalry had given them, were tearing to shreds the entire center of the British Army. Cornwallis had to stop the carnage or lose all. To the horror of his officers, he wheeled forward his artillery, loaded it with grape and trained the muzzles directly on the melee in the center, where his own men were mixed inextricably with the charging Americans. General O'Hara, who had been wounded earlier in the action and was lying by the side of the road, read his commander's intentions and was horrified.

"Stop, stop," he pleaded, "you will destroy your own men."

"We must do it to save ourselves from destruction," Cornwallis answered.

And he ordered the guns to fire. They roared out, and Cornwallis, iron-faced, stood there watching his own guns slaughter his own troops in order to halt the enemy. The inhuman strategy, born of brutal necessity, worked. The deadly grapeshot scythed through the ranks of friend and foe; it shredded, stilled the milling fury of the battle. Under the steady hammering of the guns, the Americans withdrew, slowly and reluctantly, to their own lines; and the British, with the surcease purchased by the self-inflicted slaughter, fell back spent, trying again to re-form.

This was virtually the end of the battle. Greene had the only American army in being in the South; he was in no position to risk total destruction on the chance of total victory. Reluctantly, he drew off in good order, fighting a rearguard action as he went; and Cornwallis, technically the victor, rested on the field that had witnessed the virtual destruction of his army as a fighting force. He had suffered losses he could not afford to suffer; he had paid so high a price for this Pyrrhic victory that never again could he dominate the South. In his future lay the last long march into Virginia—and Yorktown.

As for Peter Francisco, he lay among the dead, still as the dead, on the battlefield from which his comrades had withdrawn. He was found by a Quaker named Robinson, who had been searching the field to see if any still lived. Finding that

Francisco did, the Quaker took him home and slowly nursed him back to health.

While the young giant was recuperating, the story of his incredible performance on the bloody field of Guilford Court House became the talk of the Southern army. None who fought there that day apparently ever forgot the eye-filling vision of the huge soldier with the terrible sword that hacked down eleven enemies in a row. William Washington had been so impressed that he lavished his personal praise upon Francisco and urged him to accept a commission. Francisco turned down the offer, feeling unqualified because he could neither read nor write. Nathanael Greene expressed his admiration by having a handsome razor case especially made for Francisco. On it he inscribed: "Peter Francisco, New Store, Buckingham County, Va. A tribute from his comrade in arms Nathanael Greene." The razor case still exists, preserved in the Hall of History in Raleigh, North Carolina. And on the battlefield of Guilford Court House a monument commemorates the spectacular feat of Peter Francisco.

By the time Francisco had recovered from the leg-splitting bayonet thrust that had almost cost his life, the war had moved ahead of him. Cornwallis had taken his badly shattered army to Wilmington, North Carolina, and from there he had moved north to unite with a smaller British army that had been ravaging Virginia. By the time Francisco was well enough to travel, the southern war was being fought in Virginia, his own state.

Trudging north on foot, Francisco immediately volunteered his services and began to scout the countryside, then being roamed almost at will by the troopers of Banastre Tarleton and other British raiders. It was a risky service, and one day, while Francisco was stopping at Ward's Tavern in Amelia County, now Nottaway County, nine of Tarleton's dragoons clattered up the road at a gallop, surprising and surrounding him in the inn yard. It was useless to resist, and Francisco, recognizing this, stood quietly like a man submitting to his fate.

Most of the troopers went inside the tavern, but one, saber drawn, approached Francisco. The conversation, as Alexander Garden later related it, perhaps with an embellishment or two of his own, went like this:

"Give up instantly and surrender everything you have of value—or prepare to die!" the trooper thundered.

"I have nothing to give up," said Francisco with a shrug. "So use your pleasure."

The dragoon's covetous eyes were drawn to a pair of large silver buckles that Francisco wore on his shoes. These were not the expensive buckles spelling the initials "P.F." that he had worn as a boy when put ashore at City Point; those had been entrusted to Judge Winston's wife for safekeeping. In their stead, the judge had given him the plainer, but expensive silver buckles that caught the eye of the British trooper.

"Give me instantly those silver buckles on your shoes," the cavalryman ordered, waving his sword.

"They were a present to me from a valued friend," Francisco protested. "Give them up, I never will. You have the power. Take them if you see fit."

The dragoon decided to act on the invitation. He tucked his saber beneath his arm and stooped to snatch the buckles from Francisco's shoes. The dual action had the effect of presenting Francisco the trooper's saber, hilt first, sheathed beneath the man's armpit. With a speed and dexterity amazing in so huge a man, Francisco acted. He grasped the saber by the hilt, wrenched it free, and in almost the same sweeping motion delivered one of those awesome Francisco strokes—splitting the trooper's head and neck in half down to his shoulders.

Instantly all was confusion—such confusion that the accounts of what occurred next are somewhat garbled and contradictory. As far as we can tell, now, this is what happened:

The sabering of the dragoon brought the rest of Tarleton's troop rushing from the tavern. One aimed a pistol at Francisco. Francisco sprang at him with the saber. The dragoon fired even as the saber fell. The ball grazed Francisco's side—the sixth wound he had received during the war. The saber practically severed the hand that had fired the shot, and with another blow, Francisco cut the trooper down.

While he was doing this, another of the dragoons leaped to horse. Ben Ward, the tavern keeper, who had come running into the yard with the dragoons, chose this minute to cast his lot with what he fancied must prove the winning side. He grabbed a musket and passed it up to the mounted dragoon.

The trooper leveled the gun at Francisco's breast and pulled the trigger. It missed fire. Immediately, Francisco was upon him. Reaching up, Francisco grabbed the musket, wrenched it from the dragoon's hands and clubbed him from the saddle. Even as the man fell, Francisco leaped upon the horse, acquiring a post of vantage above his enemies.

He rose in the stirrups and hallooed even as he had hallooed when riding through Tarleton's troopers at Camden: "Come on, my brave boys, now's your time; let's dispatch these few!"

Backing words with action, he charged, just as if he were really at the head of a thundering troop. He cut down another of the dragoons in the inn yard, and as he did, the rest of the squad broke and fled, running in panic across the fields in all directions. Left in possession of the battleground, Francisco whirled upon the treacherous tavern keeper whose intervention had nearly cost him his life.

"I seized Ward and would have dispatched him," Francisco related afterwards, "but the poor wretch begged for his life. He was not only an object of my contempt, but pity. The eight horses that were left behind I gave him to conceal for me."

Francisco had no time to waste on the innkeeper or the horses, for the rest of Tarleton's troop, some four hundred men, had come into view in the distance, riding toward the tavern. Seeing the disturbance in the inn yard, ten of them had broken out in front of the rest, riding to cut off Francisco. He tarried no longer. Putting spurs to his captured horse, he took off down an obscure country road and, using his knowledge of the countryside, easily eluded his pursuers.

The next day, despite the continued presence of Tarleton's troop in the vicinity, Francisco rode back to the tavern and demanded the captured horses from Ward. The tavern-keeper insisted on keeping two as a reward for the risk and trouble he had incurred in hiding them. Francisco begrudged the wretch such a bounty, but he dared not linger in the neighborhood and so settled for the six horses.

"I intended to have avenged myself on Ward at a future day," he said later, "but Providence ordered that I should not be his executioner, for he broke his neck by a fall from one of the very horses he had taken from me."

Francisco kept the best horse for himself, and in memory of the manner in which he had captured the animal he renamed it "Tarleton." The other horses he sold at the Prince Edward Court House the following day, turning the funds over to the government. As for "Tarleton," this horse became Francisco's favorite mount, one he rode for years afterward.

The encounter with Tarleton's dragoons at Ward's Tavern became one of the best-known anecdotes of the postwar years, and it so intrigued the artist James Worrell that in 1814 he painted an imaginative recreation of the scene that was hung in Independence Hall in Philadelphia.

As for Francisco, his encounter with the nine dragoons was just about the last of his wartime exploits, though he was in the lines at Yorktown when Cornwallis surrendered. After this climactic victory, he turned his thoughts to other pursuits—specifically, to a girl.

According to family tradition, it was shortly after the victory at Yorktown that Francisco and his old friend the Mar-

quis de Lafayette came to Richmond. They were walking
past St. John's Church, where as a boy Peter had listened open-
mouthed to the oratory of Patrick Henry, when a beautiful
young girl came down the steps, headed for her waiting carriage. On one of the last steps, she tripped and would have
fallen except that Peter Francisco, a handy man, was there to
catch her.

The girl was Susannah Anderson, just sixteen, the daughter
of Major Anderson and already "one of the acknowledged
beauties and belles of her section." The night after the encounter on the church steps, the beautiful girl and the huge
hero of the Continental Line met again at a party at the home
of Colonel Carrington of Richmond. Susannah was all but
betrothed to George Carrington, the son of the colonel and
a suitor much favored by her father. But Peter Francisco,
badly smitten with his first case of love, was not the man to
bow meekly to parental wishes.

The emotional fireworks that had been sparked by his first,
chance meeting with Susannah evidently convinced him from
the start that his only obstacle was the father, not any un-
willingness on the part of the girl. And with the father his
illiteracy and his lack of worldly prospects were the things
that counted. But these were things, too, that could be reme-
died.

Francisco began the remedying by opening a small store and
tavern on the Willis River at New Store in Buckingham
County. He also set up a smithy on a crossroads piece of land
given to him by Joseph Curd, an army comrade. With these
projects enhancing his material prospects, Francisco turned his
attention to the art of learning. The offer of a commission in
William Washington's cavalry hadn't inspired him to try to
learn to read and write; but the lure of Susannah Anderson
proved a more potent stimulant.

Francisco began to attend a neighborhood school run by a
Mr. McGraw, and with his incentive, he quickly proved an

apt pupil. Between lessons, he sometimes demonstrated the power of the muscles that had brought him the awe of the Continental Army by picking up his schoolmaster, a one-hundred-ninety-pound man, and lifting him in the palm of one hand as easily as an average man might an apple.

Four years of study, spiced with such demonstrations of physical prowess, overcame the objections of even Susannah Anderson's disapproving parent, and in 1785 Peter Francisco and the girl he had caught in his arms coming down St. John's steps were married. For a wedding present, Judge Winston gave Susannah the Negro mammy who had helped to rear the waif who had been abandoned on the Virginia docks just twenty years before.

With marriage, prosperity came to Peter Francisco. Susannah apparently brought him the estate, "Locust Grove," at which they lived; he acquired slaves and property and became a planter and country gentleman. With money and leisure, he not only indulged his lately acquired taste for learning and but also became something of a dandy. He read avidly in ancient and modern history, treating his books carefully like treasures; and in dress, he exhibited a taste for high hats, silk stockings and bright waistcoats. He became, in the words of a contemporary, "a product of the social influence of Virginia, and as charming as those who know they are descended from England's royalty."

Whether this was the most appropriate yardstick for the height of charm with a war against England just concluded is dubious, but one thing is certain: Peter Francisco, when he put on the airs of a Virginia gentleman, did not become a foppish puppet. He remained true to himself and true to his reputation as the Colossus of the Continental Line. When any deed of seemingly superhuman strength was to be performed, Peter Francisco always seemed equal to the challenge, and as the years passed, his tremendous physique continued to supply colorful anecdotes with which to embroider the Francisco legend.

On one occasion, he was summoned to a boggy meadow where a milch cow and her calf had become stuck in the mud. Francisco picked up the cow under one arm, the calf under the other, and carried both to firm ground. Another time, on a muddy highway in winter, he came upon a heavily laden tobacco wagon stalled in the mire. Three teams of mules were straining vainly to budge it. Telling the driver to unhitch the mules, Francisco put his shoulders against the rear of the wagon, heaved and lifted it clear of the quagmire, accomplishing what six mules had failed to do.

And there were more stories of his handling grown men like toys in his hands.

Besides the fact of his lifting two, one-hundred-sixty-pound men, one in either hand, to the ceiling, there was the even more startling experience of a carpenter who had been hired by Francisco to shingle the roof of a barn. Francisco didn't like the quality of the work and upbraided the carpenter. The latter, a medium-sized man, was angered by the reflection on his ability and charged down off the roof, ready to fight. Francisco simply stretched out his huge hands, grasped the irate carpenter by neck and breeches and heaved. The carpenter flew through the air and landed right back on the roof of the barn. There, collecting his wits and attempting to marshal his dignity after the astounding thing that had happened to him, the ruffled bantam looked down at Francisco and shouted: "Well, you can whip me maybe, but I'll be damned if you can skeer me!"

Such anecdotes spread Francisco's fame far and wide through the states and made him a marked man in an age that set great store on physical strength. In a burgeoning, frontier society, the strictly male virtues counted heavily—courage and strength, the ability to work and to dare. Inevitably, male pride set an exaggerated value on sheer muscle, and in such an age, the mere existence of a reputed super-strong man like Peter Francisco represented a challenge to other strong men, unwilling to acknowledge any superior. The result was that many, incredulous of the fantastic tales they had heard, came seeking trial by sinew.

On one occasion, two farmers from a nearby county, both mighty men in their own estimations, began bragging in a local tavern that they could whip any man in Virginia. The barkeep challenged the statement. There was, he said, a man right in town who could handle both of them with one hand tied behind him; but the trouble was he was a peaceable fellow, it would be hard to get him to fight. The muscular farmers, fortified by liberal potations, scoffed at this. They'd get super-man to fight all right, they said, and they bet one hundred dollars that they could both provoke a fight and win it.

Shortly afterwards, Francisco, suspecting nothing walked quietly into the tavern. The barkeep nodded in his direction, indicating he was the man, and the two farmers sidled up to Francisco. He had walked to the fire to warm himself and was about to sit down in a chair. The strangers yanked the chair away. Francisco fell heavily, and they jumped on him.

Never did two men make a worse mistake. Francisco shook them off the way a terrier sheds water and rose to his feet with a roar of anger. He reached out his two huge hands, grasped each of his tormentors by the back of the neck, yanked them from their feet and cracked their heads together with almost skull-splitting force. Both men were knocked unconscious and fell limply to the floor. One did not come to until late in the afternoon, and the other remained insensible until the following day.

The man who could deal with antagonists with such ferocity when the occasion warranted had, however, another and gentler side to his nature. With his friends, he often used his tremendous strength as an overgrown puppy might. Typical is the story of the milk in the springhouse.

Francisco and two comrades were returning from a fishing expedition when they passed a neighbor's farm. Crocks filled with milk had just been set in a trough through which ran a stream of cold water. The fishermen were hot and tired and thirsty, and the sight of the cool milk made them even thirstier. But there was no way to get a drink because the milk was in the springhouse, and the door was locked.

While they were considering the problem, Francisco pointed out that it should be easy to get into the springhouse since it had no floor. Going to the rear of the little shack, he slipped his fingers under the framework, strained his muscles and tilted the whole building high enough for his friends to crawl under. When they were inside, he let the house down, trapping them. Then he ran to find the farmer, shouting that thieves were in the springhouse stealing his milk. The farmer, alarmed and angry, raced to the springhouse, and there, sure enough, were Francisco's fishing partners, staring out forlornly from behind a grating. Before bodily harm could be done, Francisco explained the trick he had pulled on his friends, and all concerned burst into laughter.

Such was the man. It is little wonder that he captivated three wives and became the intimate of many of the foremost men of his day. Susannah, Francisco's first wife, lived only five years after their marriage. She died in 1790 after having given birth to two sons, one of whom survived. Four years after her death, Francisco married Catharine Brooke, a relative and friend of Susannah, whom he had met during a visit to the Anderson home after Susannah's death. They lived at "Locust Grove," which Susannah had willed to her surviving son, and Catharine, before she died in 1821, bore Francisco two sons and two daughters. In 1823, two years after Catharine's death, Francisco married Mary Beverly Grymes, who had been born in England in 1782 and had come to Virginia as a girl of fifteen to live in the home of her uncle, Governor Edmund Randolph. She was the widow of a Major West and only thirty-one, just half Francisco's age, when they were married.

The much younger wife evidently found the Revolution's most awesome warrior an easily manageable human commodity. Though Francisco had always been perfectly happy in the role of a planter and country gentleman, his young wife found the country too secluded for her taste and urged him to move to gayer Richmond. Docilely, Francisco gave in to her wishes and purchased a home in the city. There he lived comfortably enough, his own resources supplemented by his soldier's pension and his pay as a sergeant-at-arms for the Virginia House of Delegates.

In 1824, when Lafayette revisited America, the two Revolutionary warriors were reunited, and Francisco accompanied Lafayette on his triumphal tour through Virginia. Two years later, Henry Clay visited Francisco. Much impressed by the still mighty muscles of the Revolutionary warrior, he asked Francisco if he had ever met his match in a test of strength. Francisco said he never had and, laughing, told a story about a man who had traveled all the way from Clay's native Kentucky to test muscles with him.

The Kentucky strong-man was named Pamphlet, Francisco recalled, and the incident occurred while he was keeping tavern at New Store. He was in the yard outside the tavern when Pamphlet rode up, inquired for Francisco and said he had come all the way from Kentucky just to whip him. Smiling, Francisco called a servant and sent him to cut some willow switches. These he presented to Pamphlet, and turning his back, he told Pamphlet to whip away so that he could go back to Kentucky and say he had carried out his boast.

Resenting the ridicule, Pamphlet insisted on trying to lift Francisco. Francisco submitted, and Pamphlet hoisted him up and down several times, none too gently, acknowledging that Francisco was indeed a mighty heavy man.

"All right, Mr. Pamphlet," said Francisco, "you've felt my weight. Now let me feel yours."

He took hold of Pamphlet, lifted him twice into the air and then tossed him, as casually as a boy might toss a ball, over a four-foot fence into the dust of the roadway. Hardly able to believe that he was where he was, lying in the dirt of the road, Pamphlet looked up and remarked, half-sarcastically, that if Francisco would throw his horse over the fence, too, he would go away convinced. Francisco promptly led the horse to the fence, put his left arm across the horse's chest and his right under the body. Then he gave a mighty heave—and over the fence went the horse.

Witnesses to the feat are said to have corroborated Francisco's account, which gained considerable circulation in the press of the day. Henry Clay, hearing the tale for the first time, evidently relished it. He was then the target of political pamphleteers, and he laughingly told Francisco that he was glad at least one member of "the pamphlet family" had been conquered.

With strength and vigor almost undiminished, Peter Francisco lived until 1831. Then he became ill with an intestinal ailment that physicians in later and medically wiser eras have surmised might have been appendicitis. He suffered for three weeks before he died at an estimated age of seventy-one. Lafayette, when notified of his death, was deeply affected and sent a letter of sympathy to Francisco's third wife. The Virginia Legislature passed a resolution of regret, and virtually every prominent official of the state from the Governor down attended the funeral service held in the General Assembly Hall.

Francisco's third wife survived him many years, inheriting his pension and one hundred and sixty acres of bounty land. She carefully preserved the letter from Lafayette and the mementos

of her famous husband. The huge broadsword, unique weapon
in the hands of a unique warrior, was passed on to Francisco's
daughter, Mrs. Edward Pescud, of Petersburg, Virginia, and
was presented by her to the Virginia Historical Society.

Despite such memorabilia, despite the well-authenticated nature of the most important of his almost incredible exploits,
Peter Francisco has remained a hero virtually unknown to posterity. After all, privates in the line are rarely accorded prominent place in official dispatches detailing military glory. Yet so
immense was the figure of the man, so challenging and tremendous his deeds, that he could not remain in complete oblivion either. Just before the turn of the century, the Daughters
of the American Revolution planted in San Francisco's Golden
Gate Park thirteen Liberty Trees, one for each of the original
Colonies, each tree nourished by soil taken from the grave of
a Revolutionary hero. Virginia's symbol was the chestnut, and
the bag of earth about the base of the Virginia tree came from
the grave of Peter Francisco.

The Revolutionary cause was a flame that attracted women as well as men. It was the only one of our wars, except for the Civil War, that was fought on our own homeland. And unlike the Civil War, in which the South almost exclusively was the battleground, the Revolution involved at one time or another during its shifting course each of the Thirteen Colonies.

The sweep of the conflict and its intensely partisan nature inevitably led to wide involvement. It is sometimes forgotten that the Revolution was not a unified rebellion against the foreign power of Great Britain, but a civil war in the truest sense, pitting neighbor against neighbor, father against son, brother against brother. One branch of a family might be dedicated patriots, another just as devout Tories. It was a war in which there were no hard-and-fast battle lines, but rather a turmoil of plot and counter-plot, with skirmishing and partisan warfare raging in areas far distant from the main armies.

In such fluid strife, civilian distinctions were often wiped out. A woman in her cabin home was as exposed to danger as a soldier with Washington's Army. Inevitably, the women became intensely involved in the loyalties of their men, and sometimes they

215

developed a passion of conviction and a fervor for the cause that left the men behind. As a result, the Revolution, of all our wars, became the one war in which women played active roles in battle.

The women who fought were, like the men, a varied crew. There was Deborah Sampson, actually a private in the Continental Line. There were the Molly Pitchers who followed their husbands to war and, in desperate moments, manned the guns. There were frontier women, battling the twin evils of Tories and Indians. And finally there were passionate patriots like Nancy Hart.

This is their story—the story of women who, in the perilous days that shaped their nation, were sometimes just as active and just as dangerous as the men.

CHAPTER VI

★

★　　★　　★

★

Women Warriors

THE LADY WAS A HERO. When she was being just her feminine self she was Deborah Sampson, a Massachusetts household drudge; but when she donned man's attire, she became Robert Shurtleff, a private in the Continental Line, a soldier twice wounded in action.

The story of Deborah Sampson is unique in American military annals. The Revolution was fought in the era of camp followers, and sometimes when the men were shot down the women manned the guns. In such circumstances, Margaret Corbin served a cannon at Fort Washington after her husband fell, and at Monmouth, Mary Ludwig Hays McCauley, one of the women water-and-grog carriers, practically appropriated for her exclusive use the generic title of her class and became in popular imagination the one and only Molly Pitcher. In the Tory-ridden South and the Indian-infested West, women sometimes became warriors. But Deborah Sampson was different from all the others. She was the only woman who enlisted in the army as a man, served as a man, fought as a man, and later received a full veteran's pension from Congress.

In the process, she lived through some novel experiences, including the embarrassment of having a pretty young girl fall in love with her under the misapprehension she was he—Robert Shurtleff, the dashing young soldier of the Continental Line.

Deborah was born at Plympton, not far from Plymouth, Massachusetts, on December 17, 1760. Her family had roots going deep into earliest Colonial America and by marriage could boast ties to such eminent historical figures as Captain Myles Standish, the doughty Indian fighter; John Alden, the timid lover; and William Bradford, early Colonial leader and historian. But by the time Deborah came along, the line had run pretty much to seed. Deborah's father was a sailor and, from all indications, a tavern roisterer who didn't concern himself about his paternal obligations. When Deborah was five, he was lost at sea, and her mother, left penniless, broke up the family, parceling the children out among friends and relatives.

Until she was ten, Deborah was shunted from house to house, an unwanted waif and burden. Then she went to live in the home of Jeremiah Thomas in Middleboro as an indentured servant. For the next eight years, her lot was the unenviable one of a jill-of-all-work about the Middleboro farm; but stirring deep in Deborah, quite evidently, was some instinctive compulsion for self-betterment. She taught herself to read, a considerable accomplishment in a period of widespread illiteracy when girls especially were supposed to know only how to keep house. Deborah, having taken the first step into the world of books, couldn't stop. Once she was freed from her indenture, she spent part of her days attending a neighborhood school. Her mind must have been first-rate, for only two years later, when she was twenty, she had acquired enough learning to fill in as a teacher when she was not working on the farm.

It was still a dull life for a young girl with romantic urges. Perhaps if Deborah had been a beauty, she wouldn't have had to worry about farm chores and teaching school. But she wasn't. She was about five feet eight inches tall, and the hard work she had performed from earliest childhood had developed more muscles than feminine curves. She had bright eyes and a pleasing animation of manner, but these attributes hardly compensated for an elongated face and a long, prominent nose.

In early 1782, with the war still going on, Deborah Sampson decided to get away from Middleboro by crossing over into the man's world. Just where she got the idea of enlisting in the Continental Army isn't clear, but what Deborah did about it is definite. She borrowed a suit of clothes from an acquaintance named Sam Leonard, went to the local recruiting office and joined up under the name of Timothy Thayer. As Timothy, she probably got the usual bounty fee of one hundred dollars, all in badly depreciated paper currency. Up to this time, we are told, Deborah always had despised "revelry, gossiping, distraction and orgies," but her first act in her enthusiasm for her new role as a male was to take one big bound into these fascinating and unexplored pastures. She marched herself down to the village ordinary. And there she hoisted a few, just as might have been expected of a stout fellow who had joined up to serve his country. The effect on the girl who had disdained "orgies" was predictably disastrous. In a word, Deborah became tipsy. In the several words taken to describe this condition in the literature of the day, she "behaved in a noisy and indecent manner" and in general comported herself in such fashion that it quickly became apparent, even to the bibulous yokels in the tavern, that she was no Timothy Thayer.

Great was the shock in Middleboro. Sam Leonard, whose clothes had been borrowed for the masquerade, was so unnerved at the thought of what his garments had covered that "he never wore them after." Just as shocked as Sam was the membership of the local Baptist Church. A model maiden before she stepped into the pants of Timothy Thayer, Deborah had been welcomed into the church's membership. Naturally, her "very loose and un-Christianlike behavior," as the elders described the scene in the local ordinary, stirred deep concern for her welfare in the hereafter. The elders wrestled mightily with the problem "without obtaining satisfaction" from the unrepentant Deborah. Then they called a meeting of the church membership, and a vote was taken to "withdraw fellowship"—in other words to excommunicate—the wayward Deborah Sampson.

This spiritual penalty had no chastening effect on Deborah. Indeed, by the time it was imposed, she had become a man again and had marched off to war, this time without any betraying stops in the local ordinary.

Having been deprived of the habiliments of the red-faced Sam Leonard, Deborah fashioned herself a new wardrobe. With twelve dollars she had saved up from her earnings as a schoolteacher, she purchased a quantity of cloth, went to work with needle and thread, and piece by piece sewed herself a suit of men's clothes. She hid each article under the hay as it was completed, and when all was ready, she made some necessary alterations in her figure. Specifically, she wrapped a tight bandage around her breasts to achieve a properly chesty but not betrayingly bountiful profile. Then she stepped into her breeches, donned her coat and departed from Middleboro. She hiked some seventy-five miles to Worcester, went directly to the recruiting office and emerged as Private Robert Shurtleff in Capt. George Webb's company of the Fourth Massachusetts Regiment of foot.

The time was May, 1782, and though Yorktown had been won the previous fall, a lot of fighting was still being done in the embattled colonies. One of the most active areas was in Westchester County, just north of New York City. Then as now, Westchester was the home of many wealthy landowners, sentiment had been sharply divided, and the entire countryside had become a kind of no man's land across which rival bands raided and plundered. Deborah and her comrades in the

Fourth Massachusetts were soon to be plunged into the thick of this skirmishing. They were ordered to join Washington's Army, based at West Point, and early in June, they set out on the long and dusty march.

Private Robert Shurtleff stepped out as stoutly as any of "his" comrades, and none of the other privates in Captain Webb's company, men who doubtless prided themselves on having keen eyes for a figure, had the slightest suspicion that their ranks contained the most fascinating and improbable of all possibilities, a woman. Their curiosity wasn't even piqued when they noticed that Robert Shurtleff had no beard and never needed to shave. This phenomenon they apparently ascribed to the lad's extreme youth; and, intent like soldiers before and since on finding a butt for their humor, they twitted Robert, calling him "blooming boy" and "Molly." They were real cards, those men in Webb's company—or so they thought.

Once settled in camp at West Point, the men of the Fourth Massachusetts were quickly dispatched on raids to the south. Private Robert Shurtleff went along. On one raid, the company crossed the Hudson at Stony Point and pressed south along the east bank of the river all the way to Harlem. Swinging back through White Plains, the raiders encountered a rival party of Tories at Tappan Bay, between Ossining and Tarrytown. A sharp melee followed, and Deborah Sampson in the role of Robert Shurtleff gave a good account of herself. The fighting was close, hand-to-hand, and Private Robert received "his" first wound, a saber slash across the left side of the head.

The wound was healing into a fine masculine scar when Deborah, back at West Point, came perilously close to exposure. A family friend visited the camp, looking for her. Her departure from the Thomas farm in Middleboro had caused consternation. One group of relatives had a horrified conviction that Deborah, just like a woman, had run off with a man; another faction was filled with an equal dread that she hadn't,

that she had committed the even worse offense of attempting
again to disown her sex. The first supposition sent a brother
chasing off to Maine in the expectation that Deborah might be
found there, living in sin; the second brought the family friend
to West Point to see whether Deborah had shouldered a musket. The army reacted with instinctive horror to the suggestion that it might have *a woman* in its ranks, and the family
friend went back to Middleboro empty-handed. Deborah, having escaped discovery, evidently felt a twinge of remorse over
the anxiety she had caused, for she wrote her mother, explain-
ing only that she had found "agreeable work" in "a large but
well-regulated family."

The "agreeable work" turned nasty a few weeks later when
Deborah's company, on another raid down the Hudson, was
ambushed by a band of Tories at East Chester. In a sharp and
bloody skirmish, the Americans fought their way clear, but not
before Private Robert Shurtleff had been knocked flat by a
musket ball that pierced "his" thigh. The delicate location of
the wound made the soldier dread contact with a physician
more than contact with Tories. He called out to his comrades
that he had been mortally wounded and should be left behind,
but they wouldn't hear of it. Lifting the wounded Robert on
their shoulders, the men of the Fourth Massachusetts carried
"him" to a field dressing station.

Others had been wounded in the fray and the doctors were
busy. Taking advantage of their preoccupation, the injured
soldier crawled off into the woods where she could treat her
wound in privacy. Deborah hid out for several days, washing
and dressing the wound as best she could. When it was healed,
she returned to camp, the musket ball still imbedded in her
thigh, a source of pain for the rest of her life.

Still undiscovered, Deborah continued her career as Private
Robert Shurtleff. In November, Washington's Army went
into winter quarters, but Deborah and her company of un-

suspecting comrades were sent north to Ticonderoga and then west to fight marauding Indians. In one frontier skirmish, Deborah was about to dispatch an Indian warrior when she discovered that he was really a white man. Instead of killing an enemy, she rescued an unfortunate captive.

Deborah must have been a good soldier, for she was transferred next to Philadelphia to serve as an orderly to General Patterson, then trying to quell a riot of drunken and unpaid troops. An epidemic that was described as "malignant fever" was sweeping through the city, and Deborah hadn't been at her new post long before she was stricken. She was taken to one of the overcrowded hospitals and deposited in a long line of the ill who were waiting for medical attention. The doctors were so overworked that it was a long time before anyone could attend the new patient. Deborah was so far gone by then that she could no longer worry about the fate of Robert Shurtleff; she was unconscious, almost dead. Finally, a Doctor Binney, making his rounds, came to her still, outstretched form, noted the name that had been pinned to the coarse homespun coat and asked one of the neighboring victims of disease: "How is Robert?"

"Poor Bob is gone," the soldier replied dolefully—a prophetic if not medically exact diagnosis.

Doctor Binney, double-checking, felt for the pulse, found it. The beat was very faint, but it was still a beat. Researching further, the doctor placed a hand inside the patient's shirt, seeking his heart—and found what no doctor should ever find in any army, the swath of bandages that had helped transform Deborah Sampson into Private Robert Shurtleff.

The shock that must have been Doctor Binney's very private and special possession has not been recorded in history. All that is evident is that the doctor must have been a man of discretion. He acted quietly and swiftly. Not telling anyone the real reason, he pretended to take a great interest in the pe-

culiar medical case of Private Robert Shurtleff, and he had the
suffering soldier transferred to his own home on the pretext
that "he" could receive better nursing care there.

When Deborah recovered, she pleaded with the doctor to
save Private Robert Shurtleff from the embarrassment of public exposure. The doctor, evidently a kindly man, agreed to
the deception for the time being, but events must soon have
given him some qualms about the quality of his judgment. For
the truth of the matter was that, while Deborah Sampson may
have been no beauty as a woman, she made a tall and rather
handsome man, and now, in the guise of a wounded hero of the
war, she began to attract girls!

One of the smitten, according to some accounts, was a niece
of Doctor Binney. Another was a young girl who began by
writing Private Shurtleff an adoring, anonymous letter. Soon
afterwards, the girl engineered an introduction to her hero,
and it wasn't long before Private Shurtleff found "himself"
closely pursued by a young girl in love. The pair took carriage rides together, and the girl made no secret of the palpitat-
ing state of her heart. One writer of the post-Revolutionary
era described the interesting entanglement in these poetic
terms: "Timorous as a young roe, yet pliant as the bending
osier, with the queen of love resident in her eyes, she re-
hearsed her plaint of love with that unreservedness which
evinced the sincerity of her passion and the exaltedness of her
soul."

Deborah Sampson, we are told, kept a straight face. It must
have been difficult.

In any event, Private Robert Shurtleff, knowing what "he"
knew, told the love-sick girl as gently and sorrowfully as possible that their great love could never be. It was one of the
tragedies of war. Duty called and Private Shurtleff had to be
off to the front. General Patterson was leading a force across
the Alleghenies into Indian-infested Ohio, and his orderly

went with him. Patterson's men—and Deborah—had some skirmishes with the Indians before returning East again. Passing through Baltimore on the way home, Private Shurtleff again encountered the girl with the love-sick heart. This persistent young lady, whose parents by all accounts were persons of some wealth, had decided to express her affection with gifts. She pressed upon Private Shurtleff six shirts, a watch and twenty-five Spanish dollars. The soldier, in a spot that many better men have been in before and since, apparently didn't know quite how to get out of the affair, and so accepted the gifts. But later, having marched safely off to Philadelphia surrounded by the protecting ranks of comrades, the soldier-hero wrote the distracted young miss in Baltimore, told her their acquaintance must end and signed the letter with the revealing words, "Your Own Sex."

This self-confession by Deborah and her obviously dangerous charm made even the patient Doctor Binney decide that it was time for the masquerade to end. He went to General Patterson and let that amazed commander in on the secret. Understandably startled, the general expressed himself in an ejaculation that seems to have put the matter rather well.

"Why," said he, "this is truly theatrical!"

Once he had recovered from his surprise, Patterson began to wonder what should be done with the first lady of the Continental Line. He decided that the problem was too big for him, and taking his orderly with him, he repaired to headquarters, where he informed General Washington of the truly incredible state of affairs. Washington kept his reaction to himself, but he quickly had discharge papers made out for Private Shurtleff.

There was one final twist, one final fillip to the story. At General Patterson's instigation, Deborah shed her private's rags and dolled herself up in unfamiliar feminine finery. Then, on the General's arm, she paraded up and down past the ranks

of her former comrades in the Fourth Massachusetts. Those
unperceptive men were still unperceptive. Not one recognized the attractively beruffled maiden as the former Private
Robert Shurtleff.

Mustered out of the army, Deborah returned to Massachusetts in November, 1783. She had been soldiering for a
a year and a half; and, though she had never indulged in
liquor and had "never wrestled nor suffered anyone to twine
his arms around her shoulders," she must have been, especially in her day and age, something of a walking scandal. Perhaps this was the reason that she still wore her uniform for a
time and went to work on a farm, defiantly calling herself
Ephraim Sampson. Came spring, however, and also love. Deborah became a woman again, this time to stay.

On April 7, 1784, she was married to Benjamin Gannett,
a young farmer several years older than herself and one who
had stayed prudently at home throughout the entire Revolution, tilling the arable portion of his one hundred acres of
land in Sharon. On the property was a two-story farmhouse
surrounded with willows, "covered with woodbine and with
roses growing up to the chimney tops . . . with brooks running through it and raspberries in the hedges and along the
stone walls." In this idyllic setting, Deborah Sampson quietly
interred that wartime cut-up, Private Robert Shurtleff, and in
due course became the mother of three children—two daughters, Mary and Patience, and a son, Earl.

The years passed, not without their problems. The wound
Deborah had received at East Chester troubled her as she
grew older. She was often in pain from the musket ball imbedded so deeply in her thigh, and she found it impossible to
do much farm labor. Medical expenses mounted. In 1792, the
Commonwealth of Massachusetts, recognizing that the state
possessed in Deborah a unique Revolutionary veteran,
awarded her an invalid bonus of thirty-four pounds. In 1805,

Congress gave her a pension of four dollars a month as an invalid soldier, and in 1818 this was doubled.

During this same period, haunted by the specter of poverty, Deborah began to capitalize on the notoriety she had achieved by the escapade of her youth. In 1802, she became probably the first woman lecturer in the United States. She toured Massachusetts, Rhode Island and New York, delivering a pat speech about her experiences as a private in the Continental Line. Her talk consisted of generalities and glowing platitudes about Liberty and the rigors of army life and the female virtues; and she usually brought her appearance to a climax by appearing rigged out in a military costume, carrying a regulation musket and performing the Manual of Arms with all the éclat of a well-drilled veteran.

Deborah died on April 29, 1827, at the age of sixty-seven, and her husband, Benjamin Gannett, who doesn't seem to have been overly endowed with gumption, fell on increasingly hard times. Aging and indigent, he began to recall all the money he had spent on doctor's bills for his wife's care, and in 1837, when he was eighty-three, he got a Congressman to introduce a bill granting *him* a pension. The measure, introduced in the Twenty-Fifth Congress on December 22, 1837, conceded that Benjamin Gannett did not exactly qualify under the Act of 1836 "granting pensions to widows in certain cases." But the bill pointed out that the committee on pensions believed "they are warranted in saying that the whole history of the American Revolution records no case like this," and they recommended that Benjamin Gannett be granted a pension of eighty dollars a year, retroactive to March 4, 1831. This was done, but Gannett never received the benefits. He died before he could collect the money, and by special act Congress granted $466.66 to his wife's heirs.

In time, the memory of Deborah Sampson became almost forgotten—almost, but not completely. A street in Sharon, where some of her descendants still live, was named after her, and on April 10, 1944, during the crisis of another great war, a Liberty Ship bearing her name slid down the ways of the Bethlehem Steel Company's shipbuilding yards in Baltimore.

The two Mollies, Margaret Corbin and Mary Ludwig Hays McCauley, were quite different from Deborah Sampson. Both were women all the way—sturdy, rough-hewn, rough-tongued women who had followed their husbands into the army and became in battle crises volunteer artillerywomen, handling the guns and keeping them firing.

Margaret Corbin has been overshadowed in history by the more famous Molly Pitcher of the Battle of Monmouth, but she deserves her own special niche as the first woman warrior of the Revolution. She was born on the Pennsylvania frontier in 1751, and five years later, her father was killed and her mother carried off by Indians. Just how she escaped isn't clear, but in 1772, when she was twenty-one, she married John Corbin, a Virginian, and when he joined the Continental Army as a matross in Capt. Thomas Proctor's First Company of Pennsylvania Artillery, Molly went with him.

Matrosses were soldiers who assisted the gunners in loading, firing and sponging the guns. Molly Corbin, like the other camp women, watched her husband at his drill and soon became as familiar with the sequence of orders as any of the men. It was well that she did, for the war had hardly begun when her knowledge was put to the test.

In the succession of disasters that followed the Battle of Long Island, Washington's Army straggled in retreat up the spine of Manhattan and on to White Plains in Westchester County. Bloodied in repeated clashes with the pursuing troops of Howe, the Americans were rapidly degenerating into a tattered and defeated rabble; and Washington, in desperation, seeking to hold somewhere, committed errors of strategy. One of these—sheer folly—consisted of committing a small garrison to hold Fort Washington on the Hudson against the over-whelming might of British warships and the encircling army of Howe.

Molly Corbin and her husband were among the troops as-signed to the defense of the fort, built on a lofty, rocky emi-nence later to be known as Fort Tryon in what is now the Bronx. Col. Robert Magaw of Pennsylvania commanded the twenty-eight hundred troops completely isolated in the midst of Howe's Hessian and British hordes. On November 15, 1776, Howe demanded the surrender of the fort, and Colonel Magaw, in a defiance that reads as though it were taken from the pages of Thomas Paine, replied: "Actuated by the most glorious cause that mankind ever fought in, I am determined to defend this post to the very last extremity." That extremity was not far away.

Howe massed his Redcoats, his kilted Highlanders, his Hes-sians—some eighty-nine hundred troops in all—against the com-pletely surrounded fort. His heavy artillery opened a can-nonade from the land side, and from the river the frigate *Pearl* trained the crashing thunder of her broadsides on the rocky crags as landing parties stormed ashore at 201st Street. One of the heaviest concentrations of fire was laid down on an exposed two-gun battery in a northern redoubt on Forest Hill, a focal point of attack. Here Molly and John Corbin were stationed. Exploding shells sprayed the redoubt with deadly shrapnel. Men began to fall. A matross manning the gun next to Corbin's was killed, and Molly caught up his rammer staff and stepped into the gap, sponging and ramming home the charge like a veteran.

Together the Corbins, Molly and John, helped to keep the guns firing—but not for long. Another shell burst, and John Corbin reeled back and fell, mortally wounded. Molly could not know how badly he was injured, and there was no time to find out. She had to keep serving her gun. Time after time, the cannon was loaded, fired, its shot plunging down the rocky slopes into the climbing, scrabbling swarm of Hessians. The plunging cannon balls cut bloody swaths through the enemy—but the stolid Hessians, resplendent in their blue coats, yellow breeches, black boot tops and high brass-mounted caps came on. The long rifles of the Virginia and Maryland sharpshooters added to the toll of the cannon; but nothing could halt the advance, the disparity in numbers was just too great. As the Hessians mounted the slopes, Howe's cannon, loaded with grapeshot, fired a final burst above their heads, and deadly pellets whirred through the embrasures of the fort, spraying the crews about the guns. Molly Corbin was hit. She went down in a bloody mass, falling almost beside her husband. One arm was mangled, nearly torn from her body; one breast was shredded. Above her, yelling hoarsely, the Hessian troops stormed across the ramparts and carried the fort.

The wounded prisoners were released by Howe and sent on a long, jolting wagon journey to Philadelphia. Somehow, Molly Corbin survived the ordeal; somehow, she recovered. But she was to remain a virtual invalid for the rest of her life. In time, she found her way back to the army and was enrolled, the only woman, in the Invalid Regiment, designed both as a refuge for those crippled in service and as a recruiting corps and military school. She became known as "Captain Molly." In 1782 she acquired another husband, also a crippled veteran of the Invalid Regiment, but he seems to have been an ineffectual shadow in "Captain Molly's" life, for even his name has been forgotten. And "Captain Molly" remained "Captain Molly" Corbin, the heroine of the defense of Fort Washington.

Pennsylvania voted her a grant of thirty dollars; Congress in 1779 granted her a pension equal to one-half of a soldier's regular monthly pay and subsequently ordered that she be given a new suit of clothes every year. In fulfillment of this last grant, the old tents of West Point were cut up on one occasion and re-sewn into garments for "Captain Molly."

All the evidence indicates that the crippled artillerywoman became a regular Termagant as the years passed. She was possessed of a sharp tongue and a fiery Irish temper, and the more helpless she became, the more quarrelsome and troublesome she was. Her hospital and commissary rations were issued from West Point, but it became increasingly difficult to find anyone who wanted to shoulder the thankless task of caring for her. It is not known just when she died, but her grave was located more than a century later on an old Hudson River estate purchased by J. P. Morgan. The remains were exhumed and reinterred in 1926 in the cemetery of the West Point Military Academy, where a marker perpetuates her fame as the first artillerywoman of the Revolution.

Better known to the general public than "Captain Molly" Corbin, however, was the second female cannoneer of the war, the Battle of Monmouth's famous "Molly Pitcher." She was Mary Ludwig, a stocky, sturdy Pennsylvania Dutch girl. When she was only fifteen, she was married to John Caspar Hays, and when Hays joined the army, his young wife went with him. Hays's first service was with the artillery, and Mary Hays, like Margaret Corbin, watched her husband at drill until she came to know as well as he the functions of sponge and rammer.

It was a knowledge she put to use on June 28, 1778, at the Battle of Monmouth. The British were retreating across New Jersey after the evacuation of Philadelphia, and Washington had made plans to cut them off before they could reach the shelter of the British fleet at Sandy Hook. The two armies met in battle on a day of insufferable one hundred-degree heat that shimmered from the rolling fields west of Freehold. Hays had now been transferred to an infantry detachment, and his wife performed the services of a water carrier. Her bright skirt fluttered as she hurried back and forth from a spring near the battlefield, bringing pitchers of water to the gasping, exhausted troops.

The turning point in the Battle of Monmouth came early. Washington had envisioned the possibility of another and earlier Yorktown, but his plans were wrecked by the pusillanimous Maj. Gen. Charles Lee. Commanding the American advance, Lee gave the order to retreat almost as soon as fighting had been joined and thus threw the entire line into confusion. As the Americans fell back, one of their field pieces was left in an exposed sector of the field in imminent danger of capture. A member of the gun crew had been felled by British shot. Hays, with his old experience as an artilleryman, grabbed up the rammer and helped to work the gun. He, too, fell wounded. The gun crew, unable to work the piece, was about to drag it to the rear when Mary "Molly Pitcher" Hays seized the rammer that had fallen from her wounded husband's hand and began to swab and load like a veteran. The gun was still blazing when Washington himself charged upon the field, dressed down Lee in expletives that, it was said, made even the leaves of the trees vibrate—and saved the day.

Monmouth ended in a drawn battle. The Americans never could regain the opportunity that Lee had let slip, and the British got away. In the desperate fighting of that day the one name that stood out was the name of a woman—Molly Pitcher. She had served her cannon and kept it blazing at the enemy to the end, and Washington himself, in appreciation of her services, issued her a warrant as a noncommissioned officer. From that moment, Mary Ludwig Hays became known to an admiring army as "Sergeant Molly."

Molly Pitcher's husband recovered from the wound he had received at Monmouth, but he died shortly after the end of the war. Molly then married another ex-soldier, George McCauley. By all accounts, he was lazy and shiftless, and it wasn't long before Molly left him. She worked as a laundress and nursemaid, supporting herself and living to the hilt her distinguished role as a battle-hardened veteran of America's greatest war.

As the years passed, "Sergeant Molly" came to act more and more like a sergeant. She smoked a pipe, chewed tobacco, enjoyed her liquor and swore like a trooper. Sometimes she watched the militia drill, shook her head in despair like a drill sergeant and allowed she didn't know what the race was coming to. It wasn't like that at Monmouth, she opined; men were men then, and if you didn't believe it, you should have seen her manning a gun. Practically won the battle single-handed. Awarded an annuity by the State of Pennsylvania, Sergeant Molly lived long and contentedly. She died on January 22, 1832, at the ripe old age of seventy-eight. And to this day, on the battlefield of Monmouth, a monument commemorates her moment of glory—the one and only Molly Pitcher manning her cannon in the hour of her army's greatest need.

Just as the careers of the two Mollies differed from that of Deborah Sampson so did the adventures of a third type of heroine differ from either. They didn't go looking for trouble; it came to them. They were women who were impelled to action by the harsh necessities of their times and their environment. They were primarily frontier women and female partisans in the Tory-riddled South.

West Virginia produced two of the well-known heroines of the frontier. The first was Betty Zane, who was credited with saving Fort Henry during an Indian raid by the much-hated white renegade Simon Girty on September 11, 1782—one of the last actions of the Revolution.

Girty had led a raiding party of some four hundred Indians across the Ohio, had burned a blockhouse some dozen miles from Fort Henry and had started to lay waste the countryside. Wheeling at that time was a scattered village of some twenty-five log huts. Its main defense was Fort Henry, a stockaded stronghold with blockhouses at each corner.

When smoke from cabins fired by Girty's raiders began to darken the horizon, a reconnoitering party was sent out from the fort. Unfortunately, Girty's marauders were a lot closer than anyone had expected. The scouts were ambushed, and most of them were killed. Swiftly, Girty swept down upon the settlement. Some of the settlers elected to defend their own cabins; the rest, a small force of less than twenty men and boys, were left to defend the fort.

Girty's Indians quickly fanned out in a skirmish line outside the stockade and trained a hot, incessant fire upon its defenders. The frontiersmen fired back. The duel continued for six hours, and at the end of that time, the frontiersmen made a horrifying discovery: they were running out of powder.

About a hundred yards from the fort was the well-defended cabin of Ebenezer Zane, one of the founders of Wheeling. Zane, as the garrison of the fort knew, had an extra keg of powder hidden in his cabin. The problem was how to get at it.

The frontiersmen held a council of war. Obviously, some-one would have to run the gauntlet of the Indians to Zane's cabin, get the powder—and then make the same hazardous journey back. It was clearly a suicide mission, and volunteers were asked for. Every man and boy in the fort stepped forward. Before a choice could be made, another and surprising volunteer appeared—Ebenezer Zane's young sister, Elizabeth.

She had just returned to the frontier after a term of schooling in Philadelphia, and she was in the group of women who had been sent into the fort for protection and who had busied themselves during the siege in casting bullets, making cartridges and loading rifles. At first the frontiersmen wouldn't listen to Betty Zane, but she insisted that she should be the one to go. She pointed out that all the men were needed to defend the fort and that anyway, no man would stand a chance; he would be shot as soon as he stepped outside the palisade, but the Indians might have other ideas about a woman.

Her logic was unassailable, and the defenders of the fort

finally agreed to let her make the attempt. The gate was opened, and Betty Zane slipped out. Exercising supreme self-control, she did not run, she walked. Now the Indians—a fact that is often overlooked today—were extremely curious folk, sometimes almost as easily intrigued as a child. And so, while they obviously wondered what Betty Zane was up to, they did not interfere. They whooped and hollered at her, but they let her go.

She reached Ebenezer Zane's cabin and darted quickly through the door. Breathlessly, she explained the plight of the garrison. Zane's reaction was instantaneous. He dragged out the keg of powder, knocked in the head of the barrel and dumped the contents into the middle of a large tablecloth that he tied up into a bundle for Betty. The girl whipped off her dress to leave her legs unencumbered, grabbed the bulging tablecloth and sidled out of the cabin. Knowing deception would be useless this time, she began to run.

The Indians spotted her at once. Rifles cracked on every side. Bullets whizzed past her darting figure, kicked up dust at her feet. Panting, she sped across the crest of a little knoll and raced down the hill to the waiting palisade of Fort Henry. The gate swung open for her, and she staggered through with her invaluable burden. The fort and Wheeling were saved.

Betty Zane lived to be an old woman. She was married twice, and among her numerous descendants in succeeding generations was the popular American novelist and teller of western tales, Zane Grey.

While Betty Zane's fame rests on her one fleet, courageous dash through the Indian gauntlet during the siege of Wheeling, the second heroine of the West Virginia frontier had a war-long career, and like Deborah Sampson, though without Deborah's deception, she dressed and lived and fought like a man. She has come down in frontier legend as "Mad Anne" Bailey, scout, courier, and Indian fighter.

"Mad Anne's" maiden name was Hennis, and she was born

in Liverpool, England, probably in 1742. As a girl, she came
to live with relatives in Virginia, and there she met and married
Richard Trotter, a born frontiersman. Trotter had survived
Braddock's catastrophe in the French and Indian War, and
after the war was over, he took his bride into the Great
Kanawha Valley, where they built their cabin. With the
Revolution brewing, Indian warfare flamed along the exposed
frontiers, and on October 10, 1774, Trotter was killed in a
battle between the frontiersmen and Indians at the mouth of
the Kanawha.

His wife, in their years together, had become as skilled
a frontier fighter as any man. She often dressed in homespun
hunting shirt, leggings and moccasins; she carried a long
hunting knife; and she was deadly with the long rifle. Another
type of woman might have sat down to mourn her husband;
"Mad Anne," on the contrary, was determined to avenge him.
Leaving her son William in the care of a frontier neighbor,
she set out on her self-appointed mission.

She was a woman who had received more than the usual
education during her girlhood in England, and she appears
to have been perceptive enough to realize that she could accomplish more by telling her story than she could blundering
off single-handed through the wilderness. And so she started
on a tour of the frontier, traveling from hamlet to hamlet,
visiting recruiting stations and exhorting men everywhere to
join up for army duty. In her strictly masculine, warlike garb,
she must have been an impressive figure, and it was not long
before she was an active courier, carrying messages—sometimes
on foot, sometimes on horseback—into every danger zone
from Staunton to the outermost fringes of the West Virginia
frontier.

Not much detail has survived regarding her actual encounters with Indians. But on one occasion, while traveling
between Point Pleasant and Charleston, West Virginia, she

encountered a band of braves upon the warpath and was almost captured. Leaping from her horse, Anne took to the woods, utilized all the forest lore her husband had taught her and finally concealed herself in a hollow sycamore log. Some of the Indians, in their hunt for her, actually sat upon the log above her without having any suspicion that she was near. Ultimately, failing to find her, they called off the search and went on their way. Normally, one would have thought that the fugitive in such a case would have felt thankful enough to travel in the opposite direction as speedily as possible—but not "Mad Anne"! She crept out of her hollow tree trunk and began to trail the Indians. She followed them right to their camp, and when night came, she waited for her opportunity, stole her horse back again and rode on her way.

Another of her adventures involved a one-hundred-mile journey through a wilderness infested by Indians, her mission the succor of a frontier fort. The tiny stronghold was called Fort Lee, and when the Indians menaced it, the fort was suffering from that most acute of all frontier deficiencies, a lack of powder. The only hope lay in obtaining a supply from Lewisburg, one hundred miles away. None of the frontiersmen wanted to volunteer for the mission, but "Mad Anne" did. She made it, too, riding one horse into Lewisburg and riding another back, laden with all the powder he could carry.

Feats such as these convinced the Indians that the woman who tracked and fought and hunted like a man was one of those fey individuals who have the protection of the great spirit in their madness. And so Anne, who had met and married John Bailey, another scout, became "Mad Anne" Bailey, a unique legend of the West Virginia frontier.

Anne's second husband died in 1802, and once more she took to the roads. This time she became a female traveling salesman—again, a distinct rarity of that time—riding on horseback to carry goods long distances to the exposed frontier settlements. In 1817, she moved with her son by her first marriage, William Trotter, into the new wilderness north of the Ohio River, and there, on a new frontier, she died on November 22, 1825, some 83 years of age.

A legendary figure fully as colorful as "Mad Anne" Bailey was Georgia's Nancy Hart. Nancy was an Amazon of un-prepossessing and formidable appearance, and the possessor of such ferocious instincts that the small stream on which she lived near the Broad River in the neighborhood of Dy's and Webb's ferries in Elbert County became known as "War Woman's Creek."

Some skeptical historians have wondered just how much of the Nancy Hart story is fact and how much legend. The question is complicated because the now-famous "war woman," a female guerilla if ever America had one, wasn't mentioned in the usual Revolutionary accounts devoted to male heroism. She first appeared in print about fifty years after the war was over, a lapse of time that makes it highly possible for vivid imaginations to have colored the actual events. The first version of the achievements of the formidable Nancy evidently saw light in a small Milledgeville paper, and whatever information it contained has now been lost. But in the eighteen-thirties Elizabeth Ellet, wife of a professor at Columbia College in South Carolina, picked up the strands of the Nancy Hart legend by talking to old-timers who had known her or known of her. That started the furor. Since then, one county in Georgia and innumerable schools, hotels, cafés and filling stations have been named after the "war woman" of the Revolution.

Although considerable fiction has doubtless become em-broidered on the Nancy Hart story, there is underneath a solid basis of fact—enough to indicate that Nancy Hart was a woman no man should ever have crossed. Her maiden name was Ann Morgan, and she was born, probably in 1735, on the

Pennsylvania or North Carolina frontier. Nancy, as she was always known, was married to Benjamin Hart. They settled first in South Carolina, but about 1771 they moved on into the sparsely settled country beyond the Broad River in Georgia. There, in the post-Revolutionary era, Benjamin Hart was to become a prominent citizen, land-owner and slave-holder; but in these first years of settlement, while Nancy's eight children were being born, they lived in a one-room log cabin. The up-country section was a hotbed of Whig, or patriot, sentiment; and Nancy Hart appears, according to the legend, to have considered her husband "a poor stick" because he didn't take a more active part in the war. Benjamin, however, was no slacker. He was a lieutenant in the Georgia militia, and he must have performed some service because in the desperate days of 1781, with the South overrun by British and Tory armies, the Georgia Executive Council came to his family's relief by granting them a bounty of twenty bushels of corn.

On the other hand, it might be argued that the bounty was a reward for Nancy Hart's services, for certainly she appears to have been the militant one of the pair. She was a woman of impressive size, about six feet tall and "very muscular and erect." She was also—and this description is handed down from a day when heroes were usually pictured as heroic and heroines as beautiful—"cross-eyed, with a broad, angular mouth, ungainly in figure and rude in speech." It is admitted, too, that she was "vulgar and illiterate," but in her favor it is pointed out that she was also courageous and hospitable—and a sharpshooter. Her cabin was decorated with antlers and bearskins to prove it. Of the many tales told in subsequent years of the "war woman's" exploits, these appear to be the best authenticated.

On one occasion, Georgia Whigs needed information about events on the Carolina side of the Savannah River, where the

Tories were sweeping all before them. Nancy volunteered for the dangerous scouting mission, built a raft by lashing some logs together with grapevines, floated across the river —and returned with the needed information. Another time, while the British were in possession of Augusta, it became similarly essential for Elijah Clarke and his Whig followers to get information about their activities and intentions. Nancy dressed up like a man and wandered into the enemy camp, acting as if she were crazy. She played the role so well that no one suspected her, and again she came back with the needed information.

It was at about this same time, while the Tories were still in possession of Augusta, that Nancy Hart performed what was probably her most daring and, in a grim way, her best-authenticated deed. It was an act that might be called "the saga of Nancy Hart and the six Tories," and to the main drama, there was an intriguing prelude.

Nancy was working in her cabin one day when she heard the sound of hard-galloping hooves. Looking out, she saw a faithful patriot whom she knew riding hell for leather, undoubtedly being pursued by Tories. Instantly, Nancy devised a ruse to effect his escape.

She took down the bars and swung open both the front and back doors of her cabin. Then she motioned the rider to gallop right through. The hard-pressed fugitive didn't pause to ask questions, but simply thundered through the house and down to the swamp by the creek, where he hid. Nancy quickly shut and barred the doors. Then she muffled her head and face in a shawl, like an old woman.

Hardly had she made these preparations when a band of pursuing Tories swept out of the forest, around a bend in the road and up to her cabin. They wanted to know if a horseman has just galloped past. Why, no, said Nancy, nobody had passed her home that day; but now that the gentlemen mentioned it, she did recall having seen a horseman who had turned off the road and taken a path through the woods some three-hundred yards back, just a few minutes before. Whirling their mounts, the Tories galloped away on a false scent and the patriot went safely on his way.

But when they got back empty-handed to Augusta and began to compare notes, the Tories suspected they had been tricked. One day shortly afterwards, a half-dozen of them rode out of Augusta, raided across the river, surprised a local militia colonel in his bed, killed him—and rode on to visit Nancy.

Sitting their horses in front of her cabin, they demanded to know whether she had deliberately tricked them and hidden the rebel rider a few days before. Nancy, who by all accounts was overly endowed with brass, bluntly told them that she certainly had. This decided the Tories. They announced they were going to stay for a time—and that Nancy was going to wait on them.

"We're hungry," the leader said.

"I never feed traitors," Nancy snapped.

"You're going to feed us."

"I ain't got nothin' to feed you with," Nancy told them. "You've stole everything, all my pigs and chickens—everything except that one old gobbler in the yard."

"All right, *that* you shall cook for us," the leader declared, shooting the turkey.

Nancy swore a round volley of oaths that should have curled the hair of the hardest trooper, but the Tories, pleased with themselves, just grinned and dismounted and took possession of her cabin. They all had muskets, and there wasn't much that Nancy could do, apparently, except to obey their orders and feed them. She appeared to recognize the inevitable and began to clean the turkey.

Even as she worked, she was thinking. Her husband Benjamin had been out in the fields when the raiders arrived. She had to get word to him. Summoning her twelve-year-old daughter, Sukey, she whispered her instructions. Then, raising her voice she told the child to go outside to the spring and fetch some water.

Sukey ran off on her mission. She quickly found her father and gave him Nancy's instructions. A conch shell had been hidden for emergencies in a "high, snag-topped stump" among the trees at the edge of the swamp. Hart was to round up some neighbors, and when Sukey blew on the conch shell, he was to hurry to the cabin, ready for action.

Unaware that more than a feast was being prepared for them, the Tories broached some liquor they had brought along and devoted themselves to some spirit-lifting exercises while they waited for the turkey to roast. Finally, the meal was ready, and Nancy bustled back and forth, serving her bibulous and famished guests. As she worked, she took advantage of certain elements of the situation.

The Tories had stacked their muskets in one corner of the room, and in the happy state at which they had arrived, they were not keeping too close an eye upon the guns. Surreptitiously, Nancy forced out a piece of pine that served as a chinking between two logs at the rear of the cabin. Then, on her trips back and forth to the table, she began to snatch muskets. She had taken two and passed them out through the chink in the logs, and she had a third in her hand, about to shove it out, when one of the Tories discovered her.

His shout of alarm brought his comrades storming to their feet. Nancy, who had already dispatched Sukey to blow loud on the conch shell, whirled and faced them, the gun in her hand.

"I'll kill the first one that moves," she said.

She gave the Tories her best cross-eyed stare, and in the circumstances it was a bit difficult to tell just who was the intended victim. One of the Tories, evidently under the misapprehension that he couldn't be the marked man, started forward. Nancy shot him through the head.

The other Tories, seeing Nancy with the discharged musket in her hand, thought she was helpless now and started for her. But Sukey came racing up to the cabin just in time, grabbed one of the muskets her mother had shoved out and passed it back in.

"Daddy will soon be here," she gasped.

Nancy, a fresh gun in her hand, faced the Tories, just as deadly as before. Again they tried to rush her, and again she fired, wounding one. As she did, she reached one hand behind her, and Sukey shoved the third—and last—loaded musket into it.

"You better surrender or I'll kill you all," Nancy Hart told the Tories in a deadly quiet voice.

While they hesitated about surrendering to a woman, Benjamin Hart and a posse of neighbors charged up, surrounded the house, and made debate academic. With the invaders trussed and helpless, the patriots were all for shooting them on the spot, but Nancy Hart demurred.

"Shooting's too good," she decreed. "Hang 'em."

Her word seems to have been the law. The Tories were dragged from the cabin, a rope was thrown over the limb of a tree in front of it, and they were all expeditiously and expertly hanged.

That is the "war woman's" story. Truth or fiction? No one can be absolutely certain of all of it—but Nancy's vendetta with the six Tories, it would seem, almost has to be judged as fact. E. Merton Coulter, a professor of history at the University of Georgia, is one of those careful historians who haven't been able to believe fully in Nancy Hart. That fifty-year-old, word-of-mouth business disturbed him, and so, a few years ago, he did the most exhaustive research that has yet been done on the birth and growth of the Nancy Hart legend. There is no proof at all, he concluded, for most of the stories of Nancy's valorous services; but when he came to consider the incident of Nancy's encounter with the six Tories, Professor Coulter did unearth one startling bit of circumstantial evidence. Long years after the Revolution, a railroad line was being extended through the region beyond the Broad River. Nancy Hart's old cabin was razed for the right-of-way. Workmen, digging up the ground to lay the foundations for the roadbed, were shocked by the discovery of bones, human bones. In the end, they unearthed entire human skeletons—six of them!

The war at sea is one of the most overlooked phases of the Revolution. Popular attention has always been focused on the important land battles, and the general impression is that the sea fighting did not amount to much. Actually, the war at sea was as desperately fought as the war on land and had its own moments of high drama.

Throughout the long course of the war, those privately armed raiders known as privateers and the warships of the infant Continental Navy scavenged the sea lanes with a persistence and daring that have rarely been equalled. The sea fighting of the War of 1812 has been much better publicized; but the well-trained, professional officers of that later era, with their far more powerful warships, seem frequently to have lacked the supreme ingenuity and audacity of the best of the Continental Navy skippers, who sallied forth in cockleshells and attempted the fantastic.

The performance of the Navy of the Revolution was inevitably a most uneven one. Hardly any of its officers and men—Nicholas Biddle was a noteworthy exception—had been trained in the tactics and tradition of naval warfare. They were almost exclusively merchant sailors suddenly given the command of fighting ships;

245

and though the average seaman of that day had to know how to handle guns and fight a battle, there was still a vast difference between warding off an attack by pirates and going out to wage aggressive warfare against the greatest sea power the world had ever seen.

Yet the sailors of the Revolution, the best of them, achieved the great transition. They carried the war into the home waters of Great Britain and to the shores of her far-flung dependencies in a manner that put to shame the efforts of the strongest nations of Europe. They snatched prizes within sight of the English Channel; they dogged, harassed and pilfered heavily protected ocean convoys; sometimes they even brought their little ships into hostile harbors, attacked forts, raided on land. They inflicted losses on British shipping that ran into millions of dollars, driving maritime insurance rates to peaks never before reached and eliciting howls of pure pocketbook anguish from Britain's wealthy and influential merchant class.

All this they did, and yet just one sailor—John Paul Jones, who waged his immortal battle with the frigate Serapis *in the shadows of the English coast—has emerged from obscurity. The other sea fighters of the Revolution have been almost forgotten. They deserve a better fate.*

Among the many who should be rescued from oblivion, the name of John Peck Rathbun stands high. He might be called the mystery man of the Continental Navy. He was so overlooked, even in his own time, that the Secretary of War, in a final compilation of Revolutionary naval officers, neglected even to include his name. He has been so poorly dealt with that even in official records his name was rarely spelled the way he spelled it, Rathbun, but was usually Rathburne or Rathbourne. He disappeared so quickly into civilian anonymity that even his final destiny remains obscure. Yet he performed two of the most audacious feats of the Revolution; and one of them, at least, was something that the entire Navy of the War of 1812 could not match—a supremely bold descent upon the fortifications of Nassau in one little sloop mounting just twelve guns and carrying a crew of only fifty men.

CHAPTER VII

★

★　★　★

★

The Captain and
the Lieutenant

THE SLOOP *Providence* was at sea under a new commander—
a tall, lanky, lean New Englander with a long neck and a
prominent Adam's apple, John Peck Rathbun. He was a
veteran sailor, a skilful mariner, and he needed to be for he
commanded a pint-sized warship.

Originally named the *Katy*, the *Providence* had been a
Rhode Island trading sloop until war came along to change
both her vocation and her name. Her one tall mast was stepped
well forward, and the long boom for her huge fore-and-aft,
gaff-rigged mainsail extended beyond her stern when her sails
were housed. Aloft she carried a large, square-rigged topsail
and a small cloud of staysails and jibs. She was narrow of beam,
fast, but lightly built and puny of armament. A single roundshot from one of the heavier naval cannons of the day would
have shattered her thin scantling like an eggshell, and in self-
defense she could only bark at her enemies with twelve

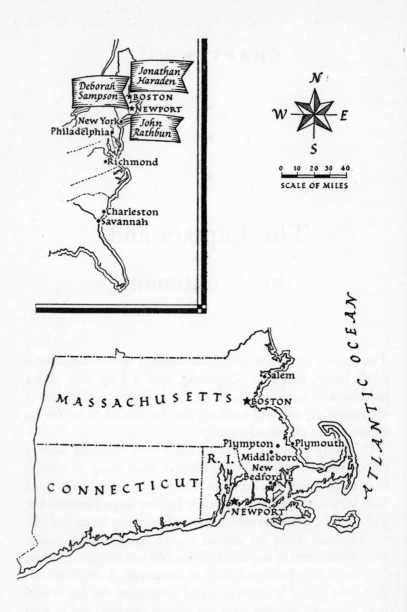

Jonathan
Haraden

Deborah
Sampson

★BOSTON
★NEWPORT

New York•
Philadelphia•

John
Rathbun

•Richmond

•Charleston
•Savannah

N
W   E
S

0 10 20 30 40
SCALE OF MILES

Salem

MASSACHUSETTS   ★BOSTON

Plympton• •Plymouth

R. I. Middleboro
New
Bedford

CONNECTICUT

NEWPORT

ATLANTIC OCEAN

four-pounders, ranged six guns to a side on her poop and open main deck.

Rathbun had drawn the unenviable task of taking this gallant but makeshift little man-of-war out on an ocean crawling with British frigates and ships-of-the-line. It was a mammoth order, for in addition to coping with the weakness of the *Providence* herself, Rathbun had encountered all kinds of difficulties, in this spring of 1777, in getting together enough men to handle the sails and work the guns, and his ship was undermanned.

In the earlier, halcyon days of the war, when hope had been bright and victory had looked almost easy, the *Providence* had carried ninety men, including a full complement of twenty-seven Marines. Now her crew was whittled down to little more than half that number, and Captain Rathbun and his lieutenant, John Trevett, had had the devil's own time getting them. The rich rewards of privateering, where a man fought only as much as necessary, contrasted unfavorably with the hazards and bad pay of the Navy, in which a man's main job was to fight and in which, after he had fought, he sometimes had trouble collecting his prize money. With the scales so unevenly balanced, the best sailors not unnaturally preferred the privateers, and Rathbun and Trevett had been forced to fall back on the much-detested press-gang tactics of the Royal Navy to get together a slim crew of some fifty men.

They made a good team, Rathbun and Trevett, and probably never did a commander owe more to his lieutenant than Rathbun, all unknowing, owed to his. For Trevett, who had a meticulous streak in him, kept a diary which he later expanded into a journal; and if it hadn't been for this, the exciting adventures of John Rathbun and the crew of the *Providence* would be largely unrecorded.

The skipper of the *Providence* was a Rhode Islander by birth and a Bostonian by choice. He was the son of Nathaniel

Rathbun and Ann Peck Rathbun, and had been born in Exeter, Rhode Island, on March 23, 1746. He had gone to sea as a boy, and in time had become the master of ships sailing out of Boston. At the outbreak of the war, he had been commissioned a lieutenant in the Continental Navy, and he had served almost continuously in the *Providence*, first under Capt. John Hazard and later under John Paul Jones himself. He knew his ship thoroughly.

Trevett, like Rathbun, had been in Navy service since the start of the war, and, like Rathbun, he had been in the first American fleet to take to sea—the squadron that doddering old Commodore Ezek Hopkins led against Nassau and brought back laden with guns and ammunition for Washington's Army. More than just the habit of service held Trevett in the Navy, however. He had a personal reason for wanting to wage war. His brother, Constant Church Trevett, the captain of a merchant ship plying between the Carolinas and the West Indies, had been captured by the British and had rotted to his death in the foul hold of the Old Jersey prison ship. Trevett, as a result, felt an almost religious, Old Testament hatred of the British, and he confided to his journal that he would "rather be taken by the Turks" than by the gentlemen of the Royal Navy.

When Rathbun took command of the *Providence* in May, 1777, she was a bit battered from a bout with a British brig in which her last commander, Jonathan Pitcher, had been badly wounded. Rathbun and Trevett saw to her repairs, then put to sea and headed for Martha's Vineyard to see what they could do about rounding up a crew.

"At Bedford I pressed one John Scranton, one of my townsmen, and three others," Trevett wrote in his journal. "We arrived at Old Town, lay there two days, got what men we could, and then ran for Sandy Hook and made it."

Lower New York harbor, when Rathbun poked the nose of the saucy little *Providence* almost into this lair of the

British fleet, was a forest of masts belonging to ships anchored inside the Hook and waiting to put to sea. Although Rathbun and Trevett could not know it, one of the vessels whose tall spars they studied was to have a special witch's lure for them, enticing them in the end into a foolhardy venture against seemingly hopeless odds. Rathbun studied the huddled merchant fleet through his glass, then stood off the coast, shadowboxing with the land in the hope that some of the ships would put to sea and give him an opportunity to snatch prizes.

Late in the afternoon, his patience was rewarded. Four vessels—ship, brig, schooner and sloop—weighed anchor and put out to sea, standing to the southeast. Rathbun, keeping them in sight just above the horizon, dogged along in their wakes. Throughout the night, he tracked his quarry, and the next day, being far enough at sea to risk action without the danger of interference from British warships in New York, he began to chase in earnest. It was three o'clock in the afternoon when the *Providence* came up with the ship, a fine vessel mounting sixteen guns. Rathbun hailed her, but got no answer. The ship simply held to her course, ploughing on across the seas with the brig, schooner and sloop ahead off her weather bow.

". . . we gave her a bow gun, intending to break her cabin windows," Trevett wrote. "We drew very near her but the wind being scant we found we could not get to windward, so we bore away and went under her lee, as near as we could, and gave her a good broadside. She immediately gave us as good a one, and run us aboard on our starboard quarter, and hung there about five minutes, until she broke all our sweeps that were lashed there.

"At the same time the brig of 10 guns and the schooner of eight guns lost no time—all three of them firing into us at once. As the ship fell off, she gave us her starboard broadside, and we shot ahead of them with our sails and rigging much cut to pieces."

The *Providence*, with her twelve popguns, was certainly overmatched. The three vessels she had fought mounted thirty-four guns in their broadsides, but Rathbun wasn't awed by the odds. He bore away, putting all hands to work repairing the rigging, but he hadn't given up the battle by any means. He had, in fact, just begun to fight.

"We had but a poor crew at this time," Trevett wrote. "Our loss was our sailing master, Capt. George Sinkins, of Newport, who was killed, and only 2 or 3 men slightly wounded. We hove him overboard, got our rigging repaired as soon as possible, and made sail for the ship.

"We came up with her just after sunset, with a determination to board her, for we well knew if we carried the ship that the rest of the vessels would fall into our hands. We ran within half pistol shot, and gave her a full broadside, but all three of them played their part so well we gave it up.

"At this time the schooner was ahead of the other vessels, and we ran her alongside and took her. We found her to be of about 140 tons burthen . . . This schooner had some horses and carriages aboard, and we ordered her for Bedford, where she arrived safe."

From the crew of the captured schooner, Rathbun learned that the ship was named the *Mary*, sixteen guns, Captain, Henry Johnson, and that she was bound to Jamaica in ballast. Having manned and sent away his prize, Rathbun resumed the chase, steering the same course the remaining three vessels had been following. They apparently changed course in the night to elude him, however, for when dawn came, the sea was clear except for one pip of sail a long distance to the southward. The *Providence* gave chase and got close enough to identify the stranger as an enemy privateer; but that was all. The privateer fled and, proving to be the faster vessel, made good her escape.

The little *Providence* kept on her southeasterly course for several days, sighted several neutral vessels, but found no opportunity to take prizes. Then came a strange encounter.

"Being in the Gulf Stream, it being meridian," Trevett wrote, "saw a sail as far as we could discover; stood for her, and at sunset found her to be a ship. Her crew appeared to act strangely; she decoyed us before the wind, and sometimes shaking in the wind, top-gallants and all sail out. About 1 o'clock A.M., it being star light, we neared her, and some of our crew said she showed lights, but the officers could not see any. We came within pistol shot and hailed her, but received no answer. We gave her three shots at once, which made a cracking on board of her, but still no answer, and no lights were seen."

As the *Providence* flitted about the weirdly silent ship, John Rathbun stood with his head thrust forward on his long neck, his eyes sharp and wary. He studied every inch of the stranger's deck, but he could see no movement, no sign of life. Carefully, he brought the little *Providence* into the wind, dead in the seas off the strange ship's quarter, his crew manning the broadside guns, ready to fire at an instant's notice. Still no gun spoke, no hail came from the stranger. Rathbun decided that this cat-and-mouse game had lasted long enough. He ordered a boat lowered away, and he directed Lieutenant Trevett to take an armed boat crew and board the silent vessel.

Both Rathbun and Trevett knew this was a risky venture. If the ship's crew were playing possum, Trevett and his men might be overwhelmed on her deck. But Rathbun gestured to the *Providence*'s ready guns, assuring Trevett of their support, and he made a grim jest of the danger, as fighting men sometimes do.

"Don't worry," he told his aide, "if they kill you, I shan't spare one of them!"

Trevett seems to have considered this poor consolation as he dropped down into the boat and rowed away into the night.

"I set out and ordered the cockswain to steer under her

stern," Trevett wrote. "I held a lantern and saw her rudder was gone, and hailed, but received no answer. I ordered the cockswain to steer around her larboard quarter, and go alongside, and I sent one man up with the lantern, and followed him.

"I found no boats on deck, but saw on the quarter-deck a deep sea lead and line. I went into the cabin and found all the beds and all the trunks full of rich clothing, and chests with their keys in them. One of our men cried out, a man! a man! I asked where, and it proved to be a small dog, that opened all the eyes he had, but could not speak our Yankee tongue.

"I then went into the hold and found her in ballast; no cargo or provisions, except bread, and 40 casks of nails, and a few cases of French cordials. I sent the chests, trunks, and what was of value aboard our sloop, but we were so lately out we could not stow away much. The ship being destitute of a rudder it would have been difficult to get her into port, so we kept the barge plying all day and until late in the evening, when we took out the dog, and for fear she would fall into the hands of the English (she being a noble ship) we set her on fire and burnt her to the waters edge."

Rathbun and Trevett deduced from the fancy clothes—the French-style ruffled shirts, the fine silk handkerchiefs and other items—that the "noble ship" was a French vessel that had grounded, all sails set, on the outer shoals of Cape Hatteras. Her crew evidently had abandoned her in haste and made for the shore in the ship's boats. Subsequently, a high tide had refloated the vessel; west winds had blown her out to sea; and there, with her broken rudder and her lone dog for crew, she had become an ocean gypsy, wandering on changing courses as the winds willed.

The encounter with the ghost ship marked the last notable incident of the cruise, and the *Providence*, much buffeted by the sea, returned to New Bedford. There she refitted and recruited a new crew. When she sailed again in November, 1777, she was undermanned as before, with only some fifty men in her complement. She ran immediately into dirty weather, and all during her first night out, she lay hove to riding the seas in a howling snowstorm. Her bowsprit sprung, she weathered the gale and sailed for the South Carolina coast. Off Charleston bar, she raised a strange sail that Rathbun took "to be a Droger, going from Charleston to Georgetown."

Rathbun and Trevett were below when, about one P.M., an officer came down to warn them that the stranger was very near—making threatening gestures.

"Capt. Rathbun and myself went on deck," Trevett wrote, "and she hailed us, and ordered 'the damn Yankee beggars to haul down the colors.' We had a foul weather Jack at the masthead. In a few minutes she run under our lee-quarter, gave us a broadside without any courtesy, and run ahead of us. Capt. Rathbun ordered the boatswain to call all hands to quarters, as still as he could, and not use his call.

"The Privateer (as she proved to be) bore away, and coming up again was soon alongside; we were all ready for them, and as soon as they made the first flash, we gave them a Yankee welcome, with a handsome broadside. They up helm and ran to the eastward, and not having a man hurt of any consequence, we made sail after them . . ."

The *Providence* had been a bit cut up aloft and dropped behind while repairs were being made. Night fell, but there was beautiful moonlight and the little sloop kept the privateer in sight. Unable to shake off the *Providence*, the crew of the fleeing privateer hung a lantern at their masthead, signaling for help. By this, Rathbun knew that a heavy British warship must be in the vicinity, but despite the risk, he kept up the pursuit. When dawn came, the lookout spotted "a large ship under the land," but though she had all the appearance of a British frigate, she was far away and Rathbun continued the chase. The *Providence* was gaining steadily now.

"About sunrise we neared the Privateer so much that the Lieut. from the roundhouse fired several times at us," Trevett wrote, "and the balls went a distance beyond us. I told Capt. Rathbun that we had without doubt as good muskets as they had. I spoke to Mr. Michael Molton and Mr. Bailey (of Boston) and requested them to go forward with me and take a shot at him, as he made a fine mark to be shot at standing on the roundhouse.

"We had not fired more then three shots before we saw him fall, and instantly the Privateer got in the wind, and we were alongside of her in a few minutes; when we boarded her and found it was her Lt. we had shot, and he fell on the man steering at the wheel.

"This Lt. belonged to the state of Va., and he expected to be punished if taken by the Americans, so he was determined to fight as long as he could. He had a handsome brace of pistols at his side when he laid dead on the deck. We found five men badly wounded on board; our shot went into one quarter and out through the other, and she was badly shattered."

The large ship that the *Providence* had sighted close inshore was, indeed, a British frigate. The officers of the captured privateer had been on board her only the day before and were to have met her the next day off Charleston bar. Since the frigate effectively blocked the way to Charleston and since, during the chase, he had run far to the east, Rathbun changed his plans and took his prize and prisoners into Georgetown, South Carolina.

Trevett was assigned to escort the captain of the captured privateer to Charleston. Rathbun followed and soon picked up the information that was to lure him into one of the most hare-brained ventures of the war. A Captain Newton, master of a trading vessel, had just come into port from the West Indies, and he told Rathbun and Trevett that a rich cargo ship, the *Mary*, homeward bound to New York from Jamaica, had put into New Providence in distress. She was still lying there, being repaired in the harbor of Nassau, and if Rathbun and Trevett sailed at once, they might have a chance of capturing her.

Mention of the *Mary* homeward-bound from Jamaica set Rathbun thinking. This was not just another rich cargo ship, but a very special ship—the identical vessel he had battled so desperately on her outward voyage from New York, the well-fought craft whose broadsides had killed his sailing master, George Sinkins. She was lying there in the roads off Nassau, waiting to be taken. An ambitious project, a truly mad project began to take shape in Rathbun's mind. Why not take Nassau by surprise? Why not seize the port—and the *Mary* with it?

"We thought the time of retaliation had come," Trevett wrote, "and we had a notion of killing two birds with one stone; so we determined to go, and take Fort Nassau, and then we should have command of the town of New Providence and its harbor, and take what we pleased."

Bold words. But the boldness was Rathbun's, not Trevett's. In fact, Trevett seems to have been a most worried confidant of his captain and, though he doesn't put it quite that way, more than a little tempted to get out of the entire project if he could. In Charleston, he had met Nicholas Biddle, one of the few trained officers in the Continental Navy and the skipper of one of its finest frigates, the thirty-two-gun *Randolph*. Biddle had just returned from a cruise, and he offered Trevett a post with him in the *Randolph*. Trevett was anxious to take it, but he pointed out that he would have to have Rathbun's permission for such a transfer. Rathbun was sitting at the time in a Charleston coffee-house, and Biddle and Trevett went there to see him.

On the way, Trevett evidently confided to Biddle the secret of Rathbun's hare-brained scheme to try to seize Nassau and the entire island of New Providence with just one twelve-gun sloop and fifty men. Biddle, the trained naval officer, was appropriately shocked. He "said it was downright presumption to undertake such an attempt," Trevett wrote—and, not a doubt about it, Biddle was absolutely right. Together he and Trevett appealed to Rathbun for Trevett's release. But Rathbun, bemused by the wildest scheme any naval officer had yet conceived, wasn't in any mood to relinquish the services of his most experienced and trusted lieutenant.

"I have made an agreement with Captain Trevett and I will not give him up," he told Biddle, evidently calling Trevett by his merchant mariner's rank.

The three shook hands, and Biddle rose to leave, shaking his head sorrowfully.

"I am sorry, for I shall never see you more," he told Trevett.

He was right, but not at all in the way he meant. Sailing from Charleston shortly afterwards, Biddle in the *Randolph* engaged in a broadside duel with the British ship-of-the-line *Yarmouth*, sixty-four guns. A hot shot from the *Yarmouth*'s broadside found the *Randolph*'s magazine and blew her to pieces, killing Biddle and all his crew, except four sailors who were found days later clinging to a floating spar.

This unsuspected tragedy was still in the future when Rathbun and Trevett hurried back to the *Providence* in Georgetown. Early in January, they sailed. Trevett evidently had done some more worrying about the magnitude of the task they were undertaking and, unable to sail in the *Randolph* with Biddle, he had made a stout-hearted compromise with fate. "I have had time to reflect on what I am about to undertake," he wrote, "and am well satisfied that we are engaged in a good cause and are fighting the Lord's battles."

It looked at the outset as if they might need an extra ration of the Lord's help. The *Providence* was barely at sea when she sighted a ship, a brig and a sloop off the coast to the eastward. All three gave chase, and the ship especially gained fast upon the *Providence*. By two o'clock in the afternoon, Rathbun

and his men could see her tier of guns rising out of the sea
and knew that she was a British warship of no mean strength.
Desperately, they struggled to get more speed out of the
Providence. Rathbun spread every inch of canvas she could
fly, trimmed the sails to catch every ounce of wind. He
ordered water, provisions, extra spars thrown overboard. Thus
lightened, the *Providence* gained a little speed and managed
to keep out of gunshot until nightfall. Fortunately, it was one
of those black nights on the sea, with no moon, no starlight
even; and Rathbun doused all lights, altered course slightly,
then swiftly stripped the *Providence* of every bit of canvas.
Under bare poles, the little sloop lay low in the water, swallowed up in utter darkness; and the British squadron went
tearing past on the course she had been following. When
they were far away, Rathbun hoisted sail and altered course
radically. Morning found the *Providence* alone upon the sea.

Rathbun now headed directly for the Bahamas. With favorable winds, the *Providence* made a swift passage. They needed
a temporary haven where preparations could be made for the
attack, and for this purpose Rathbun chose the island of
Abaco, which he had visited with Ezek Hopkins' squadron
early in the war. Abaco, then uninhabited, is on the northern
fringe of the archipelago, just forty miles from Nassau. Here
the *Providence* dropped anchor and Rathbun put his men to
work.

Water casks were filled. A scaling ladder was made. Then
Rathbun, with crafty design, set about altering the appearance
of the *Providence* so that, if she should be sighted on her
approach to Nassau, no one would suspect her of being a
warship. Her topmast and her topsail yard were sent down; her
gunports closed, the guns housed; her men hidden below
decks. When these alterations had been made, the *Providence*
looked like a dowdy island trading sloop, and relying on this
camouflage, Rathbun set out on the last stage of his incredibly
daring adventure.

The town of Nassau, now the famous Caribbean winter resort, lies on the northern shore of the island, its anchorage protected by the long arm of Hog Island lying directly off the coast. About midnight, ghosting along in a light breeze off the land, the *Providence* passed the entrance of Nassau harbor, circled Hog Island and stole in to the coast to put her landing party ashore. Rathbun had delegated to Trevett the task of surprising and storming the fort while he kept the *Providence* hovering near. Everything now hung in the balance; the whole wild scheme was about to be put to the test. Trevett wrote:

"I had picked out my lambs!—better I could not wish—all smart and active, except one lame; he said to me, 'I cannot run.' I said, 'You are the man I should choose.'

"We soon disembarked 15 men, as our barge would take no more at once, and then 12, beside myself: that made 28 all told. We [had] nothing with us to eat or drink, but filled our pockets with ball cartridges. We landed about a mile from the Fort, and got our scaling ladder and all things ready.

"I recollected that when I was at the taking of New Providence with Com. Hopkins, I left out one of the pickets of [the palisade] of the fort, and I thought this might prove fortunate if it had not been replaced. So I left my men and went myself to see, and I found it as I left it, still out. I went through, and near the embrasures, I heard talking in the fort, and instantly one of the sentinels came to the corner of the fort, and cried, All is well! and was answered from the other end of the fort, All is well! The ship that lay near the fort— her sentinel also cried, All is well!

"I lay still a few moments, as I supposed the sentinels were going their rounds. I then went back, and we came on with the scaling ladder, and lay down near the fort until the sentry should come round again, for I expected they gave the cry every half-hour, and so it was. We had been but a short time there before they came around and cried, "All is well!"

"I waited a few minutes and then placed the scaling ladder near one of the embrasures and went over, every man following me. I gave positive orders not to fire a pistol or make any noise, as I knew it would instantly alarm the town. I went on, and as I was turning round the corner of the barracks, I met one of the British sentinels full out. I seized him by the collar, and ordered him in the first barrack door; he was much frightened and exclaimed, 'For God's sake, what have I done!'

"One of our men, in despite of my orders, fired a pistol over my shoulders at the sentinel. I had hold of it, but it did no damage. I spoke a soft word, and went into the barracks and examined the prisoner and found there was only one more sentinel, and he at the other end of the Fort. I soon put him into another barrack-room and examined them apart; they both told me the same story, and said that Gov. Gambier had had sent into the fort every article necessary about three weeks before we made them this friendly visit. I asked them the reason of having only two sentinels in the fort in the time of war; they said if they had only time to fire one or two guns, that in less than 10 minutes they would have more than 500 fighting men in the fort."

This could hardly have been encouraging news for Trevett and his little band of twenty-seven men. They had seized the fort with almost ridiculous ease, but the question remained: Could they hold it? Trevett set to work to see that they did. He found that a number of the fort's eighteen-pounder cannon were fully loaded, lighted matches glowing beside them, needing only to be slapped against a touch hole for the reverberation to have awakened the town. In the magazine, he found three tons of powder, but a shortage of cartridges. He put his men to work making cartridges and tugging at the huge cannon, pulling them back from the sea wall and training them to cover the ships in the harbor and the streets of Nassau. All the time, he lulled town and ships into a false sense of security by having his men maintain the routine of the

British sentinels with the half-hourly cry, "All is well!" Each time the Americans uttered the cry, the watch on the *Mary*, lying directly under their guns, echoed it back: "All is well!"

Morning came, and with it revelation. Trevett had the flag with thirteen stars and stripes flying from the staff where, normally, the British ensign flew. While the sleepy town and the sailors on the imprisoned ships were still rubbing their eyes in disbelief, Trevett began playing a colossal game of bluff. He had two objectives: one, to get food for his men; two, to convince the residents of the town that he represented merely the advance guard of an invading force so powerful that it would be suicide to attempt to resist it.

In furtherance of both of these objectives, Trevett decided to contact an old acquaintance, James Gould, a former Rhode Islander from Newport, now a merchant living in Nassau. And so he sent a messenger carrying a white flag into the town to notify Gould he was wanted at the fort.

Gould came. Trevett had the scaling ladder lowered from one of the embrasures, and Gould climbed up into the fort. Accosting him at once, Trevett gave him no chance to observe the actual strength of the raiding party that had captured Fort Nassau. But Gould was curious. He wanted to know, quite naturally, where the American fleet was and how strong it was.

Trevett told him that Commodore Biddle was bringing a powerful squadron over to New Providence from the island of Abaco. Trevett explained that he had been sent ahead with an advance guard of thirty officers and two hundred men to seize the fort. Commodore Biddle had instructed him, he said, to assure the residents of Nassau that they would not be disturbed, that their private property would not be touched; the Americans wanted only the war supplies in the fort and the shipping in the harbor. If the residents did not resist, all would go well; but if they did, the guns of the fort would level the town. In the meantime, could Gould get together some food? He had, Trevett lied boldly, plenty of provisions for his two hundred men, but he desired a more tasty breakfast for his thirty officers. Gould promised to see what he could do, and soon after he left the fort, a bounteous supply of bread, butter, and coffee was delivered to the hungry Americans.

Having succeeded in this initial hoodwinking of the enemy, Trevett turned his attention to the next essential steps: the seizure of a smaller, little-used fort four miles away on the opposite side of the harbor, and the capturing of all the shipping in the bay.

Only bluff could serve, and Trevett bluffed boldly. He dispatched Lt. Michael Molton, accompanied by just two men, to demand the surrender of the other fort. Trevett had learned that only two sentinels were stationed there, and he instructed Molton to repeat the fairy tale about the invasion force of thirty officers and two hundred men. Molton did, and the two sentinels most agreeably yielded the fort to him.

While this was going on, Trevett turned his attention to the ships. There were five: the sixteen-gun *Mary* lying right under the guns of the fort, a brig loaded with indigo, a sloop and two American schooners that had been captured and sent in as prizes. Trevett had already found and released thirty American sailors, the crews of the schooners, who had been imprisoned in the dungeons of the fort. Now he acted to recapture their vessels and to seize the others lying in the roadstead.

He had learned that the *Mary*'s captain, Henry Johnson, was ill in the town, and so he sent a midshipman with an armed boat crew to demand the surrender of the ship from the first lieutenant. The lientenant seemed made of sterner stuff than anyone else in Nassau. He refused, at first, to let the midshipman and the armed Americans board. Trevett, leaping upon the battlements of the fort, cursed him out and threatened to blow his vessel out of the water if he didn't yield.

Behind Trevett, the American gunners waved lighted matches just above the touch holes of the eighteen-pounders scowling down at the *Mary*. The demonstration finally persuaded the obdurate lieutenant. Trevett's men boarded the *Mary* and sent forty-five men in her crew to the fort to occupy the dungeons the American sailors had just vacated.

The other ships were taken without difficulty, and Trevett, with his wafer-thin force, was now the complete master of Nassau and all the shipping in the harbor. The day was one of those beautiful, crystal-clear Caribbean days, with bright sunshine and virtually unlimited visibility. From the ramparts of the fort, Trevett and his men could look far out to sea, and about two P.M., they made out two sails heading for the harbor. The first, they recognized at once as the *Providence*. The second, according to the recently freed American prisoners, was the Jamaica privateer *Grayton*, sixteen guns, Captain Chambers—the very craft that had captured their schooners.

Rathbun in the *Providence* easily won the race for the harbor entrance and came gliding in over the bar a good two hours in advance of the *Grayton*. Trevett promptly informed him of the identity of the approaching privateer, and Rathbun decided to set a trap for her. He ordered the American colors lowered from the fort, hoping that the *Grayton* would come sailing in and anchor under its guns.

This bit of strategic deception was too much, however, for the previously docile residents of Nassau. All morning they had accepted every bit of propaganda Trevett had put out for their consumption, and they hadn't made the slightest hostile gesture. But the trap the Yankees were setting for one of their own ships was too much. Turmoil swept the town.

Men, women and children ran out along the heights overlooking the sea. The men waved their hats, the women their aprons, trying to warn the *Grayton* to stand off. The captain of the privateer, never imagining that what had happened could have happened, held on for the harbor entrance, and it was not until several men tumbled into a boat and rowed hard for the channel, waving their hats in go-away gestures, that the *Grayton* finally took alarm and went about. Trevett, in disgust, fired three of the fort's eighteen-pounders at her, and one of the shots smashed cleanly into her mainbeam, making the splinters fly. It didn't stop the *Grayton*, however. She went out around Hog Island, then circled back and came to anchor at the other end of the roadstead, out of range of the fort's guns.

Rathbun now moored the *Providence*, her guns covering the streets of the town, springs on her cables so that she could be swung quickly in any direction and could concentrate her fire wherever it might be needed. Swiftly he assessed his victory and the problems that it posed. Molton and the two men who had "captured" the secondary fort across the harbor abandoned it and rejoined Trevett after spiking all the guns and throwing the powder into the sea. All hands were then put to work loading the captured ships with the large quantity of war supplies that had been seized.

Rathbun's wild gamble had paid off. He had taken Nassau, but he and his little force still were in the most precarious of positions. The hovering *Grayton* alone should have been more than a match for the *Providence*, and in Nassau several hundred men might at any moment be flung against Trevett's twenty-eight, all that Rathbun could spare to hold the fort. Indeed, on the morning of the following day, it looked as if an attack were about to be made. "The town continued in great confusion, many of the inhabitants moving their valuable goods, and numbers of all colors under arms, around the Governor's house, and all the hills around alive with them, their arms glistening in the sun," Trevett wrote.

But Trevett and his skipper were equal to facing down the milling hundreds arrayed against them. The fort's eighteen-pounders were loaded with grape and langrage and trained on the town; the inhabitants were again reminded that theirs was the choice—to let the Americans depart peaceably or to attack and bring down upon themselves death and destruction. The bold bluff worked; the threat passed.

The next day, the third day that the Americans had held Nassau, it was not so easy. Captain Chambers began to land guns and men from the privateer *Grayton*, and the citizens of Nassau, strengthened by Chambers' fighters, suspicious now of Trevett's boasts about Biddle's non-appearing squadron, began to flex their muscles with greater determination. Gould, Trevett's former Rhode Island friend, came to him and said that he was moving his family from the town to Hog Island. Smiling, Trevett remarked that he hoped Gould wasn't afraid, and Gould replied: "No, I am not afraid, but I do not ever expect to see you again, for they have all the privateer's crew at the Governor's house, and are making every preparation to attack you tonight, for they have discovered your strength, and if I thought you had nothing but that damned bumboat [the *Providence*], I would fight against you myself."

Trevett informed Rathbun of the new threat, and the skipper of the *Providence* decided sterner measures were needed to cool the mounting martial ardor of Nassau. Jack Scranton, one of the *Providence*'s crew, was sent shinnying up the flagstaff of the fort; and there, in full sight of the town, he nailed the colors to the mast. They couldn't be pulled down then, under any circumstances. It was a gesture of defiance of that era and meant there would be no surrender. Then a stiff note was sent to the governor—an ultimatum that, if the massing troops in the hills didn't disperse in fifteen minutes, the guns of both the fort and the *Providence* would open up on the town in a cannonade without quarter. The threat worked. In less than twenty minutes, not an armed man was to be seen on the hillsides, and the night passed quietly.

Rathbun realized that the miracle he had worked in capturing Nassau was wearing thin. He determined to sail the next day, and throughout the night, he drove his men, trundling all the arms, powder and captured supplies from the fort and ferrying them out in barges to the *Providence* and the other ships in his little fleet. By morning, all was ready. The captured ships were sent out over the bar first, and the *Providence*, sails slatting in the wind, anchor apeak, lay for two hours under the walls of the fort, waiting for Trevett. That indomitable sailor spiked every gun, smashed all the rammers and sponges, destroyed every warlike implement the Americans had not been able to carry away; and then at last, his work done, rowed off with the last boatload of men to rejoin his captain.

The *Providence* flitted quickly out to sea, shepherding her prizes before her. Rathbun put Trevett in command of the stout ship *Mary* and set a course for home. The little *Providence*—"that damned bumboat," as Gould had called her—and her crew of fifty men had accomplished one of the most incredible feats of the war. They had seized Nassau and held it for three days; they had liberated thirty American prisoners and retaken their two captured schooners; they had come away with a sixteen-gun ship and a well-laden brig as prizes; they were taking home a large quantity of powder, arms and munitions; and they had achieved all this without the loss of a man—without a man receiving as much as a scratch!

More formidable than the defenses of Nassau were the rigors of the midwinter North Atlantic. The voyage home took eighteen days, and they were eighteen days filled with almost ceaseless gales, high seas, snow and bitter cold. Trevett wrote that, of his thirty men on the *Mary*, all but ten had their hands and feet badly frost-bitten and one, James Dark, was actually frozen to death. The *Mary* and the *Providence* became separated for a time, but off Nantucket they joined up again and sailed together into New Bedford.

The end of the cruise marked the end of the profitable collaboration of Trevett and Rathbun. The lieutenant transferred to another and more powerful vessel, was badly wounded in a sea battle and lost the sight of his right eye. Rathbun remained in the *Providence* for another year, then was promoted to the command of the twenty-eight-gun frigate *Queen of France*. Almost at once, he pulled off a coup.

On June 18, 1779, Rathbun in the *Queen of France* sailed from Boston in a squadron of warships headed by Commodore Abraham Whipple in the frigate *Providence* and including John Paul Jones' old sloop-of-war, the *Ranger*, now commanded by Capt. Thomas Simpson. The warships cruised to the north and east, looking for British prizes. For a time they had no success. Mid-July found them off the banks of Newfoundland, hove to, shrouded in a dense and impenetrable blanket of fog. Suddenly a signal gun boomed out.

Officers on the quarter-decks of the American ships searched the white-cotton mist. Lookouts at the mastheads strained their eyes. They could see nothing. Again the signal gun sounded, then another. The sound of a ship's bell came across the water. Clearly, the three American warships, smothered in one of the Grand Banks' densest fogs, were drifting into the middle of a large fleet—a British fleet that would certainly be guarded by huge British ships-of-war.

About eleven o'clock in the morning, the fog began to lift. The crew of the *Queen of France* gaped in amazement as a huge merchant ship loomed black and solid through the shredding mist. More rapidly, the fog bank rolled away, the horizon widened, and the Americans, staring about themselves and counting, found themselves in the middle of a fleet of one hundred and fifty sail. It was guarded by a seventy-four gun ship-of-the-line and by several frigates and sloops of war.

The American warships, of course, had no colors flying, and they had not, as yet, been discovered. The sailors of the Royal Navy had so many helpless merchantmen to shepherd that they hadn't had any time to notice that three strange vessels had been added to their flock. There was still time to escape.

Only John Peck Rathbun was not thinking of escape. Good fortune, it seemed to him, had dropped incredible riches right into his lap, and he was not the man to turn away from such bounty. His sharp eyes studied the British warships, riding quietly on the sea, and the sight inspired him to a gamble that deserves to rank with the gamble he had taken at Nassau.

Speaking a quiet order to his helmsman, he edged the *Queen of France* closer to the large, black merchantman that had materialized first out of the fog. He hailed her.

"What fleet is this?" he asked.

"British merchantmen from Jamaica, bound for London. Who are you?"

"His Majesty's ship *Arethusa*," Rathbun lied boldly. "From Halifax on a cruise. Have you seen any Yankee privateers?"

"Ay, ay, sir. Several have been driven out of the fleet."

"Come aboard the *Arethusa* then," Rathbun ordered. "I want to consult with you."

The ruse worked. Soon a boat put off from the side of the merchantman. It rounded the stern and bumped along the lee side of the *Queen of France*. A ladder was flung down, and a jolly British sea captain mounted it—and stepped over the bulwarks into the arms of waiting, armed men!

His boat crew was summoned to the deck, made prisoners, hustled quickly and quietly below. Rathbun, chuckling to himself, replaced them with a well-armed boat's crew of his own, and the boat shoved off, rowed back to the unsuspecting merchantman. The boat crew swarmed quickly up the side to the deck, and before the astonished British tars knew what was happening, their ship had been carried and they were prisoners—all without fuss, without noise, without the faintest alarm having been given!

It had been so ridiculously easy that Rathbun promptly

sailed on, repeated the same ruse again—and captured another fat, well-laden merchantman.

At this point, Commodore Whipple in the *Providence* bore down on the *Queen of France* and ordered Rathbun to follow him, edging out of the fleet to safety. Rathbun protested vigorously. He had just taken two rich ships, he told Whipple, and he didn't want to leave. He urged his commodore to join him in the good hunting. Whipple was a conventional sailor, which meant a timid one by Rathbun's standards, but he finally allowed himself to be persuaded. Working quietly, the three American warships stayed in the convoy until nightfall, and when they departed, they took with them eleven prizes.

Three of the vessels were later recaptured by the British before they could reach port, but the remaining eight—the *Holderness, Dawes, George, Friendship, Blenheim, Thetis, Fort William* and *Neptune*—were all brought into Boston safely. And there they and their cargoes were sold for the staggering sum of a million dollars—the richest single haul of the war.

Some idea of the windfall for the crews may be gathered from the fact that Andrew Sherburne, then just fourteen, a ship's boy on the *Ranger*, received for his prize share, as he later wrote, "one ton of sugar, from 30-40 gallons of fourth proof Jamaica rum, about 20 pounds of cotton, and about the same quantity of ginger, logwood, and alspice, about $700 in paper money, equal to $100 specie."

With the capture of Nassau and the raiding of the Jamaica convoy to his credit, with a stout frigate under his feet, John Peck Rathbun might normally have been expected to be little more than launched on his career in a war that still had four years to run. Instead, the curtain now fell abruptly, like a play that is cut off at the end of the second act.

In one of those blindly self-sacrificial acts that marked the mismanagement of the Continental Navy throughout the war, the Marine Committee now decided to commit almost every effective warship the Colonies still owned to the defense of Charleston. Whipple was ordered south, and Rathbun in the *Queen of France* went with him.

As it turned out, Maj. Gen. Benjamin Lincoln could not hold Charleston, and Whipple refused to give his fleet the only chance it might have had, refused to dispute the passage of the harbor channels with the British warships running past the defending forts from the sea. Bottled up, the entire fleet was lost when Charleston surrendered.

For the captured naval officers, even after they were paroled, there was no future, simply because the Navy had virtually no ships left. Rathbun returned to Boston, and there on August 4, 1781 he received a commission to command the twenty-gun brigantine *Wexford*, a privateer. What he accomplished in her, if anything, has not been recorded. He faded into complete obscurity.

But though Secretary of War Lewis Cass' list of Continental Navy officers and the ships with which they served did not even mention John Peck Rathbun, fortunately John Trevett did his old commander better justice. Before he died in 1823, a blind man of seventy-six, Rathbun's former lieutenant wrote out in his journal the full and graphic details of his service under the forgotten captain of the Continental Navy. Trevett's principal concern was Trevett, but in telling the adventures of the lieutenant, he helped to complete the picture of the lieutenant's skipper—the tall, lean and supremely daring New Englander who conceived and carried through one of the boldest raids in the Navy's long, bold history.

The efforts of the feeble Continental Navy were supplemented by practitioners of the lost wartime art of privateering. Today war is waged only by governments, but in the Revolutionary era the civilian volunteer, fighting for gain as well as from motives of patriotism, added another dimension to his nation's defense.

Lured by the prospect of rich prizes, wealthy merchants risked their money and seasoned skippers and sailors risked their lives. Vessels of all sizes and descriptions were purchased, armed with as many guns as they could carry, licensed by governmental authority and sent to sea with a prayer—the businesslike prayer that they could survive long enough on an ocean swarming with British cruisers to seize some fat British merchantmen and make a profit for their owners.

In this risky and novel warfare, the Revolution developed a class of raiders unique in American history. They were doubtless the smallest craft ever to masquerade as warships under the American flag. They were simply whaleboats.

The use of whaleboats as commerce raiders was made possible by the fact that the Revolution was to a large extent a coastal war. When the British seized New York, their huge army had to be supplied, and it could be supplied only from the sea. The same was true later in Virginia and the Carolinas. Wherever British arms seized a port, British ships and coastal traders followed. This traffic, so close to shore, was susceptible to surprise by swift-rowing whaleboats dashing out of the night.

The technique was practiced with the greatest energy and ferocity in the waters around New York, where the greatest mass of shipping clustered and where as a consequence the greatest riches lay. Throughout the Revolution, the western and southern shores of the harbor were in patriot hands, and they became the lairs of whaleboatmen raiding the shipping lanes close to their inlet hideaways. This combination of circumstances led to the emergence of two small-boat Vikings who dwarfed all others— William Marriner and Adam Hyler, in their day the heroes of the New Jersey coast.

CHAPTER VIII

★

★ ★ ★

★

Whaleboat Guerrillas

THE WATERS OF NEW YORK HARBOR were a battleground teeming with British shipping. Huge convoys under the escort of British ships-of-war plied back and forth across the ocean. Daily, swift rum- and salt- and sugar-laden schooners arrived from the West Indies. More than one hundred fifty small sloops and schooners carried the produce of Tory farms in New Jersey, Staten Island and Long Island to Manhattan, the source of the King's gold. On a single day, December 23, 1779, one great fleet of one hundred forty merchantmen, convoyed by Royal men-of-war, stood out homeward bound from Sandy Hook. "On this occasion," according to one account, "our waters are said to have presented a panorama never before equalled, as this immense fleet, on a fine day and before a following wind, passed out of the Hook and spread itself out over the open sea." When such fleets were in port, when the innumerable sloops and schooners and tenders and supply barges were crisscrossing the harbor, there were times when the sails of a thousand vessels seemed to shade the blue water of the bay with a moving canopy of white—there was rich booty for men valiant enough to seize it under the very guns of protecting British warships.

The antagonists were as unevenly matched as David and Goliath. The merchant ships that supplied the army isolated in New York were protected by some of the most powerful warships the world had ever seen—huge, three-decker ships-of-the-line with their tiers of heavy cannon; fast-sailing, heavily gunned frigates; smaller sloops of war; and, added to all these, a swarm of British and Tory privateers. Against this might, the Americans could pit only puny whaleboats.

These were sharply double-ended craft, broad-beamed, of shallow draft, some twenty-six to thirty feet in length. They carried crews of from fourteen to twenty-four men, and the largest boats mounted a small swivel gun at bow or stern, their only artillery. The swivel gun was in reality a large-sized musket, fixed on a swivel mounting that enabled it to be swung and aimed in all directions. It fired a ball weighing about a quarter of a pound at ranges far beyond a musket's carrying distance; but it was, at best, little more than a glorified small arm, not a cannon. To supplement the swivel gun, the heavy weapon in their arsenal, the whaleboatmen carried boarding pikes and muskets or duck guns; but their main reliance was on none of these. It was on their pistols and cutlasses—and the element of surprise. To be successful, they had to swarm swiftly over the decks of a surprised or sleeping foe; and once a prize was carried, the getaway had to be as swift as the attack. For the only safety for whaleboat raiders lay in flight across treacherous shoals and up winding and tricky channels where the heavier-armed, deeper-draft warships of the British could not follow.

Among the leaders in this guerrilla warfare at sea, William Marriner and Adam Hyler, both of New Brunswick, were the guiding geniuses of the New Jersey whaleboatmen. Marriner led the original forays across the harbor, beginning his operations shortly after the British seized New York in 1776; and when he was finally captured and inactivated by parole, Hyler took command and promptly proved himself an even more dynamic leader.

Marriner was a tall, large-framed man of great physical strength. Though no one would have guessed it when he roared across the bulwarks of an enemy vessel, cutlass in hand at the head of his men, he was by nature jovial; a big, relaxed man with a broad streak of humor in him. These were qualities that made him popular and successful in his normal vocation as a tavern-keeper and that, after the war, were to make him known even to Washington as a genial host.

Early in the Revolution, Marriner served as a private in the New Jersey regiment of Lord Stirling. He apparently saw some active service, but the details have not been preserved. In any event, fighting on the sea, not the land, was to be his forte. He left the army and established a tavern hard by the banks of the Raritan River on the outskirts of New Brunswick. His hostelry quickly became the rendezvous of whaleboatmen and an informal clearing-house for information brought in by patriot spies and informers concerning the movements of British warships and supply vessels in the harbor. From securing information to acting upon it was a short and inevitable step. It wasn't long before Marriner was planning and conducting raids across New York Bay with the hardy whaleboatmen who were his tavern customers.

One of his first and most daring forays was made on the night of June 11, 1777. The British command in New York had instituted a calculated campaign to round up and capture prominent leaders of the patriots in New Jersey. Tories who knew the identity of the patriot chiefs, and who were familiar as well with the roads and the countryside, engineered repeated raids, snatching patriots from their homes and confining them in the noisome holds of the British prison ships that had an-

chored off the shores of Brooklyn. The Americans had no
similarly important and influential prisoners to use as pawns in
an exchange. They determined to get some.

A raiding force to strike the Long Island shore, where many
prominent Tories had their country homes, was therefore organized under the command of Marriner and Capt. John
Schenck, a leader of local militia. Schenck knew the region
around Flatbush well as his family had relatives there whom he
had visited since boyhood. With Schenck and Marriner went
twenty-six picked men in two whaleboats. They set out from
Matawan Creek on the southwestern shore of Raritan Bay as
soon as night fell, and they hugged the dark shore line so that
their boats would blend in with the land and escape observation by British patrols on the bay.

The night was dark, with an overcast sky, a sharp east wind
blustering in from the open sea. An angry chop came surging
across the wide-open reaches of the lower bay, slapping at the
sides of the whaleboats and breaking in smothers of spray that
drenched their crews. North of the mouth of the Raritan
River, the boats sheered over to the Staten Island shore, hitting the coast just north of Princess Bay and creeping along
once more close to land. Here one of Schenck's militiamen
became seasick, and Marriner, fearful that the slightest sound
might alert the enemy, growled a low-voiced, menacing order:
"If that man lets out another yawp, heave him overboard."

Whether this threat scared the unfortunate soldier out of his
seasickness hasn't been recorded, but the sounds he made in his
misery weren't overhead. Undetected, Marriner and Schenck
slanted across the Narrows, the deep thread of a channel that
separates Staten Island on the west from Long Island on the
east and that connects the upper and lower reaches of New
York harbor. Grounding their boats on the Long Island shore
not far from the spot where the New Utrecht ferry road came
down to the bay, the whaleboatmen leaped ashore. They hid
the boats in a thicket, stationed a guard over them, and placed

three pickets on roads leading down to the beach to guard against surprise. Then they set off inland on their raid.

Marriner and Schenck had drawn up a list of prominent Tories whom they hoped to capture. Top priority was given to David Matthews, the Tory Mayor of New York. After him in order of importance came Miles Sherbrook, a personal foe of Marriner; the wealthy Jacob Suydam; Colonel Axtell; and Theophylact Bache, president of the New York Chamber of Commerce, whose brother, Richard, had married a daughter of Benjamin Franklin.

Marching their men into the shadows of a neighborhood church, Marriner and Schenck divided their little band into four raiding squads. Each was equipped with a heavy timber for use as a battering ram. Each squad would hit a selected home at the same time. If they were lucky, they would seize their prisoners quickly, return to the church, unite there and go back to their boats in a body.

The four groups of raiders disappeared into the night on their separate missions. At the outset, they encountered misfortune. The British in New York led a gay existence, with almost nightly parties, and sometimes, as on this particular night, this method of waging war had its advantages. Marriner's men quickly found that Mayor Matthews and Colonel Axtell were attending a night-long revel in the city and probably wouldn't get home before dawn. Unable to wait, the raiders swept on to the homes of other prospective prisoners. Here they had better luck.

In the Suydam home, they found Capt. Alexander Gradon, an American officer who had been captured in the fall of Fort Washington the previous November. He had been billeted with the Suydams, waiting for exchange, and Marriner's raiders promptly freed him and took him with them.

Then they began to have some success in their original objective, the taking of prisoners. Bache was found asleep in bed and dragged away, a captive. In the nearby home of George

Martense, Marriner tracked down Sherbrook, who was hiding in a garret behind a large Dutch chimney, his breeches in his hands. Not even giving him time to put them on, Marriner hauled his prisoner off to the rendezvous at the church. There, while they waited for the other squads to join them, Sherbrook managed to struggle into his pants before being led with Bache down to the waiting whaleboats.

So swiftly had the raid been conducted that there had been no alarm, no opposition. The boats were quickly launched and headed straight across the bay for home. The wind and choppy seas that they had bucked on the way to the raid were slanting from behind them now, the tide was favorable, and the little boats fairly flew across the wide reaches of the lower bay. It took them only an hour and a quarter, phenomenal time, to reach Keyport, and by 6 A.M., they were docking at Matawan.

While the Americans hadn't captured as many Tories as they had hoped to, the raid had been a daring and successful one—so successful that Marriner was lured into repeating it several times in the next few months. On one raid, he captured Lieutenant Forrest and Major Moncrieff, whose daughter, Marguerite, was to become the first love of Aaron Burr. On another, he landed again at New Utrecht, seized the noted Tories, Simon and Jacques Cortelyou, and made off with specie and property valued at five thousand dollars. All of the prisoners taken in these raids were brought back to New Jersey and subsequently exchanged for patriot leaders or officers of the Continental Army.

Marriner, as versatile as he was able, did not confine himself to these forays along the Long Island coast. When he was not raiding inland, he was leading his whaleboat crews against British shipping on the bay. On one occasion, when a fleet of small craft huddled in the cove behind Sandy Hook to seek protection from the weather, Marriner led a whaleboat fleet across the bay and captured three sloops and an armed schooner. An adverse wind and tide forced the sloops ashore, where Marriner stripped them of cargo and gear and set fire to them. While they burned, he made off in the schooner, which turned out to have a valuable cargo. His men received one thousand dollars each in prize money for one night's work.

Another cruise of Marriner's was even more striking—and rewarding. On the night of April 18, 1780 he dropped down the Raritan from New Brunswick in a single whaleboat. He had with him just nine men. They crossed the bay to Sandy Hook. Inside the tip of the hook, protecting the anchorage in the cove, lay a powerful British guardship, a three-decker named the *Volcano*. Nearby was a saucy little brig, the *Blacksnake*. She had been fitted out as a privateer by Rhode Islanders and mounted a sizable battery of eight-pounders, but she had been overtaken by the British frigate *Galatea* and sent in as a prize. She lay at anchor now, supposedly untouchable under the mighty broadsides of the *Volcano*. She drew and held Marriner's covetous eye.

Approaching through the night with the utmost stealth, the oars of his whaleboat muffled in the oarlocks, Marriner glided undetected under the stern of the *Blacksnake*. The brig was manned by a prize crew of twenty men under Capt. Cornelius French, but the disparity in numbers was more than offset by a difference in alertness. French and his crew were asleep; Marriner and his men definitely were not. They swarmed in a rush over the counter of the prize, seized and disarmed the lone and sleepy lookout, battened down the hatches, imprisoning the crew in the forecastle, and stationed a guard at the entrance of the after cabin. All had been accomplished in seconds, without resistance, without a sound.

Having captured the privateer, Marriner determined to bring her off. Quickly he cut her anchor cable, quietly shook out some sail. The *Blacksnake* began to move through the water, ghosting out of the anchorage. Nearby the powerful watchdog of the British fleet slept on; the volcano did not erupt.

Daylight found Marriner and his nine whaleboatmen well out to sea, almost out of sight of land, a stout little warship under their feet and the shipping lanes leading into New York wide-open for their hunting. Almost at once a plump pullet of the sea fell into their seeking hands. About six A.M., up from the south, scudded the schooner *Morning Star*, lightly armed with swivels and cohorns, but packed with a crew of thirty-three men commanded by Capt. Richard Campbell.

Marriner, bold as the captain of a seventy-four, brought the *Blacksnake* ranging alongside. With his nine followers manning the eight-pounders in the little brig's broadside, there was nobody left to work the sails, but Campbell and the crew of the *Morning Star* did not know that. The *Blacksnake* looked formidable to them, and they surrendered. Once the two ships had crunched together, however, and Marriner's men started to board, the British captain saw how few they were and called on his crew to fight. He and several of his followers were promptly cut down, and the rest, cowed by their fate, ratified the original surrender.

Marriner, who had started out the previous night with one whaleboat and nine men, now had a brig and schooner to handle and fifty prisoners to keep quiet in their holds. He knew that he had to get his prizes into port quickly before weariness overcame his men and the prisoners rose up and re-captured their vessels.

Running swiftly down the coast well away from the heavily patrolled waters around New York, Marriner ducked in through Cranberry Inlet (now no longer in existence) and brought his prizes into Toms River, where they were condemned and sold. This was his last major success as a privateersman. Shortly afterward, on another raid into Long Island, he was surprised, surrounded and captured. Paroled, he returned to tavern-keeping in New Brunswick. From there, on April 24, 1781, just a year after his capture of the *Black-snake* and the *Morning Star*, he wrote a letter to British officials. Rumor evidently had credited him with another raid in the bay, and Marriner wanted to set the record straight.

"In a New York paper it is said I was concerned in taking a sloop," he wrote. "Such a report is without foundation. I am on parole, which I shall give the strictest attention to. She was taken by Hyler and Dickie."

This is one of the first mentions of the man whose achievements with the whaleboat flotilla were to surpass even those of Marriner.

Adam Hyler was the son of Philip Hiler, who came to New Brunswick from Baden, Germany, about 1752. Adam was born in Germany, probably about 1735. He early learned the ways of the sea, and, according to one version of the story, was impressed for a time in the British Navy. When the Revolution broke out, he was a man of about forty and a citizen of some standing in New Brunswick. He operated his own small fleet of sloops and trading vessels between his home town and New York, and he lived in comfortable circumstances in a large, one-and-a-half story, log-and-frame house. His first wife, Christina Auble, had died, and on November 13, 1777, he married pretty, twenty-three-year-old Ann Nafey.

This is all that is known about the personal life of Adam Hyler before he burst with meteoric suddenness upon the Revolutionary scene, an unparalleled leader of small-boat men. He was, by all accounts, a shorter, chunkier man than Marriner, with powerful arms and torso. He had probably been active in the earlier years of the war in Marriner's whaleboat fleet, but nothing is known of these activities. His name did not begin to appear in the newspapers of the day until after Marriner's capture and enforced retirement, but then it quickly became a synonym for startling and ceaseless activity. Into one eleven-month span, beginning in October, 1781, Adam Hyler packed a lifetime of action.

A few desultory references to Hyler dot the record of the previous year. In November, 1780, he led the whaleboatmen in a successful foray along the Staten Island coast, snatching the sloop *Susannah* from her anchorage. In the spring of 1781, he and his raiding companion Captain Dickie evidently captured another sloop in the action for which Marriner had been incorrectly blamed. And on August 5, 1781, Hyler took a leaf out of Marriner's book by crossing to the Long Island shore in a prisoner-hunting raid. A correspondent in New Brunswick reported to the New Jersey *Gazette* in Trenton that Hyler had "marched three miles and a half into the country, and made Captain Jeromus Lott, a Lieutenant-Colonel of Militia, and one John Hankins, a Captain of a vessel, prisoners, and brought them safe to New Brunswick."

These actions were little more than tuneups for the main career of Adam Hyler. It began on a Friday night, October 5, 1781. Early in the afternoon, a patriot courier had brought word to Marriner's tavern in New Brunswick that a fat covey of potential prizes nestled inside the sheltering arm of Sandy Hook. Hyler hastily rounded up his whaleboat crews and set out, leading a tiny armada down the tortuous, shoal-cluttered Raritan. In the van was a little sloop that Hyler had christened the *Revenge;* trailing, were two whaleboats. The tiny flotilla reached South Amboy at the mouth of the Raritan, and there Hyler waited for night to fall. When an inky blackness at last shrouded shore and bay, he set out, heading east for the scene of action.

The *Revenge*, towing the whaleboats, ghosted silently toward Sandy Hook. Hyler knew that he was challenging the most astronomical odds that the whaleboatmen had ever faced. Out near the point of the hook, cannon rising in tiers up her black sides, lay the guardship, a powerful British ship-of-the-line. Five smaller vessels rocked gently on the waters of the cove, secure under the protecting flank of this behemoth. Three of the anchored craft were merchantmen, but the other two were armed and either one should have been more than a match for the *Revenge* and her whaleboats. The smaller, a sloop, mounted a three-pounder cannon and six swivels; the larger carried four six-pounders, two to a side. These guns afloat were supplemented by guns ashore, for a log redoubt, manned by Tories, squatted at the base of the Sandy Hook lighthouse, barely a half-mile from the scene of impending action.

Off the anchorage Adam Hyler brought the *Revenge* up into the light wind. Like a gull, the sloop drifted, black hull blending into black water. Softly Hyler called one of his whaleboat crews about him and instructed them to reconnoiter the anchored ships. The men departed on their mission, dropping overside into one of the trailing whaleboats as noiselessly as cats. The leather-wrapped oars moved noiselessly in their padded tholepins as the whaleboat faded off into the night, leaving not the slightest ripple of a wake. Impatiently, Hyler waited.

His men were gone a long time, but when the reconnoitering whaleboat stole back at last out of the opaque night, the word it brought was encouraging. The merchantmen looked deserted; apparently, most of their crews had gone ashore. There were men on the privateers, but their watch was lax. Hyler's whaleboatmen had nudged up almost under their counters without being detected; nobody had cried a challenge or an alarm. The whaleboatmen had not gone so close to the mighty guardship, but they reported that aboard her, too, nobody seemed to be stirring, everyone seemed drugged with sleep.

Listening to this report, Hyler decided to waste no more time but to swoop down on the anchorage at once. He assigned one whaleboat crew to board the three nearly deserted merchantmen. The second whaleboat would attack the smaller privateer. He and his men in the *Revenge* would attempt to take the stronger vessel.

The whaleboats stole off in the night. Hyler waited a few minutes to let them get in position; then he put the *Revenge's* helm over and sent her coasting down upon the anchorage. Closer and closer the little sloop groped through the night toward the indistinct shadow of her foe. The shadow grew in size, began to take shape as a ship, and the *Revenge*, hardly a ripple at her forefoot, narrowed the gap to yards, to feet, to inches. Gently she bumped against the counter of the Tory craft, and in that instant grapnels swung, biting into bulwarks, welding the two vessels fast. And in that instant, too, Hyler leaped for the enemy deck, his men pouring up and over the side behind him.

The pounding feet of the boarders woke the enemy at last. The sleeping deck watch screamed an alarm, then went down in the rush. In the forecastle, startled sailors grabbed cutlasses and pistols and tried to sally forth. Only the first few made it. Hyler and his men charged up beside the hatch, standing guard with their cutlasses and threatening to lop off the first head that showed itself. Not attracted to that fate, the rest of the crew huddled safely below.

Seeing this, the few who had gained the deck fled aft. A couple dived overboard; the others dropped into the longboat trailing by a painter off the stern and started to row frantically for shore. Resistance was over, the ship was carried—all in the space of seconds, without the loss of a man.

Elsewhere in the anchored fleet, Hyler's whaleboatmen had struck with equal swiftness and equal success. The smaller privateer had been carried, only a few of her crew escaping in the ship's yawl. The merchantmen had been virtually deserted. Aboard them, the whaleboatmen found only the sleeping watches and, in the cabin of one, a mother with four children clutching at her nightclothes.

The entire fleet of five ships had been captured with breathtaking rapidity, but the real danger lay ahead. The Tories who had fled ashore in the boats would give the alarm, the log redoubt would come to life, the huge cannon aboard the massive guardship would begin to thunder. Hyler and his men would have to work fast.

They did. Cargo from the captured vessels was trundled across the deck and dumped into the *Revenge* and the whaleboats. Guns, sails and cordage were swiftly plundered. As the whaleboatmen worked furiously, guns ashore began to speak. The first of the refugees had reached the log fort, and the garrison there started to blaze away with twelve swivel guns. The range was too great, the night too dark for the shots from the little popguns to find their mark and do any damage. But the noise they made was dangerous in itself. The whole anchorage was coming to life. Out near the point that slumbering watchdog, the Royal man-of-war, was at last arousing himself. Lights flashed from the portholes; shouted commands rang across the water. Adam Hyler, surveying the turmoil he had caused, knew that it was time to leave.

Sparing the one ship on which the woman and her four children huddled, he fired the others, shook out every rag of sail the *Revenge* could carry, and towing his whaleboats behind him flitted toward the safety of the bay's enveloping darkness. Behind him the pyres of burning vessels lit the sky; behind him, finally, the huge cannon of the guardship roared out. The waters of the bay spouted, frothed with the plunging, ricocheting roundshot; but the little *Revenge* was moving fast, she faded away like a ghost ship in the night.

Hyler's return to New Bunswick in the bright of day was triumphal. The New Jersey *Gazette*'s correspondent reported gleefully that his small ships had come back laden with prisoners, with sails and cordage stripped from the captured vessels and with other booty that included "250 bushels of wheat, a quantity of cheese, several swivels, a number of fuzes, one cask of powder and some dry goods."

The raid was a thundering prelude to a career that swept through the next few months at a furious tempo. Just eight days later, Hyler with the *Revenge* and his two whaleboats was back again, nosing around his special happy hunting ground—the cove behind Sandy Hook. One would have thought that the British, stung once, would have been alert the second time, but Hyler evidently had complete confidence in the British Navy's sublime belief in its own invincibility. He obviously reasoned that they would dismiss his first raid as a fluke, that they'd never imagine a whaleboat privateersman would be audacious or foolhardly enough to strike again in the same spot. Yet there were two schooners and a sloop, anchored just off the lighthouse fort, practically begging to be taken.

The tactics of Hyler's descent upon the anchorage were a carbon copy of the tactics he had employed the first time. There was just one difference. The second time around, it was even easier. Only two watchmen had been left behind on the three ships; all the rest of the crews were ashore. And even the watchmen were asleep. They were surprised, made prisoners before they had a chance to squawk even one startled cry into the night. Hyler, looking about him, realized that he had taken three ships so swiftly and silently that no one even knew it had happened. He determined to try to bring out the ships themselves, this time.

With his men in the *Revenge,* he had carried the larger of the schooners. He assigned a whaleboat crew to each of the other vessels. Swiftly sails were spread, the anchors catted, and the little fleet stood out silently, leaving fort and guardship in blissful and unsuspecting sleep.

Affairs had proceeded so far without the slightest hitch, but now Hyler began to run into trouble. The captured sloop proved such a dull sailor that she held back the whole flotilla, yet it was imperative for Hyler to cross the bay and escape behind the protecting shoals of the Raritan before dawn. The British, as an antidote to the whaleboat raids, had armed several fast-rowing galleys with one heavy cannon apiece. One shot from the long eighteen- or twenty-four-pounder cannon these galleys mounted would demolish any craft in Hyler's fleet, and the galleys usually maintained a close patrol about the mouth of the Raritan, the whaleboatmen's favorite lair. Hyler had no wish to encounter such formidable antagonists in the daylight, while he was encumbered with prizes; and so, three miles out in the bay, he halted his little fleet and set fire to the sluggish sloop that was holding up his progress.

Flames from the burning vessel lit up the night and belatedly woke the British to the realization that some of their ships were missing. Hyler, of course, knew that the blazing sloop would stir up British patrols in the bay, but he estimated he had such a head start that he could be safely up the Raritan before they could catch him. Everything would probably have worked out just that way, too, except that the tide was falling and off Point Comfort, at the mouth of the Raritan, the smaller of the captured schooners ran hard and fast aground on a sand bar. There was no time to try to refloat her, for one of the British galleys from Staten Island, alert at last to what was happening, came rushing up out of the night like an angry terrier, barking with her heavy twenty-four-pound thunderbird as she came.

Swiftly, Hyler's men stripped the stranded schooner of stores, sails and cordage, then set fire to her. Shepherding his whaleboats and his one remaining prize, Hyler went on up the Raritan while behind him sailors from the British galley put out the flames aboard the stranded schooner. When high tide came again, the craft was refloated and towed back to the Hook. As for Hyler, he reached New Brunswick with his prize, described as "a remarkably fine, fast-sailing Virginia-built pilot boat, mounted with one four-pounder."

With two successful raids in eight days to his credit, one might have thought that Hyler would have been content to give both his own boat crews and the British a rest. But he wasn't. With hardly a pause, he went right back into action again. The *Gazette* correspondent in New Brunswick told of it in a dispatch dated October 29, 1781.

"On the 24th inst.," he wrote, "Capt. Hyler, of this place, went down with one gun-boat to surprise the Refugee-Town near Sandy-Hook, where the horse thieves resort. He landed within three-quarters of a mile of the light-house, but found that they were out in the country of Monmouth stealing horses. The Captain, however, fell in with six other noted villains, whom he brought off, and they are now lodged in a safe place."

This skirmish failed to sate Hyler's restless urge for action, ever more action. Early in November, leaving his whaleboats behind and packing all his men aboard the *Revenge*, he slipped out of the Raritan, veered to the north and coasted along the Staten Island shore until he came to the Narrows. Audaciously poking the *Revenge*'s nose inside the channel, he discovered a good-sized cargo ship, the *Father's Desire*, lying in the anchorage close to the Staten Island shore.

Drifting down upon her in the night, Hyler laid the *Revenge* aboard, and his raiders swept across the bulwarks before the startled British crew of fifteen knew what was happening. The watch was overpowered and the crew imprisoned below before the alarm could be given. Investigating, Hyler found that the *Father's Desire* had a most desirable cargo of pork and Jamaica rum, and decided to bring her back to New Brunswick.

Sail was made and the *Revenge* and the *Father's Desire* stood back through the Narrows, then cut across toward the New Jersey shore. Again, the trouble was that the tide was falling, and in trying to cross the shoals between the Staten Island ship channel and the Raritan River channel, the *Father's Desire* ran aground off Ward's Point. Hyler had no choice but to strip and burn her. He loaded the *Revenge* with all she could carry, some thirty barrels of pork and twenty hogsheads of rum; took aboard his fifteen prisoners and a captured Negro slave named Will; and sailed on up the Raritan, leaving the *Father's Desire* to burn to the waterline behind him.

This was Hyler's last action of the year. For the rest of November and all of December, his whaleboat crews apparently remained inactive, but about the first of the new year, a report reached New Brunswick that sent him off on a new venture. Patriot spies had learned that a heavily laden cargo ship was anchored just inside the Narrows. Hyler decided to try to cut out the rich prize and hastily assembled the largest flotilla he had yet commanded, seven whaleboats manned by well over one hundred men. Leading this squadron in the *Revenge*, he sailed from the Raritan and made for the Staten Island shore. On the way he encountered two Tory sloops, returning from a trading voyage to New York. Hyler and his whaleboatmen promptly gave chase, overhauled the sloops and captured them. The prizes were remunerative ones. Both vessels were loaded with dry goods, and the whaleboatmen found some fifteen hundred dollars in cash aboard them. And among the prisoners was one John "Shore" Stevenson, a notorious Tory.

So much time had been consumed in chasing and capturing the Tory sloops that Hyler decided to abandon his projected attack on the rich cargo ship in the Narrows. Instead, he returned to New Brunswick with his prizes, his booty, and his prisoners.

Hyler by this time had become a much-wanted man. His incessant raids were an ever-increasing irritant to the British high command, and with his capture of Stevenson, influential Tories began to demand counter action to wipe out the whaleboat nests along the New Jersey coast. British strategists listened to the outcry and decided to strike directly at Hyler's home base of New Brunswick. An attacking force consisting of several hundred veteran British and Tory troops was assembled and ferried across the bay in whaleboats and barges. Shortly after midnight on the morning of January 7, 1782, the assault force was spotted about two miles from New Brunswick, ascending the Raritan. The alarm was sounded.

Only a small number of militia was available to oppose the

invaders. Townsfolk, thrown into panic, fled. A few volunteers came forward, and these and the militia tried to prevent the landing. But a driving rain and sleet had dampened many firelocks, and the British and Tories came charging ashore with a loss of only two men killed. The amateur American soldiers, at the sight of the rows of oncoming bayonets, decamped, and the British quickly took possession of the town. They burned the whaleboat fleet, and then, their mission accomplished, retired down the river.

The British had, however, failed to find and capture Hyler. Just where he was at the time of the raid isn't clear, but there are some indications that he was away cruising in the *Revenge*, for the little sloop seems to have been the only one of his vessels to escape destruction. In any event, after the British had gone, Hyler set about building new craft. There was no time to construct another fleet of whaleboats, but Hyler did succeed in building one large barge and one huge, thirty-oared whaleboat. With these and the *Revenge*, by the time spring came, he was ready for action. It was good that he was.

The British had continued their sweep down the Jersey coast, landing in raid after raid and burning and destroying whaleboats and shipyards. In the course of this punitive expedition, they had committed one final atrocity. In early March, they stormed the blockhouse at Toms River and captured Capt. Joshua Huddy, one of the boldest patriot leaders in Monmouth. Huddy, taken in battle, deserved to be treated with all the honors of war, but he was turned over to a Tory leader, Richard Lippencott, who transported him to Sandy Hook and hanged him out of hand.

The wanton execution became a *cause célèbre*. Washington was so angered that he ordered lots drawn for a British officer to die in retaliation. This brought a storm of protest from the British camp, and while diplomats and generals hashed over the issue, Hyler decided to act. He determined to invade New

York and attempt to capture Lippencott, the murderer of Huddy.

So daring a scheme required elaborate preparation. Hyler contacted patriot agents on Staten Island, which had been securely held by the British and Tories ever since the invasion of New York in 1776, and asked them to steal for him the uniforms and accoutrements of a Royal Navy press gang. He knew, of course, that he and all his men would be hanged as spies if they were caught in enemy uniform, but he knew, too, that it was the only way he could hope to land boldly in New York and march up to the front door of the home of Richard Lippencott.

Hyler's Staten Island agents managed to pilfer the equipment he needed and even managed to steal a longboat belonging to one of the anchored British warships. Informed that all was ready, Hyler took a picked handful of men and rowed across to the Staten Island shore on a night in early April. There Hyler donned the uniform, cocked hat and greatcoat of a British lieutenant; his men attired themselves as Royal Navy sailors. Then, with the bogus British tars at the oars, Hyler launched the stolen longboat, took the tiller and, sitting arrogantly erect in the stern, steered his way up the harbor through the thick of the British fleet.

Even after nightfall, British boats were constantly plying these waters on many different missions and, just as Hyler had expected, nobody paid any attention to one press gang more or less. Unchallenged, he and his men completed their long row up the harbor, turned their longboat into the East River and swung boldly in to shore just to the east of the South Ferry landing stages.

Detailing one of the men to remain on guard with the boat, Hyler led his squad in a tramping march up Broad Street. On land as in the harbor, the Americans in Royal Navy garb attracted no particular attention. British press gangs were always roving the streets, shanghaiing tipplers from the grog shops to help satisfy the voracious demands of the fleet for manpower. The outcries of impressed victims were a commonplace, so routine that they were usually ignored by passersby, and it was on this that Hyler counted heavily in the event of Lippencott's calling for help.

It was not yet eleven o'clock when he reached the Lippencott mansion, mounted the steps and hammered authoritatively on the door. He waited, clutching a pistol concealed beneath the folds of his greatcoat.

A Negro servant opened the door, and in a few brief words dealt the death knell to Hyler's audacious enterprise. Lippencott wasn't home. He probably wouldn't be home until morning. The British officers were all attending a big party somewhere in town, didn't the lieutenant know?

The lieutenant obviously didn't. He excused himself as best he could, telling the Negro he would see his master later. Then he turned and went back down the steps, back to his waiting "press gang" in Broad Street. In a few whispered words, Hyler acquainted his men of the mischance that had ruined all their hopes; then, putting a haughty British lieutenant's face on the matter, he stepped out briskly at their head, retracing the route they had just come, returning to the longboat waiting at the water's edge near the ferry stages.

They climbed aboard and pushed off, heading out into the stream. And there in front of them, anchored in the fairway, was a rum-laden sloop just in from the West Indies. Hyler studied her, and his eyes narrowed.

"Boys," he whispered, gesturing, "we might's well have something to show for our night's trouble. Let's take her."

The boat crew bent to the oars, and in a trice the longboat slid alongside the sloop, whose master was astonished to see a British lieutenant and his press gang come swarming up the side at that time of night. He was more astonished in the next few minutes, however, by what this strange-acting British lieutenant did. Why, the man simply ordered the cable cut, the sails hoisted and headed out the East River, making off with the whole sloop!

Before the stunned British master or any of his sailors could make an outcry or protest, sharp cutlasses gleamed at their throats, and the bogus Royal Navy tars revealed themselves for the Americans they were.

The wind was favoring from the northeast, but Hyler figured the risk was too great to attempt to run the gauntlet of the entire British fleet in the bay and slip through the heavily guarded Narrows. Therefore, he pointed the sloop's prow farther to the west and ducked into the Kill Van Kull, a narrow thoroughfare that separates the western edge of Staten Island from the New Jersey shore. At Elizabethport, he ran the sloop aground. Wagons were procured, the casks of rum broken out, the sloop stripped. The loot was then hustled away inland, and the sloop, gutted to a shell, was set afire and burned to the water's edge.

The bold attempt to kidnap Lippencott signified that Hyler was again on the warpath; and in the weeks that followed, in a swift succession of actions, each capping the achievements of its predecessor, he left no doubt of it.

The first blow was delivered on a Friday night late in April when Hyler took the *Revenge* and his newly built barge into the Narrows. There he surprised and captured a formidable privateer, a British cutter mounting six eighteen-pounders and ten nine-pounders. Wind and tide being unfavorable, he burned the prize at her moorings. Immediately afterwards, he seized a trading sloop, ransomed it back to its owner for four hundred dollars and returned to New Brunswick laden with booty and prisoners.

Next, in his large new barge, with twenty-five men, he stole back to the Sandy Hook anchorage where he had made things so hot for the British the previous fall. A heavily armed cutter lay at anchor, almost under the guns of the guardship. Fortunately, a thick fog blanketed the bay. Creeping through it, Hyler nudged his barge alongside the cutter, led his men in a pounding charge across the deck and quickly overpowered the sleepy crew. He herded forty prisoners into his barge and the cutter's small boats. Then, keeping the fastest of the cutter's boats under the counter, he sent his barge and the other boats away into the night. Quickly he laid a powder train to the cutter's magazine, touched a fuse to it and scrambled over the side. As his waiting men rowed him away into the fog-shrouded night, the cutter blew skyward behind him, showering the bay and the nearby ship-of-the-line with flaming debris.

Just a few days later, near the end of this busy month of April, Hyler took the *Revenge* out to sea on a cruise, and in the Atlantic, barely out of sight of the Sandy Hook lighthouse, he came up on the fast cargo sloop *Alert*, bound from New York to Bermuda with a valuable lading of clothes, shoes, medicine, tea and tools. He snatched the prize and convoyed her into Toms River to be sold.

Riding the crest of success, Hyler now suffered one of those strokes of misfortune that sometimes, by perverse irony, shadow triumph. The sketchy accounts of the day do not make clear exactly what happened, or how it happened. But Hyler was wounded, the ball from a pistol passing through the flesh of his leg near the knee. The wound was an accidental one—received, one account says, as Hyler picked up a pistol to clean it—and the ball apparently splintered no bones. As the events were to show, Hyler was far from incapacitated. But even trifling wounds, in those days of primitive medicine, could often breed tragic results.

At the time the bullet-bite didn't even seem to slow Hyler down. Continuing his cruise down the Jersey coast in the *Revenge*, he encountered the schooner *Speedwell* off Egg Harbor in early May. The *Speedwell*, a taut little craft of twenty-two tons, had belonged to the American firm of Moore & Stratton, but had been captured off the Virginia

Capes by the British privateer *Sukey*. She was on her way to New York, with a British prize crew aboard. Hyler promptly recaptured her and sent her into Toms River to be sold.

With the seizure of the *Speedwell*, Hyler's luck seemed to run out. He spent some time off the South Jersey coast without a rag of sail showing over the horizon. Provisions started to run low, and he headed the *Revenge* for home. Off Long Branch, he captured another schooner and took her with him through a no-longer-existing inlet called the Gut, which then linked the Shrewsbury River directly with the ocean. Hyler's presence in the Shrewsbury soon became known to Tory spies and, through them, to the British command in Sandy Hook. An expedition was promptly organized to capture the daring privateersman who had tweaked the nose of the Royal Navy with such impunity.

Captain Johann Schaak, of the Fifty-seventh Regiment, was the man selected to snare Hyler. Schaak took a large whaleboat with a swivel mounted in its bow, and with twenty-five regulars rowed down the coast to cut off Hyler's retreat through the Gut. Other forces were to be assembled as quickly as possible and sent down both the bay and ocean sides of the Hook, completing an armed noose from which there would be no escape. But Hyler did not wait for the noose to be drawn.

Learning from his own informants that Schaak had arrived and taken up a post at the Gut, he determined to surprise the enemy while they were still under the delusion that they were surprising him. He loaded a dozen of his best men into a boat, dropped down the river in the dark and crossed over to Sandy Hook Island (as it was then), landing in Schaak's rear. Advancing stealthily, Hyler crept up on Schaak unobserved and placed his dozen men in ambush about the unsuspecting British camp. As dawn broke, the *Revenge* dropped down the river, stood in close to shore and sprayed the waterside with a deadly hail from her muskets and swivels. While Schaak and his men were preoccupied with this threat from the water, Hyler leaped to his feet in the underbrush behind him and shouted: "Give them a volley, boys, and charge!"

The bushes exploded with musket fire. The heavy balls, fired at close range, tore into the milling figures of the startled regulars. Then the whaleboatmen grabbed their cutlasses and charged the British soldiers with the same impetuosity they used in storming across the decks of unsuspecting merchantmen.

The British, blasted from the inlet by the *Revenge*'s swivels, attacked from the rear by the cutlass-wielding whaleboatmen, threw down their arms and fled. The rout was swift, complete. Hyler, left in possession of the field, captured Captain Schaak and eight of his soldiers. Four others lay dead. The remaining thirteen, some of them badly wounded, escaped into the dunes and underbrush.

Hyler's victory had insured his escape to sea through the Gut, and he wasted no time. He put his prisoners aboard the *Revenge*, gathered up fifteen stands of arms that the British regulars had left behind them in their flight, and took in tow the swivel-armed whaleboat in which Schaak had come to capture him. Then he stood out to sea, waited for the cover of night and, in the dark, slipped back past the Hook and across the bay to New Brunswick. There the *Gazette*'s correspondent chronicled his latest victory, describing with obvious relish the discomfiture and defeat of British regulars and adding pridefully: "Captain Hyler, previous to this encounter, accidentally met with a hurt, otherwise, it is probable he would not have let a man escape."

The "accidental hurt" may have slowed down Hyler, but it certainly didn't drydock him. On the last day of June, he joined forces with another whaleboat raider, Captain Storer of Woodbridge, and set out on another foray. In the *Revenge*, trailing two whaleboats, he crossed the harbor to Gravesend Bay on the Long Island shore. There he captured two Tory

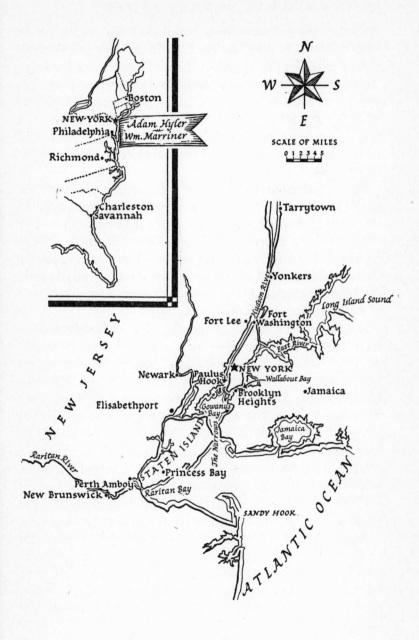

N

W   S

E

SCALE OF MILES
0 1 2 3 4 5

Boston

NEW-YORK

Philadelphia

Richmond

Adam Hyler
Wm. Marriner

Charleston
Savannah

Tarrytown

Yonkers

Hudson River

Long Island Sound

Fort Lee   Fort
Washington

East River

N E W   J E R S E Y

Newark   Paulus
Hook   ★ NEW YORK
Wallabout Bay

Brooklyn
Heights

Jamaica

Elisabethport   Gowanus
Bay

Jamaica
Bay

STATEN ISLAND   Princess Bay

The Narrows

Raritan River

Perth Amboy

New Brunswick   Raritan Bay

SANDY HOOK

ATLANTIC OCEAN

trading sloops and put prize crews aboard. Slipping out to sea past the Hook, he sailed down the coast and brought his prizes through the Gut into the Shrewsbury. He anchored just inside the inlet and sent his two whaleboats up the river. They captured two more Tory sloops, laden with sheep. When the whaleboats returned, Hyler detached one of them to escort his four prizes down the coast to Toms River. Then, with the rest of his men, he prepared for a new and more ambitious undertaking.

Word had come to him that a fast-sailing privateer, the schooner *Skip Jack*, mounting six large carriage guns and several swivels, was lying at anchor inside the Hook, about two miles from the guardship. She was lightly manned, waiting to take on her full complement before setting out on a cruise. If she could be attacked before her crew was at full strength, she might be carried. Hyler, assessing the chances, determined to make the attempt—at once, in daylight!

For so daring a project, camouflage was obviously needed. Hyler, a man never at a loss for a stratagem, decided to disguise the *Revenge* as a coastal trader. Sending his men ashore, he put them to work cutting lengths of cordwood. These he stacked on the *Revenge*'s deck. His crew was to hide among the piles of wood. The remaining whaleboat was lashed tight against the *Revenge*'s starboard side, where the little sloop's hull would hide it from suspicious eyes as she went up the coast, and Hyler stood out to sea at ten A.M. July 2, 1782, headed toward the tip of the Hook.

Rounding the point in full sight of the ship-of-the-line, still keeping his whaleboat hidden on the *Revenge*'s off-side, Hyler brought his little sloop about and lazed down toward the anchorage in the cove. Aimlessly, blunderingly, he drifted in toward the *Skip Jack*. No clumsy trading sloop could have been handled more ineptly. The crew on the *Skip Jack* suspected nothing until finally, close aboard, Hyler swung into action.

At his shouted order, the cordwood stacked on the *Revenge*'s deck suddenly crawled with men. A full crew tumbled overside into the whaleboat, slashed it loose and pulled for the *Skip Jack*. The *Revenge* in the same instant, waltzing on her heel, swung sharply under the stern of the *Skip Jack*, laying her aboard.

It happened so fast that the twelve men on the privateer hardly had time to cry the alarm. Boarders from the whaleboat swarmed up the side; Hyler led another rush across the stern. In one swift moment of action, the *Skip Jack*'s crew were prisoners, their ship taken.

But Hyler knew that he had not a second to waste exulting over his victory. There was no time even to loot. The attack had been made in full sight of overwhelmingly superior enemy forces afloat and ashore, and already the decks of the Sandy Hook guardship were stirring with men, milling like a swarm of bees in a ruptured hive.

Hustling his prisoners aboard the *Revenge*, Hyler fired the *Skip Jack* in half a dozen places. Then he cast off and spread the *Revenge*'s white wings in flight, as flames leaped from deck to rigging aboard the blazing privateer.

Behind him as he fled there sounded a familiar diapason. The guns in the log fort ashore barked angrily, the mighty batteries of the guardship thundered in deep-throated and futile menace—just as they had so many times in the past. Flames wreathed the doomed *Skip Jack*, lapped at her carriage guns, exploded them one by one. Then a spark reached the *Skip Jack*'s magazine, and the world seemed to erupt in one awesome explosion. Flaming rigging and long black spars and huge sections of deck and bulwark were flung skyward, hung suspended for an infinitesimal second, then came raining down in a shower of debris about fort and guardship. It was an awesome and blazing climax—and fittingly so. For this was the last great raid of Adam Hyler.

A couple of lesser expeditions later in July marked the finish of his career. On July 11th, he captured a couple of fishing boats near the Narrows. And on July 21st, he and Captain Dickie in three twenty-four-oared whaleboats attacked one of the heavily gunned Royal Navy galleys off Princess Bay on the Staten Island coast. The galley put an eighteen-pound shot through the stern of one of Hyler's boats, shattering the craft. The crew escaped to the Staten Island shore, and Hyler landed, fought a sharp action with British troops, and brought his men off. With his two remaining boats, he escaped into the Raritan, but off South Amboy another British galley spotted him and put a twenty-four-pound shot through Hyler's boat, sinking it. Transferring all of his men to the one remaining boat, Hyler limped home to New Brunswick, bringing with him as a prisoner Gen. Jacob Jackson, whom he had captured at South Bay before the fireworks with the galleys began.

Hyler now was seriously ill. Medicine was then far from an exact science, and the accounts of the day are confused as to the nature of his ailment. One says he suffered a "tedious and painful illness" from the leg wound he had accidentally inflicted upon himself in April. It would seem that such a wound either would have healed or incapacitated him before three months had passed, and so a second version gained currency at the time and seems even today to possess some validity. According to this account, a Tory tavern wench in South Amboy slipped poison into the drink of the doughty whaleboat captain, and while the poison didn't kill him instantly, its effects were such that he never recovered from it. He died at his home in New Brunswick on September 6, 1782 and was buried in the old Dutch burial ground. Ten days later, his wife, Ann, bore him a son—a boy named Adam, who was to grow up to become a skipper and to sail his own ships across the waters of New York harbor on which his father had fought.

All Revolutionary sailors ran risks. But the risks of whaleboat privateersmen who plied their trade close to shore, with the safety of tricky inland channels a relatively short distance away, were more limited than those of the skippers who took full-sized ships to sea and prowled the ocean lanes that for years had been the almost exclusive preserve of the Royal Navy.

Many a privateering cruise ended almost before it started—in the hold of a British prison ship. Many privateers were successful for a time; but for most there came a day when they could not run, when they were trapped under the guns of a British warship and had no choice except to fight or to surrender. Faced with this alternative, a good number meekly surrendered.

The explanation is not hard to find. The main job of the privateer was to take prizes; it was not her purpose, if she could avoid it, to fight a pitched battle. The spirit of the profession was to raid and run, and this did not develop the tradition of battle, the esprit de corps *of fighting men. The result, of course, was often that meek surrender mentioned above: some privateersmen simply refused to fight, abandoning their guns and fleeing into the sanctuary of the hold. On the other hand—and to their credit*

—this was by no means invariably the case. Many ships fought with a determination and skill that would have done credit to the best navies in the world.

Why the difference? The answer is usually to be found, not in the crews, but in just one man: the captain.

A ship is never any better than her captain, but in regular navies a ship can be pretty good without a captain of exceptional ability to make her so. Discipline and drill insure a certain proficiency. In the privateers, this simply was not so. Privateersmen became awesome fighters of the sea only when they were led by captains of high skill, gifted with the ability to inspire blind faith.

The Revolution took place in the age of the heroic example. The man who got men to follow him was the man who went into the thick of bullets with a brazen disregard for death, who faced the sharpest fire with a calm they-can't-kill-me attitude. On land and on sea, this was the tradition of leadership, and nowhere did the tradition count for so much as on the exposed deck of a privateer where one erect and dauntless figure quite literally could knit an entire crew together.

The sea history of the Revolution is studded with the names of many successful privateersmen, but of them all, a special palm must go to Jonathan Haraden of Salem. He was a man with ice water in his veins; a man who, like Lord Nelson in later years, deliberately donned his gaudiest waistcoat when going into battle, as if defying enemy sharpshooters to kill him. His composure became the rock on which his fighting crews founded their confidence, and throughout the long course of the Revolution, the composure never faltered, the rock never cracked. The result was that Jonathan Haraden, who is now thoroughly forgotten, became one of those rarities in any war—a captain who led only to success.

CHAPTER IX

★

★ ★ ★

★

Jonathan Haraden

THE TWO SHIPS LAY BROADSIDE to broadside, only their topsails visible above the billowing pall of powder smoke—a grayish-white shroud that smothered the hulls under the disembodied tops; a shroud rent periodically by angry, stabbing flashes of red as the carriage guns roared. Barely a pistol shot apart, the two ships drifted slowly across the Atlantic swells, while their powder-blackened, half-naked crews, worked feverishly on the great guns whose efficient service would decide their lives and destinies.

For four glasses—four hours in modern terminology—the American privateer and the Royal mail packet of his Britannic Majesty George III had turned this sector of the ocean into their own private bit of hell. For four glasses, they had slugged each other with heavy round shot propelled from the belching throats of their cannon; they had peppered each other with deadly pellets from the muskets of sharpshooters in their tops; they had brandished pikes and cutlasses when the vessels surged so close that hands could almost touch above the bulwarks.

And still there was no end. Still the deadly struggle went on and on, a test of endurance in which, it seemed, there could be no victor, only mutual annihilation.

As the battle mounted to its crisis, a tall and lanky man paced the quarter-deck of the American privateer, as serene amidst the deadly hail as a pastor in his pulpit. He had light-colored, close-cropped hair, keen blue eyes on either side of a beaked, hawk's nose. When he gave an order, it was always with an air of quiet mastery, and when he paused in his pacing, he stood erect, an inviting target in a vivid scarlet, gold-braided waistcoat by the taffrail nearest the enemy.

The deadly danger that he seemed to court, he disdained with the monumental calm of a man convinced of his own invulnerability. Jonathan Haraden had been engaged in literally hundreds of sea battles; he was known as one of the greatest sailors ever to hail from Salem, that port of great sailors; and he was fast solidifying his reputation as the John Paul Jones of Revolutionary privateersmen, a dogged battler and inspired strategist who almost as a matter of routine triumphed over odds that lesser men would never have challenged.

The ship with which he was now locked in a death grapple was one of the most heavily armed private ships on the seas, a fast and efficient King's packet bound to England from the West Indies. Haraden knew from the fiery explosions that lit her sides that she carried nearly twenty guns and she must berth a crew of sixty to eighty men. His own swift raider, the *General Pickering*, carried only sixteen six-pounders and forty-five men and boys. His ship had maintained the unequal battle for four hours, but now she was badly cut up. Great rents gaped in her sails where round shot had sheered the canvas; severed ends of the running rigging whipped in the air; splinters carpeted her decks. Another few broadsides and she might become an unmanageable hulk, impotent in battle, incapable of flight. In such circumstances, even Haraden recognized the necessity of discretion and reluctantly gave the order to sheer off.

Slowly the *General Pickering* drew away from the equally battered Royal packet. The guns fell silent, the pall of powder smoke shredded into drifting wisps in the breeze, and peace descended temporarily upon the seas. Feverishly, the crews of both ships utilized the interval to make the repairs that would permit new battle. The running rigging was spliced, new sails bent, the decks cleared for action. In the midst of this activity, the crew of the *General Pickering* made a nerve-shattering discovery. They were almost out of powder. All they had left was a charge for one broadside.

Jonathan Haraden received the news impassively. He was a man who had demonstrated many times that he was most dauntless and dangerous when the odds were almost astronomical; but even John Paul Jones in his near-hopeless battle with the *Serapis* had at least had sufficient powder for his guns. Without powder, only one course of action, obviously, was possible for Haraden—flight before the heavily armed packet discovered his true helplessness. But Haraden did not instantly make that seemingly inevitable decision. Instead, he stood with his thin, sloping shoulders stooping a little and stared out at the Royal mail packet; and when he spoke, in a voice whose calm might have been envied by a father at the breakfast table, he gave an astounding order.

"Very well," he said. "One charge will be enough. Load and shot the guns."

The crew of the *General Pickering* had had occasion previously to suspect that their skipper became slightly fey when lured by that wanton witch called danger. But never had they been so sure of it as they were now. Under another commander, they might have rebelled; under Haraden, they merely muttered.

Swiftly, the *General Pickering* turned her prow toward the

waiting packet. Jonathan Haraden, oblivious to the mutterings behind him, leaped into a commanding position in the lower mizzen shrouds above his quarter-deck. He looped one arm through a backstay and swayed there, a lone and challenging figure. Every eye on both ships was upon him as the *General Pickering* bore down upon her foe.

The range narrowed to musket-shot distance, but not a musket was fired, the great guns were still. On both ships, the crews waited, wondering, tense, attention riveted on the silent figure that swayed above them, dominating the scene.

Then across the seas came the voice of Jonathan Haraden, trumpeting an audacious, an impudent ultimatum.

"I will give you five minutes to haul down your colors," he bellowed to the British skipper. "If they are not down at the end of that time, I will fire into you and sink you, so help me God."

Ignoring the stares of his own dumbfounded crew, he drew from his pocket a cumbersome timepiece. Clearly, like a referee counting over a fallen prizefighter, he began to toll off the minutes of doom.

"One—"

A pause.

"Two—"

"Three—"

Before he could utter "Four," the British flag fluttered to the deck in surrender. An incredibly bold psychological bluff had worked the miracle that broadsides had failed to accomplish.

A boat, quickly lowered from the *General Pickering*, raced across the narrow strip of water before the Englishmen could change their minds. An account subsequently compiled from eyewitness stories by Haraden's men says that the prize crew "found blood running from her scuppers, while the deck appeared more like the floor of a slaughter house than the deck of a ship. On the quarter-deck, in an armchair, sat an old Gentleman, the Governor of the island from which the packet came. During the whole action, he loaded and fired a heavy blunderbuss, and in the course of the battle had received a ball in the cheek, which, in consequence of the loss of teeth, had passed out through the other cheek without giving a mortal wound."

Such a triumph—over a foe most captains wouldn't even have tackled, in circumstances that seemed to promise defeat—was typical of the long Revolutionary War career of Jonathan Haraden. He frequently challenged odds of three-to-one as if they were no more than an even match; he captured vessels that mounted an estimated total of one thousand guns; he never lost a battle. Yet, because he was not a naval officer but an exponent of the extinct profession of privateering, his name has been almost completely obscured by time. A four-piper destroyer was named after him in World War I, but this ship has since vanished into the oblivion that, by some special perversity, seems the fate of Jonathan Haraden.

Despite this public neglect, specialists in sea lore unite in according to Haraden a niche among the immortals, honored ranking in that exclusive gallery of super fighting men like Jones whose refusal to admit defeat time and again has turned hopeless cause into stunning victory.

Born in Gloucester in 1745, Haraden lived almost all of his life in Salem. His parents, Joseph and Joanna Emerson Haraden, moved to Salem when he was quite young, and as soon as he was old enough to ship out as a cabin boy, he began his career upon the sea. When the Revolution broke out, he enlisted in the Army, and on July 11, 1775 was commissioned a second lieutenant in one of the most famous commands of the war—Col. John Glover's Marbleheaders, marching seamen who became known as the "web-footed infantry" for their feats in ferrying Washington's Army across the East River, after the debacle on Long Island, and across the ice-choked Delaware to the war-reviving surprise at Trenton.

Before these events, however, Haraden had left the infantry for the kind of fighting for which he was best equipped, the war on the sea. Massachusetts, like many of the other Colonies, had built a state navy to prey on British commerce, and on June 3, 1776 Haraden was appointed first lieutenant under Capt. John Fisk of Salem aboard a brigantine with the ferocious name, *Tyrannicide*. The *Tyrannicide* mounted fourteen guns and carried one hundred men; under Fisk and Haraden she quickly became the scourge of British commerce off the Massachusetts coast.

Ten days after Haraden joined her, she captured the British packet schooner *Dispatch*, and in the next few months five additional prizes hove to under her guns. Then, on February 20, 1777, Fisk left the *Tyrannicide* to command a larger vessel, the brigantine *Massachusetts*, and Haraden was promoted to captain. One of the most colorful careers of the Revolution had begun.

The records of the Massachusetts Board of War detail Haraden's notable success. On March 14, 1777, the Board of War ordered Haraden in the *Tyrannicide* and Fisk in the *Massachusetts* to cruise to the coasts of Ireland, England and France. The two captains sailed on March 24, and on April 2, in latitude 41 degrees 20 minutes North and longitude 45 degrees West, they captured the ship *Chalkley* bound from Honduras to Bristol with a cargo of mahogany and logwood. This was the first rich prize in what was to be a successful and sometimes hair-raising cruise.

The ocean lanes were crawling with British merchant ships, some separated by wind and storm from their convoys, and Fisk and Haraden snapped up the strays, as busy as a pair of foxes in the henyard. Haraden took the snow (a type of Revolutionary vessel) *Sally*, bound from London to Quebec, and sent her safely into Salem. On April 8, Fisk in the *Massachusetts* went off to chase a strange sail, and while he was gone, Haraden located a fine prospect of his own, the five hundred ton *Lonsdale*, three times the size of the *Tyrannicide*. Undismayed by the odds, Haraden laid the *Tyrannicide* close to her huge antagonist, and for three hours the two ships dueled broadside to broadside. Then the *Lonsdale* surrendered.

Haraden put a prize crew aboard and sent the *Lonsdale* back to Boston. Next he snatched the brig *Eagle* and the barque *White Haven*, and sent them off to America. The hunting was so good that Fisk and Haraden spent days sweeping slowly back and forth across the shipping lanes as they worked their way slowly eastward. And so, two weeks after Haraden's battle with the *Lonsdale*, they ran headon into a heavily armed British convoy.

In a laconic report to the Board of War, Haraden later conveyed a graphic picture of the two little American brigantines virtually thumbing their noses at an entire fleet. He wrote that they "fell in with a fleet of 9 sail bound to the Westward, one of 60 and one of 14 Guns, British Ships of War, with 7 Transports from Plymouth for New York. Being a Fresh gale we could not bare down on them; however, finding one Brig to lay astern, we took the liberty to take her under Convoy. She had on board 63 Troops, Hessens Chussers, with their accountrement compleat."

With the Hessians dispatched to an American prison camp, Haraden and Fisk sailed on and soon brought their cruise to an exciting climax. Fisk slipped the *Massachusetts* into the French port of Nantes on May 21st and promptly wrote the Board of War that he feared Haraden and the *Tyrannicide* had been captured. He reported that "on the seventeenth Instant at Nine in the Morning we gave chase to a Ship standing to the Eastward and came up fast. At three got within two miles of the ship, then saw three Sail in the N.E. bearing down to us; one of said Sail brought our chase to & hoisted English colors. I bore away and made sail from them; the Ship gave me chase. Capt. Haraden bore away also; the ship came up with us fast. At Nine at Night I haul'd my Wind; Capt. Haraden bore away before the wind. At half after nine, lost sight of Capt. Haraden and soon after, lost sight of the Ship. At ten, saw three flashes of Guns, which I suppose the Ship fired at Capt. Haraden and I am afraid the Ship took him, as I have not heard or seen anything of him since."

Fisk need not have worried. Haraden, finding himself pursued by a heavy frigate, had exercised every stratagem known to his wily sailor's mind to escape. The *Tyrannicide*'s sails were doused so that the canvas would retain every breath of air; stores were brought up from the hold and pitched overboard; even the carriage guns were trundled one by one into the sea. Thus lightened, denuded of most of her armament, the little brigantine found the wings to outspeed the frigate and scuttled to sanctuary in the Spanish port of Bilbao.

There Haraden refitted his raider. Stores were replenished, a makeshift battery mounted, and in a few days Haraden was back roving the seas. He scored almost at once. On May 31st, he captured the brigantine *Trepassy*, one hundred and sixty tons, Capt. Isaac Follett, and sent her to Boston, where she arrived on June 25th.

After his return from this European cruise, Haraden made one more sortie in the *Tyrannicide*. He spent the winter of 1777–78 on a cruise to Portugal, the Madeiras and the West Indies, and a steady stream of prizes flowed back to American ports. Returning to Salem in early May, 1778, Haraden became involved in a dispute with the Board of War over the number of shares he was to be allotted in the distribution of prize money, and on June 25, 1778, he resigned his commission in the Massachusetts State Navy. On September 30th, he took command of the *General Pickering*, the privateer he was to make famous.

The *General Pickering* had been built by a group of Salem merchants and had been fitted out as a cruiser. She was only one hundred and eighty tons and originally was rigged as a brigantine; but Haraden altered her to a full-rigged ship to increase her speed. Originally, too, she was commissioned as a letter of marque—that is, a commercial ship carrying cargo to foreign ports but armed and commissioned to take prizes along the way. The cargo-carrying put a limitation upon the armament the ship could pack so that, during her early cruises, the *General Pickering* mounted only fourteen six-pounders. Later, when she became a full-fledged privateer, with the sole task of preying on enemy shipping, two guns were added to her broadsides.

In the archives of the Essex Institute in Salem, as carefully preserved as if they came from the captain's cabin only yesterday, are the log books of two of Haraden's cruises. One deals with his last voyage home in the *Tyrannicide;* the other, with his first venture in the *General Pickering*. The terse day-by-day entries give a vivid picture of the daily hazards of life at sea aboard a pint-sized warship in the Revolution.

Take, for example, this brief epitaph to a seaman in the *Tyrannicide*'s log of April 9, 1778:

At 5 P.M. Samuel Wylie died of the Small Pox.
At 7 P.M. Buried him.

Or take this stripped, hour-by-hour account of the *General Pickering*'s struggle for survival in a howling Atlantic storm on November 27, 1778, just ten days after she had sailed from Salem for the West Indies:

4 P.M. Close-reefed topsails, double reef mainsails.
8 P.M. Handed both top sails.
Half past 9. Hove to Under Reeft topsails, head to the wind.
Half past 10. Wore ship to the Eastward.
6 A.M. Bore away. Handed the Torn Sail. It blowed a hard gale & very High Sea.
8 A.M. More moderate. Close Reeft torn Topsails.

On January 4, 1779, a one-line entry in the log reported the capture of a schooner from Nova Scotia, and on the next day, a succinct paragraph described how the *General Pickering* flitted through an entire British convoy, drawing the fire of a large warship and escaping unscathed. The entry reads:

> Saw a sail to windward. Got all things ready for engaging & Hove about after Her & fetched to the windward of her. She fired Several Shot at us. In running for her we saw several more Sail. We run through a fleet of 11 Sails but could see no prospect of taking any of them, they had so strong a Convoy. The ship that fired at us We supposed to be a two-decker as she fired from her forecastle and quarter deck.

Haraden brought the *General Pickering* into St. Pierre on January 30th. Here the guns were hoisted out, the ship heeled over and her bottom scraped. A new mainmast was stepped to replace the one that had been sprung in the storm, and provisions and cargo were taken aboard.

Four of the hands were sent ashore to fill forty-eight water casks. Bread, pork and beef—the shipboard staples of the day— were purchased, and day-by-day entries show that the *General Pickering* took on a diversified cargo. The log lists ten hundredweight of coffee, twenty-three kegs of nails, two hundredweight of dry goods, two barrels of pewter, three casks of cutlery ware, seven bales of dry goods, eleven bales of cotton, six more bags of coffee. Each day's entry in the log ended with the notation, "Broacht cask of water and barrel of beef [or pork]"—evidently, one day's supply for the crew.

Heavily laden, the *General Pickering* sailed back to Salem, buffeted by a succession of midwinter Atlantic storms. With her safe return to her home port, the log ends. Later logs detailing Haraden's more warlike cruises subsequently fell into enemy hands and were destroyed, and so one has to rely on the stories his seamen later told those Salem chroniclers, Capt. J. P. Felt and Freeman Hunt, for descriptions of dramatic battles like the one in the fall of 1779 when the *General Pickering*, alone and unaided, tangled with an entire flotilla of British privateers.

The enemy squadron was led by the ship *Hope*, mounting fourteen guns, followed by the brig *Pomona*, twelve guns, and the cutter *Royal George*, twelve guns. Almost any captain, finding himself outnumbered by three to one and outgunned by virtually the same margin, could have been forgiven for trying to sail elsewhere as expeditiously as possible. But Jonathan Haraden calmly surveyed the opposing fleet through his telescope and held to his course.

His crew, despite their faith in his reputation as a commander whose every deed was blessed with success, began to mutter and look askance at the quarter-deck. Ignoring both murmurs and looks, Haraden calmly ordered the men to battle stations.

Then he took a stroll along the deck, an erect, lean figure as serene in mien as any good citizen of Salem out for a walk on a quiet Sunday afternoon. Almost casually, he spoke to his men.

"There's good prize money there, lads," he said, nodding across the seas in the direction of the enemy. "You stand to your guns and do your duty, and I will make you a little promise. We will take all three of them."

Had anyone but Jonathan Haraden made such a seemingly foolhardy decision, the crew might have balked, for the history of privateering in the Revolution is replete with cowardice as well as bravery. But Haraden wore the halo of victory; and so, though his sailors might quiver inwardly at the three-to-one odds they were facing, they still put their trust in his calm assurance, his infallible touch in battle. They stood to their guns and their duty.

The *General Pickering* held the weather gage, and this Haraden nursed with all the skill of a master of maneuver. As long as he kept to windward, the British ships would have to beat up toward him; he could maintain position, battling one at a time or, if he chose, he could sweep down suddenly to carry an exposed craft by boarding.

The British formed in battle line behind the *Hope*, and as

the range narrowed only the *Hope* was in position for her guns
to bear. This was just as Haraden wanted it, and he spoke a
final admonition to his men:

"Aim low, boys. We will give her a few broadsides and
board."

The *General Pickering*'s six-pounders exploded in one running sheet of flame. The *Hope* staggered under the impact.
Again and again, the *General Pickering*'s guns roared out, and
the *Hope* made only feeble response. Sensing that this was no
stout-hearted adversary, Haraden swooped like a hawk. A
touch of the wheel sent the *Pickering* plunging through the
wall of powder smoke, sent her crunching and grinding
against the hull of the enemy. Brandishing cutlasses and pistols,
the Americans swarmed over the bulwarks and poured in an
irresistible tide along the British deck.

In a few minutes, with hardly a blow struck, the *Hope* was
theirs. Leaving a prize crew aboard to keep the stunned British
sailors under control, Haraden quickly cast off. The odds
against him were still two to one. The *Pomona* and *Royal
George* were closing in, and should they combine to pour their
two broadsides into the *General Pickering*, Haraden and all his
crew might be captured.

Only a lightning stroke could save them. Realizing this,
Haraden plunged straight for the *Pomona*. Again his gunners
poured out a deadly broadside; again Haraden sent the *Pickering* boring through the shroud of powder smoke, intent on
carrying the *Pomona* before the *Royal George* could get into
action. Once more there came the grinding impact of the hulls,
the storm of yelling boarders across the decks. And once more
the demoralized British sailors threw down their arms and fled
below in panic.

With two ships carried, Haraden hastily recalled his men to
their guns and bore down on the sole survivor of what had
appeared to be, just a few short minutes before, an overwhelmingly superior squadron. The *Royal George*, shocked by the

swift disaster that had overtaken her consorts, had no stomach
to fight. She turned to flee, but the *Pickering* was the swifter
ship. Brought to bay, the *Royal George* traded a few ineffectual broadsides and surrendered. Jonathan Haraden had defied
odds of three to one and had captured the entire fleet arrayed
against him. It had taken him just thirty minutes.

The victory was a rewarding one in more than a patriotic
sense, as is shown by the fact that the *Pomona* was brought
into Salem and sold on October 23, 1779 for eighty-nine hundred British pounds, the equivalent of some fifty thousand
dollars.

Even before Haraden's men had a chance to claim their
prize money, their wily commander had added to the booty
by luring another good-sized British privateer to surrender
under his guns. Haraden himself described this capture in a
letter to Timothy Pickering from Cape Henlopen, October 1,
1779. He wrote:

"I left the Capes at Sundown on Tuesday last, and at Sun-
rising on Wednesday Morning I discovered Two sail to windward. The Winds being light I hove out two Draggs to keep
my Ship from going ahead and made all the Sail I could, as
though I was running from them. They both gave Chace and
at 5 P.M. they got nigh enough to discover that I was a cruising
Vessel.

"They both hove about and haul'd their Wind. I immediately hove about after them, they crowded all the Sail they
could and Rowed at the same time. At sundown the Wind
breezed up a little and as Night came on, I kept Sight of them
with my Night Glass; at 8 P.M., they parted, one stood to the
Northward & the other to the Southward. I kept in chace of
the largest and at 9 P.M. She Hove about, being to the Windward; as she past me I hail'd her, but had no answer. Then I
gave her a Broadside, but without any effect that I could perceive; then I Tackt Ship and gave her another Broadside and
hail'd her. She answered from N. York. I Order'd her to haul

down the Colours, which they obeyed instantly; very peaceable people like the Hope, though they had 14 6 & 4 pounders and 38 men."

Such tricks and tactics dot the career of the fighting man from Salem. Once, while he was cruising in the vicinity of Bermuda, he was annoyed by two lightning-fast Bermuda sloops. They flitted around the same sector of ocean in which Haraden was cruising, keeping a discreet distance away from his guns, but recapturing some of his prizes before they could get safely on their way to American ports.

Haraden decided to set a trap for these pesky foes who were depriving his crew and himself of their hard-earned prize money. He waited until nightfall. Then he put his sailors to work to change the *Pickering* into a floating booby trap. He sent down the fore topgallant yard and mast, altering the appearance of the ship aloft. Along the sides of the privateer he spread a painted canvas screen, concealing the gun ports. Next, he hove out drags astern to reduce his raider's speed and to complete her transformation into a lumbering-appearing merchantman. When the arrangements had been completed, Haraden headed back for the area where the Bermuda sloops had been making themselves obnoxious.

He had not long to wait. Shortly after daybreak, the sloops sighted Haraden's camouflaged warship and spread their white wings in an eager dash for booty. Haraden watched them from his quarter-deck, a grim smile playing about his lips. Not until the first sloop foamed up directly under his quarter, barely a pistol shot distant, did he give his orders.

"Drop that screen, men," he shouted. "Give her a broadside."

The canvas screen was whisked away like a false face on Halloween, and the dark row of the *Pickering*'s gun ports gaped ominously at the audacious sloop. Almost at the same instant, the broadside roared out, sweeping the deck of the smaller Bermuda privateer with death and destruction. The tricked enemy did not wait for a second deadly dose from those well-served guns. Instead, they threw down their arms and surrendered.

The second privateer, which was some distance away, was still bearing down on the scene of action. Haraden decided that a little more deception might help to lure her, too, into his trap. Therefore, he ordered the British ensign bent to the halyards above the Stars and Stripes on the *General Pickering*. This convinced the unsuspecting Bermuda skipper that the firing he had observed must have ended quickly in the capture of a fat merchantman. Eager to claim his share of the loot, he drove straight on and ran his sloop beautifully under the waiting guns of the *General Pickering*.

Successes such as these would have been sufficient to distinguish any captain and set him apart from his fellows, but they were little more than a prelude to the real drama in the career of Jonathan Haraden.

In the spring of 1780, the *General Pickering* was loaded with a cargo of sugar and dispatched for Bilbao, a favorite Spanish rendezvous for American privateers in European waters. Haraden had a new and, to some extent, a green crew. This, combined with the fact that the *General Pickering* was so deeply laden that she was not her usual swift self, made him decide to waste no time in cruising, but to head directly for Europe to get rid of his cumbersome cargo.

The voyage, consequently, was peaceful enough until May 29, 1780 when the *General Pickering* encountered a British privateer mounting twenty guns. The *Pickering* was still carrying only fourteen, and Haraden had a crew of only forty-seven men and boys. Despite the odds, he fought a savage battle. For an hour and forty-five minutes, the two ships traded broadsides, and then the Englishman, badly battered, sheered off and went looking for easier quarry.

A few days later, tacking into the Bay of Biscay, Haraden encountered an even more formidable adversary. This was the

British privateer *Golden Eagle*, carrying twenty-two guns and a crew of sixty. Night was just falling when the *Golden Eagle* was sighted, and a prudent captain might have taken advantage of the darkness to give the more powerful vessel the slip. But prudence was not the key to the character of Jonathan Haraden; he delighted in the audacity which, when it works as it did for him, is safer than prudence. He spread all sail in chase.

It was a black night, the kind of night in which sea and sky blend into one inky mass and objects looming suddenly out of that opaqueness play tricks upon the eyes and assume weird dimensions. Such an object was the *General Pickering*, foaming boldly, confidently out of the enveloping blackness; looking with her sudden, swift emergence at least twice life-size. Quick to embellish the false image, Haraden seized a speaking trumpet.

"Ship ahoy!" he bellowed. "This is an American frigate of the largest size. Strike your colors, or I will sink you with a broadside."

The British captain, evidently just an ordinary man whose limited imagination could not grasp the possibility of such superb audacity, believed every word of the empty ultimatum and struck his colors without firing a shot.

John Carnes, of Salem, was put aboard the *Golden Eagle* as prize master, and the English captain was rowed, a prisoner, to the *General Pickering*. Only then did he discover his error. Only then, too late to rectify the blunder, did he learn that he had capitulated so meekly to a ship scarcely two-thirds his size.

With this daring coup to his credit, Jonathan Haraden in the *General Pickering*, trailed by the *Golden Eagle*, squared away once more for Bilbao. The two ships were nearing port on the morning of June 3rd when they sighted a large vessel working out of the roads toward them. She carried a vast spread of canvas and was obviously twice the size of the *General Pickering*. The British skipper who had so meekly surrendered to the *Golden Eagle* stared at the headsails of the stranger with the eye of a practiced mariner and broke into smiles of undisguised glee. Haraden, observing his reaction, remarked:

"I gather you recognize that sail, Sir. Could you tell me what ship is that?"

"Gladly," beamed the Englishman. "That is the *Achilles*, one of the most powerful privateers ever to sail out of London. She mounts forty-two guns and carries a crew of one hundred and forty men."

"Is that so?" murmured Jonathan Haraden in the mildly interested tone in which a man greets a bit of curious trivia.

The British captain, who had expected his announcement to bring dismay, gaped in astonishment at the unruffled Haraden. Reading the look, Haraden kept his eyes on the towering headsails of the *Achilles* and spoke quiet words that further increased the British captain's astonishment.

"Be that as it may," he said, "and you seem sure of your information, I shan't run from her."

Boldly, the *General Pickering* stood in for the land, ready to match her fourteen guns against forty-two; her thirty-seven men and boys—ten were aboard the prize—against the one hundred and forty men on the *Achilles*. As the day advanced, the wind died away, and the vessels were virtually becalmed. The *Achilles*, with her taller masts and larger spread of canvas, held the whisper of breeze longer than the *General Pickering* and the *Golden Eagle*. Slowly she crawled across the water toward Haraden's prize, which finally she brought under her guns and easily recaptured.

Then the wind died completely, and the vessels rocked gently on a nearby lifeless sea.

Word of the impending naval battle spread along the coast, and by sunset thousands of spectators blackened the Spanish cliffs and headlands. When the wind died before battle could be joined, the deferred drama lured still others from their homes, and through the night the expectant crowds swelled until it was estimated that one-hundred-thousand persons clung to vantage points along the coast or put out in small boats to get close to the scene of action.

The disparity in size between the *General Pickering* and the *Achilles* made the outcome seem inevitable. One eyewitness, Robert Cowan, wrote that "the General Pickering in comparison to her antagonist looked like a long boat by the side of a ship."

The Spanish spectators quaked for the fate of the American privateer, but aboard "the long boat" itself there prevailed an incredible air of self-confidence. Haraden himself, by every word and look and action, was the personification of unruffled calm, and his supreme assurance communicated itself to his crew. Satisfied that the dead calm would last the night and that battle could not be joined before morning, he turned to his first officer and said:

"I'm going below and get a little rest. Call me if she tries to close."

The night passed quietly, and at dawn, when a breeze came up and the *Achilles* headed for the *General Pickering* again, Haraden was found so soundly and blissfully asleep that he had to be shaken from slumber.

"He calmly arose and went on deck as if it had been some ordinary occasion," a contemporary account says.

Ordering the *General Pickering* cleared for action, Haraden went forward to address the sixty prisoners captured in the *Golden Eagle*. With his own crew depleted, he had barely enough men to handle the sails and work the guns. He needed recruits, and as so often happened in the Revolution—a war marked by frequent changing of sides and allegiance—he sought them in the ranks of the captured enemy.

The exact words that Haraden used have not been preserved, but he must have been eloquent as he stressed a dual theme. He urged the British sailors to join their American brethren in the cause of liberty, and at the same time he held out to them the allure of a tempting cash reward in the form of a full share of prize money should the *General Pickering* be victorious. The prospect of prize money, considering the tremendous odds against the *Pickering*, could not have been very promising, but so convincing was Haraden that a British boatswain and ten men stepped forward, volunteering their services.

His crew thus restored to normal strength, Haraden made a final tour of the deck, talking quietly to his men.

"She's bigger than we are, lads," he told them, "but we've beaten worse odds before. Just stand firm and ready, and we'll take her. Aim low. Don't throw away your fire."

To the marksmen with small arms in the tops and on the quarter-deck, he gave this advice: "Aim at their white boot tops."

Having completed his preparations for battle, Haraden utilized the morning breeze to work the *General Pickering* in close to shore, picking his battleground with wily forethought. A series of shoals extended out from the coast, and Haraden placed the *Pickering* in the deep water between them. This meant that the *Achilles*, to get at him, would have to advance almost head-on up the narrow channel between the shoals, exposing herself to a near-raking fire, with her far heavier batteries unable to bear fully upon the *Pickering*.

Along the decks of the *General Pickering*, the crew clustered near the open gunports, making ready for the first broadside. As the *Achilles* swept toward them, narrowing the range, the orders ran down the deck:

"Cast off tackles and breechings."

"Seize the breechings."

"Unstop the touch-hole."

"Ram home wad and cartridge."

"Shot the gun-wad."

"Run out the gun."

"Lay down handspikes and crows."

"Point your gun."

And then the final, all-important command: "Fire!"

The seven six-pounders in the *General Pickering*'s broadside spoke as one voice, and their iron hail swept over the water to crash against the stout sides of the *Achilles*. The huzzahs with which the British had swept into action died out, and the forward guns of the *Achilles*, the only ones that could be brought to bear, roared a deep-throated reply.

Thus was the battle joined, much to the delectation of the excited mob of spectators who swarmed along the nearby coast. Again and again the *Pickering*'s guns roared, firing so rapidly that the thunderclap of one broadside seemed to roar from the dying echoes of its predecessor. Desperately, the British captain tried to drive his ship through the deadly storm, seeking to close and board so that he could sweep the *Pickering*'s deck with an irresistible tide of superior manpower.

But Jonathan Haraden was not the sea fighter to let himself get caught in such a trap. Exercising all his genius, he kept maneuvering the *General Pickering* between the shoals, kept that strip of blue water between him and the enemy, kept those deadly broadsides thundering. Through it all, he stood in his favorite battle position—by the rail of the quarter-deck on the side nearest the enemy. Round shot and musket balls flew past his tall, erect figure, and he seemed to take a perverse delight in their ominous winging. It was a demonstration that so impressed his crew that one of them wrote years later: "All the time he was as calm and steady as amid a shower of snowflakes."

Though Haraden stood untouched, unharmed, the deadly storm that swept across the hull of the low-lying *Pickering* took its inevitable toll. One round shot carried away the head of the British boatswain who had volunteered for battle; eight of the crew were wounded. Still the doughty men of Salem labored unflinchingly at their guns, pouring an accurate fire into the towering sides of the man-crowded *Achilles*. For two hours, the British captain endured the unequal contest, trying to bore through the iron hail to close with his elusive foe. Still he could not succeed, and finally, despairing of ever laying the *General Pickering* aboard, he ordered his ship swung broadside to the American in the narrow lane of deep water. There at last all of the *Achilles'* mightier armament could be brought to bear, and the battle raged to a fierce crescendo.

For fifty-five minutes more, the ships dueled, broadside to broadside, three guns thundering on the *Achilles* to every one on the *Pickering*. These were crushing, overwhelming odds; yet, for the Americans, there were some slight compensations. The *General Pickering* was so heavily loaded that she sat low in the water and was hard to hull, while the high-sided *Achilles* loomed over the gun sights, an ideal target. Shot after shot from the *Pickering*'s guns crashed through the hull of the British privateer, tearing great gaps near her waterline. Still the stubborn British battled on. And now the Americans faced a new crisis. They were running short of round shot.

Haraden, typically, was undismayed by the discovery that soon he would be without cannon balls to fire at his huge foe; that then he would lie helpless, unable to reply, and must suffer in silence the full weight of the *Achilles'* heavy broadsides. Ever the master of the eleventh-hour improvisation that so often turns defeat into victory, Haraden now made a characteristic decision. If the round shot was running low, he would use something else.

"Load with crowbars," he shouted to his men.

They obeyed, and the next broadside from the *Pickering* showered the decks of the *Achilles* with a deadly hail of these crude, powder-propelled javelins. The crowbar broadside did what round shot had failed to do. The *Achilles* had taken a fearful battering; she was truly in desperate plight. Her hull was so badly riddled that if she fought on she might sink; her rigging was so cut up that if she fought on, soon she might not be able to flee. Then, from the skies, the crowbars plunged like spears, skewering many of her crew and driving some of the gunners from their battle stations. It was the last straw. The *Achilles* had had enough. Orders rang out, and the huge British privateer spread all the canvas she still could carry, swung about and fled for the open sea.

Haraden, his fighting blood at fever heat, did not care in this moment of victory that he had beaten off a vastly superior foe, that the port of Bilbao and safety lay open before him. He wanted the complete and final triumph, he wanted a prize; and he spread all sail in pursuit.

The *General Pickering* in pursuit of the *Achilles* resembled nothing so much as a fox terrier chasing a great Dane, but Haraden had no doubts about the outcome should he once catch up with his thoroughly vanquished and demoralized foe.

"Another share of prize money to any gunner who can bring down a spar!" he shouted.

His marksmen tried, but their shots ripped through sails and rigging and plunged on into the sea without splintering the masts of the *Achilles*. The fleeing privateer, with a mainsail described by eyewitnesses as one "as large as a ship of the line," drew rapidly ahead. Haraden was compelled to give up the chase, but he consoled himself by swinging around and re-taking his original prize, the *Golden Eagle*, which had tarried over-long as a spectator at the scene of battle.

Among all the thousands who had witnessed the spectacular sea fight, no one was quite as thunderstruck by the outcome as the second lieutenant of the *Achilles*, who had been put aboard the *Golden Eagle* as prize master. He had questioned John Carnes before the battle was joined about the size and strength of the *General Pickering*, and Carnes had answered him truthfully. The Englishman had rubbed his hands in delight, anticipating a quick and easy victory. As the battle wore on and it became obvious that the *Achilles* had caught a Tartar of Tartars, the British officer's jubilation died in amaze-ment, and he swung upon Carnes and taxed him with practicing deception about the size and armament of the *Pickering*. The Yankee smiled wryly and replied:

"If you knew Captain Jonathan Haraden as I do, you would not be surprised at this. It is just what I expected, and I think it not impossible that the *Achilles* will be beaten off, and I shall have command of this prize again before night."

Haraden made his second officer a perfect prophet, for before nightfall the British lieutenant was Carnes' prisoner and the *Golden Eagle* was anchored beside the *General Pickering* in the port of Bilbao.

The Spanish populace, thrilled by its grandstand seat at the amphitheater of war, made Haraden its idol and its hero. The *General Pickering* and the *Golden Eagle* anchored about a mile from shore, and before they had swung in the roads for half an hour, such a solid mass of spectator boats formed about them that, eyewitnesses averred, it would have been possible to walk all the way to land by stepping from one boat to another. And when Haraden went ashore so great was the admiration of the people that they lifted him aloft on their shoulders and bore him in an impromptu triumphal procession through the streets of the city. Later he was feted with an almost unending round of dinners and public receptions.

So sensational a victory could not help but enhance the Haraden legend. His name, awe-inspiring before, now became so formidable that sometimes victories were won as much by the name as by the broadsides of the *General Pickering*.

Accounts of the day tell how Haraden even captured a British war brig subsequently, almost without firing a shot, "just by the mere terror of his name." The incident occurred off the Capes of the Delaware. Haraden had taken a prize and put a prize crew aboard to run the gauntlet of the British blockade up the Delaware to Philadelphia. Before the prize could slip into the Delaware Bay, however, she was overhauled and retaken by the British brig, and the members of the

American prize crew were hauled as prisoners aboard the British warship.

Among them was a young cabin boy, a devout worshipper at the Haraden shrine. To the boy, the captain appeared invincible, capable of capturing any warship smaller than a ship-of-the-line. Therefore, when a sail was sighted and the boy recognized the rigging of the *General Pickering*, he began to skip about the deck.

"What's the matter with you?" an English bo'sun growled.

"That's my master in that ship, and I'll soon be with him," the boy predicted confidently.

"Your master?" asked the bo'sun. "And who the devil is he?"

"Why, he's Captain Jonathan Haraden!" cried the boy. "Don't tell me you've never heard of him! He takes everything he goes alongside of, and he will soon have you."

This prediction of the cabin boy was relayed to the captain of the brig, who promptly summoned the boy aft for questioning. There, on the quarter-deck of the British warship, the young hero-worshipper launched into a long recital of the epic of Jonathan Haraden. All the time he talked, Haraden was driving to the rescue under every rag of sail the *General Pickering* would carry. It is not quite clear from the legendary accounts of the day exactly what transpired on the British quarter-deck, but it is obvious from the event that either Haraden's cabin boy was the greatest storyteller since Scheherazade or the British captain was a complete dunder-head. For by the time the fascinated Briton tore himself away from the Haraden story and devoted his attention to the very real business of war, he had been completely out-foxed and out-maneuvered.

The day was blustery, with a high wind and a choppy sea. These weather conditions altered the circumstances in which a ship to windward normally held all the advantage, and Haraden deliberately chose to attack from the leeward side. He swept up within musket shot of the British warship, which was heeled over so far by the wind that the seas swept along her lee gunports. Any attempt to open the gunports would bring the seas surging over the decks. The *General Pickering*, on the other hand, was not so handicapped. She was presenting her weather battery to the enemy, and all that she had to do was to depress her guns and sweep the exposed deck of her foe.

"Haul down your colors or I will fire into you," Haraden bellowed.

Trapped, the English sailors tried briefly to make a fight of it. They popped away at the *General Pickering* with small arms and swivel guns attached to the bulwarks, but it took only one broadside to convince them that such toys were no match for Haraden's heavier cannon. The British colors were struck, and the next day the British warship was anchored as a prize beside the *General Pickering* off Philadelphia—an event that fulfilled to the letter the rash forecast of the young cabin boy when the *Pickering*'s headsails had first come into sight.

Such triumphs, one following swiftly on the other, marked the year 1780. In swift succession, Haraden captured a veritable fleet of enemy vessels and sent the bulk of them safely into port enriching his vessel's owners and earning himself and his crew precious prize money. The ship *Rodney*, one-hundred and twenty tons, was sold in Salem for ninety-thousand pounds— about $450,000. The brigantine *Myrrh* brought twenty-five thousand pounds, and the brigantine *Venus* twenty-thousand pounds—sales that give a good idea of the rich rewards of successful privateering.

Then came 1781, and the only ill-starred adventure in Jonathan Haraden's long career. He was captured. But it took an entire British fleet to do it.

Haraden had sailed on a West Indies cruise on November 16, 1780. He cut his usual swath across the busy ocean-shipping lanes until, early in the new year, off the Dutch island of Saint

Eustatius in the West Indies, he captured a ship that was to cause him more trouble than any enemy warship.

The prize hailed from Boston. She had been captured by the British. Before she could make port as a British prize, Haraden drove alongside and retook her. So far all was well. But now Haraden made a fateful decision. He decided to take his prize and the *General Pickering* into Saint Eustatius.

The two vessels had barely gotten safely into port when, on February 3, 1781, Admiral George Brydges Rodney descended upon the island with a powerful British fleet. Bottled up in port, Haraden had no chance to escape, and the Dutch were too weak to resist. The island fell, putting some fifteen million dollars in loot into the pockets of Rodney and his men; Haraden, the *General Pickering* and the Boston vessel so recently snatched from British hands were all captured.

From this misfortune developed one of the weirdest legal tangles ever to enmesh a gallant seaman. The owners of the Boston ship that Haraden had had the bad luck to recapture sued him for damages. They contended that, once having retaken their vessel, he had cost them the vessel by exercising bad judgment in taking her into Saint Eustatius just at the time that Rodney was coming along. If he had sent the vessel into an American port, all would have been well, the owners argued, blandly ignoring two major facts—that Haraden could hardly be held responsible for not being able to read Rodney's mind and intentions and that there was no guarantee the ship, if sent to an American port, might not have been seized again by the British on the way.

Common sense would seem to have argued that such a suit for damages should be laughed out of court, but law suits are not always decided by common sense. Solemnly, the courts ruled that Haraden was responsible for the lost ship and that he would have to pay. Accounts of the time do not reveal how many thousands of dollars were involved in the verdict, but the total doubtless represented a crushing financial disaster for a sea captain, even for one as well-heeled with prize money as Haraden.

The captain from Salem, however, was not a man to surrender meekly either to enemies on the sea or to legal leeches. Finding himself boxed into a tight financial corner, he came up with a stratagem of his own. He asked the owners of the *General Pickering* to indemnify him for the amount of the judgment. He argued that he had gone to the West Indies on the orders of the *Pickering*'s owners, that he had been simply their agent, and that, if he was to be held responsible for the loss of the Boston ship, they should be responsible because he had been acting for them. Though Haraden had made fortunes for the owners of the *Pickering*, they were businessmen; past profits weighed less with them than current loss. They were chagrined as it was over the loss of the *Pickering* in Saint Eustatius, and they were in no mood to come to the financial rescue of their captain. They refused to pay. Haraden sued.

The case, pitting against each other two dramatic opposites—the hero whose courage, skill and invariable success had made him a popular idol and the merchants who had remained snugly at home, profiting from the hero's ability— quickly became the *cause célèbre* of the day in Salem. When the trial opened, Salem was thronged with crowds debating the issue, and the courthouse was packed with spectators. The evidence was submitted, and when the last legal argument had been heard, the court ruled in Haraden's favor, a triumph of sailor-hero over merchant that met with complete public approbation. Cheers rocked the courthouse at the news, and again, as in Bilbao, Jonathan Haraden found himself hoisted aloft on stout shoulders and carried along the streets, the hero of the day.

Important as the legal and pecuniary triumph was to Haraden, it would seem inappropriate if the career of such a warrior of the seas were to end with any victory so tame as one wrought by lawyer's words in court. It should end as it began, to the rolling crash of broadsides and the shouts of armed seamen swarming across the decks of a helpless enemy. And so, indeed, it did in real life.

The old records are not clear on exactly how long Haraden remained a prisoner of the British after the fall of Saint Eustatius. But he was back in Massachusetts before the end of 1781, and on May 3, 1782, he was made the commander of the two-hundred-ton ship *Julius Caesar*, mounting fourteen guns and manned by forty men. Soon he was off harrying the seas again, preying on commerce that, then as now, represented the very life blood of England.

On June 5, 1782, Haraden in his new privateer fell in with a British ship of eighteen guns and a brig of sixteen. Instantly, he engaged in another of his statistically lopsided battles, sending the *Caesar*'s broadsides crashing first into one enemy ship and then into the other, all the time maneuvering so skillfully that they could never bring the combined weight of their two broadsides to bear on him at once. For five glasses, the unequal battle raged; and then, as Haraden wrote drily, in what must stand as a classic of understatement, "both parties separated, sufficiently amused."

Actually, both British ships were so battered that they had to concentrate all their energies on just staying afloat, and the *Julius Caesar* was so cut up in spars and rigging that Haraden had to make extensive emergency repairs at sea.

Once these were completed, he continued on his voyage to the West Indies; and on July 18, 1782, off Bermuda, he encountered almost identical two-to-one odds. The two were British brigs, one mounting twenty guns, the other sixteen. Though either should have been more than a match for the *Julius Caesar*, the British privateers kept their distance and refused to fight. Haraden, disgusted at such faint hearts, chased and overhauled a schooner one of the brigs had just captured, retook the prize under the very noses of his timorous foes and sailed on his way, consoled that he had made at least some small profit out of the encounter.

He finally brought the *Julius Caesar* safely into port in the French island of Martinique. An American there wrote to a friend in Salem of Haraden's arrival, related the details of his battles and added: "Capt. Haraden was subsequently presented with a silver plate by the owners of his ship, as commemorative of his bravery and skill. Before he reached Martinico he had a severe battle with another English vessel which he carried thither with him as a prize."

Sailing for home in the fall of 1782, Haraden encountered a huge four-hundred-ton vessel that had served as a storeship for Lord Howe, laid her close aboard in another thundering duel of broadsides—and captured her. He convoyed this rich prize into Salem on December 31, 1782, and with this act, as seamen say, he swallowed the anchor. He decided to call it a career.

Haraden was a part-owner of the *Julius Caesar*, and when the privateer went to sea again, she was under the command of Haraden's former first officer. Haraden himself remained ashore, content to take his part-owner's profits from the *Caesar*'s new ventures while he devoted himself to a new life with a new bride.

Haraden had married for a second time on March 11, 1782, just before he sailed for his final cruise in the *Julius Caesar*. His first marriage on June 8, 1767 had been to Hannah Deadman. Following her death, he married Mrs. Eunice Mason, the widowed daughter of the Rev. James Diman, of Salem. Haraden and his second wife lived together happily for fourteen years until her death, on November 17, 1796, again made him a widower. A year later, on October 12, 1797, he married another widow, Mrs. Mary Scallon.

During these post-Revolutionary years, Haraden went into business for himself, making rope in Salem. In an advertisement in 1795, he offered "Cables and Cordage of First Quality." And it was in Haraden's rope walk that workmen rove most of the rigging for one of America's most famous frigates—the *Essex*, the pride of Salem, the fighting ship in which, in the War of 1812, Commodore David Porter was to harry British shipping in his historic cruise into the Pacific. Long before this triumph of the *Essex*, however, Haraden had fought—and lost —his last battle.

His long years at sea had taken a toll of his health, and the last years of his life were beset with business worries (for the rope walk did not prosper) and with increasing physical debilities. He was saddened, too, by the death of his only two surviving children, though their loss was compensated for in part by his affection for his favorite nephew, Stephen Haraden, whom he reared and who in later years was to write a narrative that helped to perpetuate, locally at least, his uncle's fame. In these circumstances, Haraden died in Salem on November 23, 1803.

The character of the man and the flavor of his deeds were such that he remained a local legend. His former seamen and officers told and retold the stories of his famous cruises, and some of them, like Stephen Haraden, even preserved the more priceless anecdotes in written narrative for the use of those chroniclers of Salem lore, Capt. J. P. Felt and Freeman Hunt. Relying heavily on these eyewitness accounts, which seem to be amply supported by the written records of the times, Hunt summed up the career of Jonathan Haraden in this eulogistic paragraph:

"So great was the confidence he inspired that if he but looked at a sail through his glass, and then told the helmsman to steer for her, the observation went round, 'If she's an enemy, she's ours.' His great characteristic was the most consummate self-possession on all occasions and in the midst of perils, in which if any man equalled, none ever excelled him. His officers and men insisted he was more calm and cool amid the din of battle than at any other time; and the more deadly the strife, the more imminent the peril, the more terrific the scene, the more perfect his self-command and serene intrepidity. In a word he was a hero."